Being Dakota

Alanson B. Skinner and Amos E. Oneroad, September 1922

Being Dakota

Tales and Traditions of the Sisseton and Wahpeton

AMOS E. ONEROAD
and
ALANSON B. SKINNER

Edited by Laura L. Anderson

MINNESOTA HISTORICAL SOCIETY PRESS

www.mnhs.org/mhspress

The Minnesota Historical Society is a member of the
Association of American University Presses.

Manufactured in the United States of America

10 9 8 7 6 5 4 3 2 1

International Standard Book Number 0-87351-530-7 (paper)

∞ The paper used in this publication meets the minimum requirements of
the American National Standard for Information Sciences—Permanence for
Printed Library Materials, ANSI Z39.48-1984.

Library of Congress Cataloging-in-Publication Data

Oneroad, Amos E. (Amos Enos), b. 1884.
  Being Dakota : tales and traditions of the Sisseton and Wahpeton /
  Amos E. Oneroad and Alanson B. Skinner ; edited by Laura L. Anderson.
      p.   cm.
  Includes bibliographical references and index.
  ISBN 0-87351-530-7 (alk. paper)
    1. Wahpeton Indians—Social life and customs.
    2. Sisseton Indians—Social life and customs.
    3. Wahpeton Indians—Folklore.
    4. Sisseton Indians—Folklore.
    I. Skinner, Alanson, 1886-1925.
    II. Anderson, Laura L., 1950–
    III. Title.
E99.W135 O54 2003
978.004'9752—dc21

                                                    2002151743

To Dorothy and Arlene

For the Dakota
as Maḣpiyasna and Tehaŋ intended

Being Dakota

Sisseton and Wahpeton Tales and Folklore

Preface

The collection that I chose to investigate one afternoon several years ago was a portion of anthropologist Alanson B. Skinner's library housed at the Braun Library at the Southwest Museum in Los Angeles. The archivist directed me to a manuscript that seemed untouched. He had singled it out knowing my interest in the Dakota people.

Skinner had developed a close, kin relationship with Amos E. Oneroad, a Sisseton-Wahpeton Dakota. During their years together, Oneroad collected the information from various men and women and wrote the manuscript I was holding. Such a find was exciting because Oneroad was fluent in both Dakota, his native language, and in English. This made Oneroad's work more of a "first-hand" account than that of Black Elk, the famous spiritual leader of the Lakota people, literally a decade or more before Black Elk spoke.

The Oneroad-Skinner manuscript was as fascinating in what it did not say as in what it explicitly did say. The manuscript, the collaboration of Oneroad and Skinner, and the collection raised a multitude of questions in my mind. I sought information on Skinner, thinking him the primary author. I researched the history of the Sisseton-Wahpeton people specifically, as opposed to other Dakota groups. I sifted and searched for information on Oneroad, trying to build his biography in order to understand his working relationship with Skinner. My research led me to the realization that the major portion of the monograph was the work of Oneroad. Skinner had placed his name on the manuscript following Oneroad's as a facilitating adviser and editor.

During my research, I had put the events and the people of Oneroad and Skinner's experience in the historical past. That changed when I met and was interviewed by community and family members of someone I had grown to know only through research. The encounter with the descendants enlivened their ancestors' experience. Theirs were uncomfortably familiar conversations, sharing knowledge of the same ancestors, still being strangers, yet making the connection to a grandson, nephew, or an event. Their questions were probing and their answers revealing. Yet generally they spoke to me with the same restraint, the same repressed fear, the same frustration, the same sense of humor as used by their ancestors. The tension, which revealed itself partly by what was left unsaid and partly by how what was said was phrased, remained. Sharing the manuscript with them manifested a connection of knowledge known but not written—until the return of this monograph. Therefore, I was unprepared for the life it took on when in the hands of the Sisseton-Wahpeton elders. I was unaware how fresh the events I considered history remained in the minds of the Dakota. I did not realize the impact the monograph would have on being returned to the community, that it would be seen as affirming oral history from yet another source, would stimulate confessions of practices and beliefs that survived decades of hiding, would spark remembrances of people and of things past.

I am grateful to all who have helped me with this project. Early on at the Newberry Library, Calvin Fastwolf, David Miller, and Bill Swagerty encouraged my work on the Dakota language. Professors Barbara Johnstone in linguistics and Sylvia Grider in folklore at Texas A & M University supported my graduate studies and work on the Dakota. Professor Joseph Whitecotton at the University of Oklahoma helped hone my work in cultural anthropology and encouraged me to publish this manuscript. Editor Sally Rubinstein at the Minnesota Historical Society Press has patiently guided me through many revisions. The generous contributions of Dorothy One Road Ackerman, Arlene One Road, and their family have enriched and complemented their father's work. Publication of this text from the Alanson Skinner Manuscript Collection (MS.201) is possible through the courtesy of the Southwest Museum, Los Angeles, California. There are many others who provided lodging, shared their research, and sent me citations and photocopies; I deeply appreciate their insight. Throughout the years of research as I sought answers to the questions about Oneroad and Skinner, Gary Anderson, my husband, has been unflagging in his support.

Introduction

At the beginning of the twentieth century, as the United States government strove to suppress Indian cultures and religions, a few members of the Sisseton-Wahpeton Dakota community in northeastern South Dakota who were living in the white world quietly worked to preserve the customs and stories of their ancestors. Amos Oneroad, a son of one of those families, was educated in the traditional ways and then sent east to obtain a college degree. For most of his life he moved in two worlds. By a fortunate coincidence he met Alanson Skinner, a student of anthropology and kindred soul, in New York City. The two men formed a bond both personal and professional, collaborating on anthropological studies in various parts of the United States. But the project closest to Oneroad's heart was the collection and preservation of stories, traditions, and hand-crafted pieces obtained from his relatives and friends. Oneroad shared the stories with Skinner. The men intended to polish the resulting manuscript on eastern Dakota ethnology and folklore and publish it, but Skinner's untimely death thwarted their plans. The manuscript, which survived almost unnoticed in a California library, succeeded in fulfilling its authors' intent. It conveys these long-ago stories and traditions to the children and grandchildren in Oneroad's voice.

THE SISSETON-WAHPETON COMMUNITY

The setting of the story of the Sisseton and Wahpeton Dakota is the Coteau des Prairies, the "hills of the prairies," between the James and Big Sioux Rivers. The Coteau is about one hundred miles wide and two hundred miles long and rises seven to eight hundred feet above the surrounding prairie. From its crest, one can see Big Stone Lake, Lake Traverse, and far into the distance to the east. Its steep sides are cut by ravines and heavily wooded. Many springs feed streams and lakes. For generations this land was the home of the Sisseton and Wahpeton people. They hunted in the woods, fished the lakes, harvested the fruits and berries, and planted crops on the bottomlands. They sheltered in the wooded ravines from winter's icy blast, from summer's scorching heat, and from enemies who sought their destruction. From the Coteau, they had an excellent vantage point to spot approaching danger.

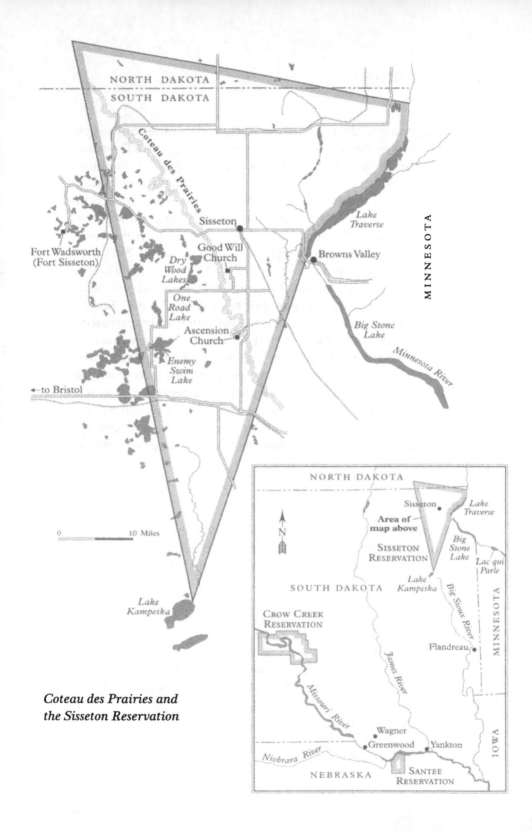

NORTH DAKOTA

SOUTH DAKOTA

Coteau des Prairies

Sisseton

Fort Wadsworth
(Fort Sisseton)

Good Will
Church

Dry
Wood
Lakes

One
Road
Lake

Ascension
Church

Enemy
Swim
Lake

←to Bristol

Lake
Traverse

Browns Valley

Big Stone
Lake

Minnesota River

MINNESOTA

0   10 Miles

Lake
Kampeska

*Coteau des Prairies and
the Sisseton Reservation*

NORTH DAKOTA

N

Sisseton

Area of
map above

SISSETON
RESERVATION

SOUTH DAKOTA

Lake
Kampeska

Lake
Traverse

Big
Stone
Lake

Lac qui
Parle

Big Sioux River

Flandreau

James River

MINNESOTA

CROW CREEK
RESERVATION

Missouri River

Wagner

Greenwood

Yankton

IOWA

Niobrara River

NEBRASKA

SANTEE
RESERVATION

While a history of the Sisseton and Wahpeton can be pieced together from written documents, it is important to consider these documents as a fragmentary sketch of those events regarded as important
enough to be recorded by non-Dakota or outsiders. Such history relates
the outsiders' perception of Sisseton-Wahpeton history, not the Dakota
ehaŋna woyakapi or "long ago" recounting. The Dakota probably
would not have selected the same events; nevertheless, the Euro-
American information has some value.[1]

The Dakota people organized traditionally into the Oćeti Śakowiŋ
or Seven Council Fires. Each council fire represented a tribe or closely
related group. This ancient league, which was in a state of decentrali-
zation by the early nineteenth century, divided geographically into
the Eastern Dakota with four councils and the Western Sioux with
the remaining three councils. The Eastern Dakota, who lived in the
Minnesota-Mississippi River area, included the upper councils of the
Sisseton and Wahpeton, near the headwaters of the Minnesota, and the
lower councils of the Mdewakanton and Wahpekute, closer to the Mississippi.[2] The Teton, who spoke Lakota, and the Yankton and Yank-
tonai, who spoke Nakota, lived farther west toward the Missouri River.

The nineteenth century brought many changes that caused tension
and splintered the community. The tide of white settlement swept over
the land and forced the Sisseton and Wahpeton to forsake the old ways.
The system of government, religious beliefs, cultural practices, and
economic pursuits were permanently altered.

Through a series of treaties, the Dakota relinquished their lands.
The primary one was the Treaty of Traverse des Sioux in 1851 that located the Sisseton and Wahpeton on a reservation on the upper reaches

1. "Dakota" is the term meaning "friendly" that the Dakota used to refer to
themselves. "Sioux" is an outsider term credited to a French corruption of the Ojibwe
(Chippewa) term for "snake." "Siouan" is a linguistic term applied to the language
family of which the Dakota language is a member.

2. William Watts Folwell, *A History of Minnesota* (St. Paul: Minnesota Historical Society, 1956), 1:182–83; James Owen Dorsey, "The Social Organization of Siouan
Tribes," *Journal of American Folklore* 4 (1891): 257–63; James Henri Howard, *Reprints
in Anthropology: The Dakota or Sioux Indians* (Lincoln, Nebr.: J & L Reprint Co., 1980),
2–6; Gary Clayton Anderson, *Kinsmen of Another Kind: Dakota-White Relations in the
Upper Mississippi Valley, 1650–1862* (Lincoln: University of Nebraska Press, 1984; St.
Paul: Minnesota Historical Society Press, 1997); Clifford Allen, *History of the Flan-
dreau Sioux Tribe* (Flandreau, S.Dak.: Tribal History Program, Flandreau Santee
Sioux Tribe, 1971), 9.

DAKOTA DIACRITICAL MARKS

The use of Dakota accents varied from person to person and over time. An effort was made to follow the use as it appeared in the source. The following guide to pronunciation is adapted from Stephen R. Riggs, *A Dakota-English Dictionary* (Washington, D.C.: GPO, 1889; St. Paul: Minnesota Historical Society Press, 1992).

Ć / ć
is an aspirate with the sound of English ch, as in chin

Ġ / ġ
represents a deep guttural gh

Ḣ / ħ
represents a strong guttural kha

Ŋ / ŋ
denotes a nasal sound similar to the English n in drink

Ś / ś
is an aspirate having the sound of English sh, as in shine

Ź / ź
is an aspirate having the sound of the English s, as in pleasure

of the Minnesota River, from Yellow Medicine to Lake Traverse, where the government opened farms for them.[3] The more traditional members of the band, who refused to give up the hunt, settled at the head of Big Stone Lake and Lake Traverse, remaining off the reservation in bands led by Tataŋkanaźiŋ (Standing Buffalo) or with Waanata (The Charger). They frequently took the annuities offered on the reservation by the government, stayed only until they received food, and then returned to their hunting grounds to follow the buffalo.

Many other Dakota responded to the arrival of Christian missionaries in 1834. By 1837 the Presbyterians Thomas S. Williamson and Stephen R. Riggs settled at Lac qui Parle, on the Minnesota River two hundred miles west of Fort Snelling, and opened the mission station of Peźihutazi or Yellow Medicine. Two Indian villages sprang up nearby, one led by the Christian sympathizer Iŋyaŋgmani (Running Walker), a Wahpeton leader, and the other by Maȟpiyasna (Amos Oneroad's great-grandfather). The majority of the Dakota converts were from their bands.[4]

The Sisseton and Wahpeton who lived at the head of the Coteau resisted the acculturation evident in the bands living closer to the missions. It was not the planting they opposed but the individualized farms, fences, and houses. Missionaries encouraged the farmers to hoard food, to wear pants, and to cut their hair, all of which signaled a break with tradition. Yet, in fact, some traditionalists put on pants, accepted allotments and houses, and began farming. And some farmers put on the breech cloth, leggings, and blanket, attended dances and feasts, and practiced conjuring.[5]

Tensions mounted in response to the threat of change, leading to a revival of ritual dances and societies.[6] Some Sisseton formed a soldiers lodge in 1861 to enforce more equitable annuity distribution and to harass Dakota farmers. Acculturation, white encroachment, and change

3. Roy W. Meyer, *History of the Santee Sioux: United States Indian Policy on Trial* (Lincoln: University of Nebraska Press, 1967, 1993), 80–87.

4. Samuel W. Pond, *The Dakota or Sioux in Minnesota as They Were in 1834* (St. Paul: Minnesota Historical Society Press, 1908, 1986); Thomas S. Williamson to Selah B. Treat, June 8 and 30, 1852, American Board of Commissioners for Foreign Missions (ABCFM) Papers, copies in Minnesota Historical Society, St. Paul (hereafter MHS).

5. Williamson to Treat, November 18, 1859, ABCFM Papers.

6. Brown to Cullen, Oct. 25, 1860, SED no. 1, 36th Congress, 2nd session, serial 1078, 278; "Reminiscences of Thomas A. Robertson," Thomas Robertson Papers, Minnesota Historical Society (hereafter MHS); Anderson, *Kinsmen of Another Kind*, 238.

divided families. But the overarching concern was the dwindling food supply.

Each summer the Dakota congregated at Yellow Medicine to receive their annuities. In 1862, seven thousand Dakota arrived on July 10 for immediate payment of money and food. The cash had not yet arrived, and the agent waited to distribute both food and funds at the same time. Meanwhile the traders sold vast quantities of food to the Dakota, who amassed huge credits that were to be paid from the annuity money. On August 4, some Sisseton-Wahpeton lost patience, broke into the storehouse, and distributed sacks of flour to the hungry families. They were diverted only after the army, present to oversee the payment, aimed a cannon at the hungry plunderers.[7] Amazingly, a disgruntled kind of calm prevailed. Yet only fifteen days later, an unrelated incident farther south among the Mdewakanton sparked the Dakota to war.

The 1862 Dakota War lasted six weeks, involving several hundred participants and taking five hundred white lives and at least as many Indian lives. The conflict further divided the Dakota into active participants in the war, passivists who were present at battles but refused to fire a shot, friends of whites, and pacifists. Most Sisseton under Tataŋkanaźiŋ and Waanata were pacifists, and many members of Iŋyaŋgmani's band came to the aid of those fleeing hostility.

A military court tried more than three hundred Dakota for participation in the war and condemned 303 to death. On December 26, thirty-eight, who had not received a presidential pardon, were hanged in Mankato. The remaining prisoners were sent to the federal prison at Davenport, Iowa. In 1863 the army conveyed the Dakota from Minnesota to a new reservation at Crow Creek on the Missouri River in present-day South Dakota. Two years later, of the 1,318 taken to Crow Creek, only 1,043 remained alive.[8]

Some of the Dakota men enlisted as military scouts with Gabriel Renville (Tiwakaŋ). The scouts were a U.S. Army auxiliary group used to control the Dakota camps, to bring in fugitives, to identify the active participants in the war, and to be trackers for the 1863–66 military expeditions. The members of the scouts' extended families were in Davenport, Crow Creek, or with the roving bands, while their immediate families were often at the scout station. The military provided specific

7. Winifred W. Barton, *John P. Williamson: A Brother to the Sioux* (Chicago: Fleming H. Revell, 1919), 41; Anderson, *Kinsmen of Another Kind*, 250-51.

8. Meyer, *Santee Sioux*, 145, 153.

orders for the scouts to carry out, regardless of the obligations the scouts felt toward their families. They understood that any redemption of the Dakota people, any benevolence on the part of the government, and any hope of return to their homeland depended on their performance for the army. In many ways the scouts were an outgrowth of the soldiers lodge, where the welfare of the community depended on the structure and regulation of the lodge to control men's actions in war and on the hunt.

By 1864 various Sisseton bands began returning to the Coteau. That same year the government started to release some of the prisoners held at Davenport. By May 1865 nearly two hundred lodges with six hundred warriors came to the area of Fort Wadsworth, the military post established in 1864 on the Coteau.[9] In 1866, the government moved the Dakota from Crow Creek to a new reserve on the Niobrara River in northeastern Nebraska Territory. The Dakota who went were impressed by the bleakness of these successive locations and depressed by the uncertainty of their tenure.

In 1867 sixteen Sisseton, including Wakaŋto, went to Washington to negotiate for a new reservation. The treaty of 1867 created the Sisseton Reservation, a triangular reserve on the Coteau that extended from Lake Kampeska on the north to the James River on the west to Lake Traverse on the east. The federal government recognized Gabriel Renville as the leader of the people residing around Lake Traverse.

The intent of the 1867 treaty was to force the Sisseton and Wahpeton to become self-sufficient farmers. To that end the government issued agricultural supplies. The agent kept track of who worked and who did not, and the storekeeper issued supplies to those who qualified. In 1872 nearly half of the 1,496 families were considered poor, but over the next several years many people moved off the poor list.[10]

In the 1870s Riggs and Williamson resumed their missionary work and began to organize churches and schools on the new reservation. No longer anticipating gradual incorporation of the Dakota into white society by assimilation, they aimed at a policy of separatism. While they wanted the Dakota to accept white lifeways and standards, they also began to believe that keeping them isolated from the vices of whites was the only way for them to succeed.

9. Paul M. Edwards, "Fort Wadsworth and the Friendly Santee Sioux, 1864–1892," in *South Dakota Historical Collections* 31 (Pierre: South Dakota Historical Society, 1962), 121.

10. Meyer, *Santee Sioux*, 198–200, 209–10.

If the missionaries felt ambivalent about their goals, the Sisseton and Wahpeton were in an even more precarious position. The government was using food and other supplies to force them to change their economic way of life, and the missionaries, working with the government agent, were insisting on abandonment of their religious beliefs. The Sisseton and Wahpeton responded in a variety of ways.

Gabriel Renville and the scout party opposed the missionaries' church party and generally preserved customs of polygamy and dancing, yet they were some of the most progressive farmers. Daniel Renville, a cousin of Gabriel, was the leader of a church group. In 1869 he sought help from the agent, Benjamin W. Thompson, for building a church, as the Dakota had been holding services in their homes. In cooperation with Riggs, the group built Good Will Church.[11] That same year the Grass Dance was introduced.

Nevertheless, Daniel Renville became the native pastor, and in 1870 a school opened with classes in both English and Dakota. Another church was build at Ascension and John B. Renville, Daniel's brother, was the native pastor. John Williamson, son of Thomas Williamson, wrote that six hundred people came to a meeting at Good Will Church on June 21–24, 1872. Williamson was surprised by the "earnestness and ability" of the Indians in discussing questions, and although it was a quiet meeting there was a "stillness that was powerful."[12]

Notwithstanding the factionalism, the Sisseton Reservation had the look of a stable and growing enterprise in the 1870s in spite of the short tenure of agents and the lack of progress in farming. Indeed, the reservation was often considered exemplary due to its acculturative success in the federal program of making Indians self-sufficient. In 1880 only one-fourth of the Indians' subsistence was provided by the government, and after 1882 no subsistence supplies were issued, except to school children.

The government's next move in making the Dakota self-sufficient and to destroy the communal land base was to implement the Dawes Act of 1887 and allot the reservation land, giving each family 160 acres and selling the rest to create a fund whose proceeds would be used for community expenses. The Sisseton Reservation was one of the first reservations to be allotted. The Dakota received 309,904 acres in 1,339 patents; the schools 32,840 acres, and the church and agency 1,347 acres;

11. Meyer, *Santee Sioux*, 204–5.
12. John Williamson to John Lowrie, August 8, 1872, John Poage Williamson Papers, microfilm, South Dakota State Historical Society, Pierre.

presidential proclamation opened the remaining 574,678 acres to white settlement at $2.50 an acre on April 11, 1892.[13]

The Indian Appropriations Act of 1902 furthered the destruction of the reservation community by permitting the sale of inherited land. The Burke Act of 1906 authorized the secretary of the interior to issue patents to any Indian competent to handle his own affairs, thus enabling him to sell his allotment. Five years later 90 percent of the reservation land base had been lost, mostly to aggressive white neighbors. Still the government in its wisdom sponsored a farmer's club and reservation fair to encourage the Indian farmer.[14]

The Sisseton-Wahpeton were good farmers and, according to the Indian agent reports, showed promise for self-sufficiency. Yet they faced a host of obstacles; competition with local businesses, settlers greedy for land, over-regulation of the Dakota economy, shackling of civil liberties, and spiraling costs of operation. Unfortunately, the late-nineteenth-century vision of a gradual process toward self-sufficiency culminating in the allotment of individually owned tracts of land became a disaster. In the haste to establish self-reliance, the government oversimplified, demanding acculturation yet refusing civil equality.

The Dakota language continued to be the daily medium of communication on the reservation. Between 1885 and 1888 the commissioner of Indian affairs issued a series of regulations aimed at limiting the use of native language, particularly on government property. Williamson fought hard to establish exceptions, declaring that the government had no right to interfere in privately funded reservation schools. Even so the Sisseton agent complained in 1890 that the Presbyterians' Good Will School "did not insist on speaking of English enough."[15] It had long been the missionaries' conviction that "if you would teach an Indian boy English, the easiest way is to teach him his own language first. . . . Add to this the discipline and the [white] culture thus secured, and it will readily appear that teaching in a vernacular tongue is, in the beginning, the most profitable teaching."[16] Native ministers used Dakota exclusively and taught school in Dakota and English.

The government simultaneously made efforts toward ending the "heathen practice" of native dances or any dance reminiscent of the

13. Meyer, *Santee Sioux*, 216.
14. Meyer, *Santee Sioux*, 218.
15. Meyer, *Santee Sioux*, 317-18.
16. United States Commissioner of Indian Affairs, *Annual Report, 1890*, 67.

Ghost Dance or Sun Dance. The idea was to encourage Indians to stay productively at home, take no part in the give-away associated with the dance, and avoid lengthy visits in encampments from which white society inferred transmission of disease and loose morality. Dancers merely avoided detection by moving the dances farther from the agent's headquarters. Ironically dancing survived at fairs and exhibitions, supported by local merchants who made money from tourism. Consequently objections diminished, provided dances were held in the daytime. Young Dakota were not permitted to be dancers or even be spectators, however; only "old scouts" were allowed to dance at fairs.[17]

The Dakota Presbytery for its part identified three major problems on the reservations: liquor, gambling, and dancing. In their annual meeting at Crow Creek Presbyterian Church in 1878, the elders went to great length to condemn the Grass Dance: "The Grass-wisp Dance works evil in the case of the flesh." They listed the chief offenses: giving away wives, horses, and clothing, killing oxen received from the government, starving themselves, losing two or three days' work for every dance, dancing in Indian costume and telling war stories in the dance, and hunting women at night. The meeting minutes continue that the dance polluted souls, drew away many church members, caused the Sabbath to be disregarded, and exhibited prayer to idols.[18] By 1889 the Dakota Presbytery had narrowed the problems to two— liquor and dancing.

In 1883 the Bureau of Indian Affairs as part of the Court of Indian Offenses policy formulated the Religious Crimes Code that essentially outlawed the traditional ceremonies and practices of the Dakota.[19] The Oneroad family remembered that:

17. Stephen R. Riggs, *Tah-koo Wah-kan: or, The Gospel among the Dakotas* (Boston: Congregational Publishing Society, 1869), 409.

18. Meyer, *Santee Sioux,* 303; William K. Powers, "Plains Indian Music and Dance," in *Anthropology on the Great Plains,* W. Raymond Wood and Margot Liberty, ed. (Lincoln: University of Nebraska Press, 1980), 212–30.

19. "Courts of Indian Offenses," *U. S. Office of Indian Affairs, Regulations of the Indian Office, Effective April 1, 1904* (Washington: GPO, 1904), 584–91. In 1883 the secretary of the interior assigned the Indian police the additional duty of serving as judges of newly established Court of Indian Offenses. Congress provided funds to employ Indians who would serve only in a judicial capacity, hoping the courts would discourage certain religious and social practices. See William T. Hagan, "United States Indian Policies, 1860–1900," in *Handbook of the North American Indians,* William C. Sturtevant and Wilcomb E. Washburn, ed. (Washington, D.C.: Smithsonian Institution Press, 1988), 4:58.

Severe penalties and punishment could include incarceration either at Fort Sisseton or at the Sisseton Agency jail as well as loss of properties should they be caught practicing such traditional religious ways.... Missionary control of Indian education and the entire reservation was very strong in 1884, and the prohibitions and pressures against practicing traditional religious ceremonies were extreme.... At that time, searches were made of all households on the Lake Traverse Reservation [Sisseton Reservation], and such sacred religious objects as Pipes, medicine bundles, and altars were seized, then burned and destroyed. It was not uncommon for federal troops from Fort Sisseton to accompany the federal Agent on these searches for traditional religious objects and articles in the households of the Sisseton and Wahpeton people according to what we learned from our father and our elders as they would whisper such information to us, when we were small children.[20]

Tribal members were themselves upset with a decline in traditional morals. Oneroad family members noted that photographs taken at Fort Sisseton in the late 1860s and well into the 1870s reveal groups of teenage Sisseton-Wahpeton girls dressed in tight-fitting blouses. Boarding schools also threatened Dakota womanhood. They interrupted the primary method of transmitting traditional ways of life and values—from woman to woman within the family and community. Instead the schools created a whole novel mystique around these "lady graduates of the boarding schools."[21]

The Court of Indian Offenses undertook further efforts to eradicate traditional life. It established a tribunal of three nonpolygamist Indians approved by the agent to be judges in a tribal court. It outlawed the Sun Dance and other dances, prohibited polygamy, required men to support their families, forbad practices by "medicine men," banned destruction of property as a sign of mourning, and proscribed use of liquor or a man and woman living together without being married by

20. The Oneroad family recalled that three members of the committee, who executed this ruling of the Dakota Presbytery, were themselves known to be good dancers throughout their lifetime; *Amos E. Oneroad (1884–1937): A Sisseton Wahpeton Man For All Seasons* (N.p., n.d.), 5. Family information comes from this booklet, a tribute written by Arlene One Road and Dorothy One Road Ackerman, who are the surviving children of Amos Oneroad and are Sisseton-Wahpeton Tribal Elders.

21. This is another example of conflicting aesthetic or social values; tailored blouses conveyed prim and proper neatness to white society but a lack of modesty to the Dakota. Edward Milton Lyle Red Owl, *Project: Traditional Dakotah Womanhood* (Sisseton, S.Dak.: Red Shield, Inc., 1991), 10.

an ordained clergyman. Anyone wishing to leave the reservation or sell craft items needed a permit from the agent. The court established fines and terms of imprisonment for infractions. These regulations were to be read publicly throughout the reservation.[22]

World views of Dakota and Euro-Americans were in direct conflict. Agents and missionaries demanded that the Sisseton-Wahpeton comply with the white standards, leaving traditionalists no alternative but to suppress their convictions and maintain them covertly, leading to a public "white" life and a private "Dakota" life. Tribal unity was dying, and the Sisseton Reservation was becoming an aggregation of families and scattered individuals.

In the haste to establish self-reliance, the federal government ignored the complications of change and of cultural difference. Contrasting concepts included: the inclusivity or exclusivity of kinship; the collective or individual base of the social economy; the holistic view of time or the segmentation of past, present, future; the holistic view or secular-religious division of their world view; the respect for the dead and ancestors in continuity of the past or the elevation of the present and living individual; the reaping and sharing of the fruits of the earth or the storing and hoarding of these same fruits as insurance against the future. Dress codes symbolized more specific clashing values: pants, tailored blouses, and cut hair, which white society found neat and civil, were unmasculine, immodest, and a sign of grief to the Dakota. Zealous whites found dancing licentious, whereas Dakota valued it as a worshipful act.

The first thirty years of the twentieth century brought the rapid reduction of the Indian land base, the disappearance of visible native culture, gradual diminishing of government services and supervision, and the awareness of a void resulting from repression of tradition. Dakota individuals faced these challenges in multiple ways.

The demarcation between traditional and acculturated Dakota became blurred by the combinations possible from the traits associated with Dakota society, missionaries, farmers, white society, and government standards. Many Dakota elected to adopt these traits without accepting the Euro-American ideals or the entire culture set, retaining and re-creating their own cultural identity while adapting to change. Others adopted more from Euro-Americans, making traditional Dakota suspicious and signaling "civilization" to zealous whites. A few Dakota made more drastic alterations, but all change was subject to

22. "Courts of Indian Offenses," 584–91.

judgment by others—the self-appointed guardians, especially the government agents and officials and missionaries.

An unintended result of this scrutiny by missionaries and agents was the documentation of four generations of Amos Oneroad's family. By studying the language used by white observers and looking at the subjects covered, it is possible to see over time a change in attitude. Riggs in the mid-nineteenth century, for instance, was free to comment on the dances, albeit in an ambivalent, condescending manner. Four generations later, even the performance of a dance was roundly condemned by missionaries and government officials. When Oneroad and Skinner talked to the Sisseton and Wahpeton, they often heard tales of the same events witnessed by Riggs. But the descriptive language and the purpose of their telling were different.

The oldest generation interpreted by whites was that of Ptehotoŋpi (Lowing Bull), one of Amos's great-great-grandfathers on his mother's side.[23] Ptehotoŋpi was with Iŋyaŋgmani's Wahpeton band in 1853–55 but with a Sisseton band led by Waanata in 1858. Riggs, who met Ptehotoŋpi when he was the "high priest and prophet at a Social Dance," described him as "bald-headed, not tall but of considerable breadth and weight"[24] and called him a great medicine man and war prophet. On a cold November day at Lac qui Parle, Riggs related that:

> The night previous had been spent by old Lowing Buffalo [Bull] in what is best expressed by the phrase, making *wakan*. The rattling of the gourd shell, together with singing over the heated stones, was quite necessary to bring the old man into connection with the spirit world.

Riggs's lengthy description was full of details and skepticism but not condemnation.

23. During the initial years of written Dakota, many names in Dakota and in their English translations were recorded as if they were one word, like Matomaza or Ironbear and Taśinahotawiŋ or Greyshawl. Later, in the twentieth century, the pattern changed and words were broken up, like Mato Maza or Iron Bear, and Ta Śina hota Wiŋ or Her Shawl Grey Woman (translating each part narrowly and giving it the status of a word).

24. *Amos E. Oneroad*, 1. See also Edward Milton Red Owl, *Shepherd Family* (N.p., n.d.), 1, transcribed from the records of Hazen Preston Shepherd. Stephen Return Riggs, "Dakota Portraits," *Minnesota History Bulletin* 2 (1918): 513–17; he described this ceremony, which in a footnote he called a Circle Dance. Riggs first remembered Lowing Bull in 1838 at Lac qui Parle. It is unclear in "Dakota Portraits" when Lowing Bull died, but it was most likely between 1853 and 1858 because he was on the annuity rolls. Annuity Rolls for the Sioux (1853–1858), National Archives Record Group 75 (NARG), Washington, D.C.

Oneroad and Skinner collected an anecdote about Ptehotoŋpi offering his wife to any Dakota man as a show of his generosity and his strength of character. However, his willingness to give away his most valued possession only resulted in her being reclaimed by her insulted brothers. This display split their families thereafter.

The second recorded generation was that of Amos Oneroad's maternal great-grandfathers, Maḣpiyasna (Jingling Cloud), for whom Amos was named, and Matomaza (Ironbear) of Waanata's Sisseton band. Maḣpiyasna married Waŋmdiśuŋ Waśtewiŋ (Good Eagle Feathers Woman); seven children were born to them. This was the last generation to have minimal white intrusion into their culture and to be described by missionaries in a positive way for being traditional Dakota. In 1838, Joseph N. Nicollet, the French mapmaker, while at Lac qui Parle listed Maḣpiyasna in his journal as one of the four chiefs of the Kit Fox society, whose secret title, he stated, was "Wowapi wakan okondakitchie, the company of the friends of the holy book (the Bible)."[25]

Riggs reported that Maḣpiyasna was the head soldier of the Wahpeton leader Iŋyaŋgmani, then at Lac qui Parle. He described Maḣpiyasna as tall and boastful, deserving to be counted among the brave, and said that he had given away more horses in his day than all that the Wahpeton had owned. Once Riggs witnessed Maḣpiyasna's Sun Dance. He commented that Maḣpiyasna came from "worshipful stock" because he was the son of Ptehotoŋpi and was "in all things very worshipful." The missionary claimed that Maḣpiyasna did not believe in a future state and that when he died it would be like an ox dying and that would be all of him.

Riggs told how Maḣpiyasna disciplined a member of the band. A young man had violated a compact of peace by killing an Ojibwe man. The soldiers' lodge determined that the offender must die, and when no one else would volunteer to carry out the order, Maḣpiyasna consented to do it. Within an hour, the deed was done. Duty to the band itself took precedence over any feelings of personal friendship or family loyalty. Another version of this tale from the Oneroad-Skinner collection adds that Maḣpiyasna thereafter took on the responsibility of providing for the widow of the Ojibwe man. It also mentions that a song board from the Ojibwe commemorated his sense of justice and

25. Joseph N. Nicollet, *Nicollet on the Plains and Prairies*, Edmund C. Bray and Martha Coleman Bray, ed. (St. Paul: Minnesota Historical Society Press, 1976), 277–78.

leadership. Riggs finished his account by relating that at Lac qui Parle in October 1842, after drinking too much whiskey, Maḣpiyasna went to his tent to clean out his gun before duck hunting. The gun discharged, killing him. Riggs questioned whether it was accidental or intentional, as Maḣpiyasna had seemed to be in a melancholy mood ever since his last "dance to the sun."[26] Riggs's comments were ambivalent toward this generation, part admiration, part suspicion, and part condemnatory where Dakota practices clashed with his Christian ideology.

The third generation experienced the white intrusion and became aware that their culture was in direct conflict with white values. This generation included Amos Oneroad's maternal Wahpeton grandmother, Hannah Shepherd (Taśinaḣotawiŋ, Her Greyshawl Woman), and Amos's paternal grandfather, Wakaŋto.[27] Hannah possessed knowledge of "long ago" history, the medicine feast, and medicinal herbs, including the serpent's root. She had been a member of the missionary-sponsored Hazelwood Republic in 1857; the Indian agent reported her on the annuity role as having nine children in her lodge but "no man," indicating no hunter. While the depth of Hannah's relationship with the missionaries is unknown, it is clear that she retained traditional knowledge. Her year at Hazelwood was a peak year

---

AMOS ONEROAD'S MATERNAL GRANDMOTHER'S FAMILY

Taśinaḣotawiŋ (Hannah Shepherd)
   m. Maḣpiya Hotaŋka
1. Wamnonhna Koyakewiŋ (Nancy Shepherd) (1848)
2. Itohnakeduta (Smiley I. Shepherd) (1852–1881)
3. Itehdugo (Joshua I. Shepherd) (1855–1878)
4. Tawohduzewanjena (1858–1858)
5. Hdonicawin (Jennie H. Shepherd) (1861–1891)
   m. Śicaya Ohaŋ
6. Maggie Shepherd (1867–1872)
7. Sutayati (Joseph S. Shepherd) (1870–1905)

---

26. Riggs, 1918: 509–13. See "War Charms" page 71, below. Song boards were a means of recording music with symbols; Skinner and Oneroad included this one in their collection. See also Skinner's Sun Dance article and Gideon Pond's article "Maḣpiyasna and the Sun Dance."

27. Red Owl, *Shepherd Family,* gives Hannah Shepherd's dates as 1829 to 1918. Her siblings were: Cancega Yuha Hiyeyewin (Carrying Drum or Jane Shepherd), 1817–95; Marpiya Wicasta Sni (No Man Cloud), 1826–43; Wanske (Fourth Born Daughter), 1832–36; Marpiya Kahominine (Turning Cloud), 1835–37; Tate Sica (Bad Wind), 1838–41; Wasicuduta (Red White Man), 1841–42.

for the potato crop, which helped to feed her nine youngsters; perhaps it was the abundant crop rather than the church that drew her to Hazelwood.[28]

Hannah Shepherd was married to Maȟpiya Hotaŋka (Big Voice Cloud), who was reportedly killed at Wood Lake in the 1862 Dakota War.[29] Because of scanty documentation, it is impossible to make assumptions about Big Voice Cloud's involvement with the missionaries. Neither did his association with a battle in the Dakota War signal the degree of acculturation or resistance as neatly as assumed by white society.

In 1860, Hannah Shepherd apparently sent her eldest son, Smiley I. Shepherd (Itohnakeduta), to the boarding school; records show him being with the Williamsons at Yellow Medicine when he was seven years old.[30] Nancy, his older sister by four years, was not listed in the records. Some Dakota individuals of Hannah Shepherd's generation elected to adopt some elements of white society that were practical in their lives. It did not signal acculturation, as so desperately desired by agents and missionaries.

In 1866 Hannah married Śicaya Ohaŋ (Mischievous One), her second husband. That same year, her daughter, Nancy (Wamnonhna Koyakewiŋ, Wears A Shell), married Peter Oneroad (Caŋkuwaŋzidaŋ). Amos Oneroad was one of their ten children. Peter Oneroad's mother was Toicuwiŋ (Takes Green), and his father was Wakaŋto (Blue Spirit or Blue Holy).[31] Wakaŋto was a medicine man, succeeding Sleepy Eye as the leader of the Lower Sisseton.

The fourth generation recorded were the parents of Amos Oneroad, Nancy Shepherd and Peter Oneroad, as well as Peter's brother White Lodge (Wakayaska). This generation suffered defeat in the struggles over values and acculturation. Amos Oneroad's immediate family

28. See the serpent's root, page 87, and the medicine feast, page 83, below. Skinner claimed in the "Medicine Ceremony of the Menomini Iowa and Wahpeton Dakota," *Indian Notes and Monographs,* vol. 4 (1920), that the medicine feast had not been performed by the Wahpeton near Sisseton since the 1860s. Hazelwood Republic, a quasi-independent political structure of Dakota farmers, gained recognition as a Dakota band in 1857. They stressed acculturation, discarded their medicine sacks, and turned from Dakota tradition to integrate into white society and gain citizenship. Annuity Roles (1857), NA RG 75; Williamson to Treat, November 18, 1859, ABCFM Papers.

29. "Trial and Prison Records," William W. and Marion P. Satterlee Papers, MHS.

30. "Boarding School Students," 1847–59, Box 4, Stephen R. Riggs Papers, MHS. Also listed at the school was David Ortley, brother of Edward Ortley, the father of Amos Oneroad's first wife, Etta Ortley.

31. *Sisseton Centennial Yearbook 1992,* 625; *Amos E. Oneroad,* 1.

AMOS ONEROAD AND HIS SIBLINGS

Wamnonhna Koyakewiŋ (Nancy Shepherd)
　m. Caŋkuwaŋzidaŋ (Peter Oneroad)
1. Wahcankato (Charley W. Oneroad) (1867–1956)
2. Matomaza (John M. Oneroad) (1870–1943)
3. Benjaman Oneroad (1876–1898)
4. William Oneroad (1878–1888)
5. Jacob Oneroad (1881–1925)
6. Amos Oneroad (Maḣpiyasna, Jingling Cloud) (1884–1937)
7. Keziah Oneroad (1886–1896)
8. Hattie Oneroad Dumarce (1888–1923)
9. Louis Oneroad (1891–1892)

---

members were absent from the attendance rolls of the mission school and were mentioned infrequently by the missionaries, leading one to believe that they were more traditional. Or the omission could have a political base. The Oneroads had marriage and family ties to the Renvilles and the scout party, many of whom had been in disputes with the missionaries. Nancy Shepherd's brother Smiley married Gabriel Renville's daughter Sarah. Amos's first wife, Etta, was the daughter of Henry Ortley, who was a scout. Smiley Shepherd's son also married a member of the Ortley family.

Peter Oneroad was most likely a passivist (having met his Dakota obligation by being present at battles but not firing a weapon) in the Dakota War, since the record of his trial, Number 195, resulted in an acquittal, a verdict reported in only 10 percent of the cases. The record stated that he said, "I was at the last battle and I didn't fire a shot."[32]

Meanwhile, remnants of Dakota families were scattered. White Lodge, among many others, fled to Canada, fearful in the aftermath; he died there in 1870. Oneroad's family believed Peter Oneroad briefly joined his relatives in Canada. A few refugees, including Peter, later returned to the Coteau. Wakaŋto, who remained in the states, was listed as consistently loyal to the whites.[33]

---

32. Original Transcripts of the Records of Trials of Certain Sioux Indians Charged with Barbarities in the State of Minnesota, Senate Records 37A-f2, National Archives, Washington, D.C. See also Satterlee Papers; Marion P. Satterlee, *A Detailed Account of the Massacre by the Dakota Indians of Minnesota in 1862* (Minneapolis, 1923).

33. Dorothy One Road Ackerman telephone conversation with Laura L. Anderson, December 1994. See also Minnesota Valley Historical Society, *Sketches Historical and Descriptive of the Monuments and Tablets Erected by the Minnesota Valley Historical Society in Renville and Redwood Counties, Minnesota* (Morton, 1902), 75.

Peter Oneroad was a scout at the camp called Buzzard's Roost or Hawk's Nest on a hill overlooking the James River Valley southwest of Fort Wadsworth near present-day Bristol, South Dakota. Because the food supply remained scanty in the mid-1800s and buffalo were becoming increasingly scarce, the discovery of a herd of three thousand head was the highlight of 1865. Gabriel Renville led a hunting party of nearly a hundred to the vicinity of Buzzard's Roost. Gabriel killed sixteen buffalo, Charles Crawford killed fifteen, and Samuel Brown emptied his gun on a large buffalo that turned on him and chased him all the way back to camp. There those who had been watching in fun finally killed the animal. Oneroad's account in the "Legend of Hoop Ravine" wove in fragments of this event.[34] During the feast following the hunt, the area around Fort Wadsworth was declared the "Tataŋka (Buffalo) Republic" and the fort "the capital to rule the woolly buffalo and wily Sioux."[35]

Another scout with Peter Oneroad at the Buzzard's Roost camp was Solomon Two Stars (Wicaŋħpinoŋpa). Solomon, who was the son of the Wahpeton leader Maħpiyawićaśta (Cloudman), was selected as a head scout by his cousin Gabriel Renville. Early in 1865 Solomon and four scouts, Wahaćaŋkaitetoŋ, Kampeska, Tataŋka Waŋzidaŋ, and Peter Oneroad, took the lives of three men from a group that had entered Minnesota, killed the Jewett family in Blue Earth County, and were on their way to the Missouri River when the scouts intercepted them. Jack Campbell, the favorite nephew of Solomon, was among the perpetrators. Under strict orders not to take prisoners, Solomon Two Stars ex-

34. The "Legend of Hoop Ravine," page 156, below, emphasized how rare buffalo herds had become in South Dakota (Roberts County). The buffalo that turned on Samuel Brown was given emphasis in the tale because a fierce male buffalo had special significance. Oneroad's father witnessed or heard firsthand accounts of the event, which he wove into the Hoop Ravine legend. The last buffalo hunt in Roberts County is said to have taken place in 1879 with eight buffalo taken.

35. See Elijah Blackthunder, *Ehanna Woyakapi: Sisseton-Wahpeton Sioux of Lake Traverse Reservation* (Sisseton, S.Dak.: Sisseton-Wahpeton Sioux Tribe, Inc., 1973), 49; Clement A. Lounsberry, *Early History of North Dakota* (Washington, D.C.: Liberty Press, 1919), 36–37; and Paul M. Edwards, "Fort Wadsworth and the Friendly Santee Sioux, 1864–1892," *South Dakota Historical Collections* (Pierre: South Dakota State Historical Society, 1962), 31:99–100. Fort Wadsworth was also called Fort Sisseton. Lounsberry reported that the hunt was near Hawk's Nest, while Buzzard's Roost is claimed as the site by Karen Karie, *Fort Sisseton (Fort Wadsworth) 1864–1889: Our Living Heritage* (Sisseton: South Dakota Department of Game, Fish, and Parks, 1979), 19–22. Both English names refer to the same place, called Hecaoti by the Dakota; Louis Garcia to Laura L. Anderson, January 31, 1994.

pediently and dutifully executed his sister's son, "before my tears should blind me," in what he lamented as "the awfullest moment" of his life.[36] Performing a soldier's duty exacted a new loyalty, as indicated by a note summarizing the action: "To Major Rose [at Fort Wadsworth], this action was an indication of the value of the surrendered Sisseton and Wahpetons and . . . the '100 men of this class now employed as scouts are more valuable for the particular service in which they are engaged than would [be] a regiment of cavalry.'"[37] Every scout, including Peter Oneroad, no doubt felt ambivalent about his new duties.

Peter Oneroad was reported as being the one responsible for bringing the Grass Dance or Omaha Dance to the Dakota in 1869.[38] This dance became the regular "give-away." Euro-Americans believed the dance involved an unreasonably lavish exchange of gifts, encouraged the neglect of individual crops and farms, and was detrimental to accumulation of individual capital and thereby subversive of self-sufficiency. Oneroad and Skinner reported that local lodges conducting the Omaha Society and Grass Dance were established at Enemy Swim Lake, Browns Valley, and the surrounding area. Peter Oneroad was the "kettle charger and server" of the Sisseton order of the Grass Dance, which would have put him at odds with the missionaries and the agents on the reservation if they had been aware of his role.[39]

Peter Oneroad and Nancy Shepherd probably established a home southeast of Drywood Lake sometime before 1876. On July 10, 1897,

36. Jack Campbell was the son of Solomon Two Stars's sister and Scott Campbell. See *Wi-Iyohi*, June 1965, p. 6; Doane Robinson, "The Fight at Webster," *Monthly South Dakotan* 3 (1901): 324–27; and Thomas W. Milroy, "Solomon Two Stars (We-cah-npe-no-pah) Peace Warrior," *Minnesota Archaeologist* 47, no. 2 (1988): 62–63. There is a marker located off U.S. Highway 12 west of Webster, S.Dak., for "The Fight at Webster"; Garcia to Anderson, January 31, 1994.

37. Karie, *Fort Sisseton (Fort Wadsworth)*, last page of Chapter 4.

38. See "Omaha or Grass Dance," page 78, below. This may be one reason that Riggs, in his otherwise thorough documentation of native missionaries, so infrequently mentions Oneroad as a native pastor.

39. Garcia to Anderson, December 13, 1994, included a portion of the Thomas Robertson Manuscript on officers of the "Lodge of the Order of the Grass Dance." The kettle that Peter Oneroad was to charge represented the enemy in the form of a puppy. The officers were: Mahpiyatokahena, keeper of the drum or chief; Peter Renville, James Long, Tamniage, and Cekpa (source of information for Oneroad and Skinner), the four assistants; Zitkansa, Rnumna, Wicakamdece, and Hoksinamaza, the four second assistants; Ohitinaka, kettle charger; Pan, feeder; Wakinyansapa, door opener and keeper; and Canka, Howakisake, Matowanyakapi, Mazainajin, Madusa, and Taniyanna.

Roberts County granted a petition signed by twenty-one legal voters organizing One Road Township. The township was high in the Coteau, about ten miles southwest of Sisseton. The largest lake in the township was named One Road Lake or Wambduska Ota Bde (or Mde) because the family's land was on its shores.[40]

A century after the lifetime of Iŋyaŋgmani, the descendants of the same families, who had appeared in Euro-American accounts, were living together on the Sisseton Reservation in South Dakota. Amos Oneroad's family centered around One Road Lake, Good Will Presbyterian Church, and Sisseton, South Dakota. Although family members moved and lived in other places, it was at the head of the Coteau des Prairies that the heart felt at home.

AMOS ENOS ONEROAD (MAĤPIYASNA)

Amos Enos Oneroad (Maĥpiyasna, Jingling Cloud) was born January 15, 1884, near Drywood Lake. According to his daughters, "At the age of 7 years, in November, 1891, our father was enrolled at the Goodwill Presbyterian Mission School at Agency Village, South Dakota. He told that he had been strongly admonished by his grandfather, Wakaŋto (Blue Holy) and his father to study hard and to learn all that he could."[41] Amos grew up bilingual, in large part because his classes at the mission school were taught in both Dakota and English. Starting October 13, 1895, he attended the Red House (Tipiśa) school at Sisseton Agency.[42] On November 13, 1905, he enrolled at the Haskell Institute in Lawrence, Kansas, graduating in agricultural sciences and practices on June 16, 1909.[43]

40. See "One Road Township," *Sisseton Centennial Yearbook*, 625–26, for notes on petition and formation of the township. This was in Roberts County, some nine miles west of Peever and ten miles southwest of Sisseton. "Wamduska" means "snakes," "ota" means "many," and "mde" (Dakota) or "bde" (Lakota) means "lake" or "lake of many snakes." The Sisseton-Wahpeton and most Eastern Dakota used the Dakota dialect in their own writings until sometime during the 1920–40s when the Lakota dialect became more prominent. This usage is evident in early Dakota letters, including Amos Oneroad's, and the present-day spellings.

41. *Amos E. Oneroad*, 2.

42. Tipiśa or Red House was so called because it was painted a reddish brown, while the government school, built later, was called Tipizi or Yellow House. See H. S. Morris, *Historical Stories, Legends and Traditions: Roberts County and Northeastern South Dakota* (Sisseton, S.Dak.: Sisseton Courier, 1939), 30.

43. *Amos E. Oneroad*, 2.

Amos's education probably included reading the *Iapi Oaye*, a Dakota-language newspaper published by the Presbyterian-run Santee Normal Training School in Santee, Nebraska. Among the articles the newspaper and its English-language counterpart, the *Word Carrier*, published were ones on current ethnology and folklore of the American Indian. Amos might have read Alanson Skinner's 1910 study of the Winnebago, Alice Fletcher's treatise on Indian music, or works by archaeologist Arthur C. Parker (Gawasowaneha). One story was about the visit of an unnamed Dakota to the Indian museum in New York where, he said, he saw more Indian things than he had in his own community in his lifetime.[44]

Sometime after leaving Haskell, Amos, at the urging of his father and grandfather, went to New York City to study. On September 28, 1913, he entered the Bible Teacher's Training School and School of Divinity at Columbia University and graduated May 28, 1917.[45] While in New York, he visited the American Museum of Natural History. The *American Museum Journal* noted: "This young Wahpeton Sioux is in the city studying in the Bible Teachers' Training School. Although only twenty-six years of age he has a surprising amount of knowledge concerning the customs of the Eastern Dakota. Accordingly Mr. Alanson Skinner and Dr. Robert H. Lowie found it profitable to take down from

44. The *Iapi Oaye* was edited by missionary Alfred Riggs. Amos often aided in translating articles for the *Iapi Oaye* and talked about the interplay of missionaries and anthropologists. A. C. Parker's articles on Indian archeology and on government Indian schools appeared in the *Word Carrier* in 1894 and 1910. Parker, a Harvard-educated Iroquois, was the New York State archivist. In 1911 he became one of the first members of the Society of American Indians, founded by Dr. Charles A. Eastman. See Hazel W. Hertzberg, "Indian Rights Movement, 1887–1973," in *Handbook of North American Indians*, Sturtevant and Washburn, ed., 4:306–9.

45. The Bible Teacher's Training School, also called Biblical Theological Seminary, New York Theological Seminary, Union Theological Seminary, and Dr. Whyte's (also White's and Wright's) Bible Institute, held classes first at the Broadway Tabernacle on Broadway and 56th Street in New York City and later at an optician's office across the street from Grand Central Station, between Lexington and 3rd Avenue. The nondenominational Protestant seminary was founded in 1900 as the Bible Teachers College in Montclair, New Jersey, by Wilber Webster White (1863–1944), a minister of the United Presbyterian Church. John Wright was associated with the ecumenical institute in 1921, contributing to the confusion in spelling. It moved to New York City in 1902. See Kenneth T. Jackson, ed., *The Encyclopedia of New York City* (New Haven: Yale University Press, 1995), 846. A 1935 memo on Rev. Amos Oneroad provided by Stephanie Muntone of the Presbyterian Historical Society in Philadelphia stated that he attended for two or three years.

his dictation notes on many subjects of ethnological interest such as war customs, terms of relationship, social usages and ceremonials."[46]

Oneroad was the kind of person an anthropologist hardly expected to find. He was a member of a traditional Sisseton-Wahpeton family, he was not old, he spoke English, he was studying in New York City, and he was sightseeing at the Museum of Natural History. No wonder Lowie and Skinner expressed surprise both at finding young Amos in their midst and that he knew so much about Dakota customs.

Oneroad soon began working with Lowie, Skinner, Parker, Mark Harrington, Harlan Smith, George Bird Grinnell, Melvin Gilmore, George A. Dorsey, and others on "authentic" culture. Oneroad was truly a participant-observer because of his knowledge of the language and his South Dakota connections. He was able to provide descriptions of material items that had none and interpretations of the traditions and tales that lacked them. Perhaps because he was so far from his Sisseton-Wahpeton home, he was able to represent his own culture with the same objective approach that the anthropologists used. He sparked curiosity in many acquaintances; the museum and the YMCA asked him to deliver lectures while dressed in "full Siouan costume."

In 1914 Oneroad and Skinner went on a field expedition for the Museum of Natural History and stayed with Oneroad's family while they investigated Eastern Dakota material culture and collected some folktales. The museum journal noted that, "These people [at Sisseton] ... have given up almost everything that pertained to the old Indian life and are now actively engaged in farming. Some very old and unusual specimens were obtained however from people who had kept them as relics of the past."[47] One member of Oneroad's family recalled that they had the impression that Oneroad and Skinner were earning money through their museum work in order to pay for their classes at Columbia.[48]

While pursuing his education, including taking classes at Columbia University and learning about anthropological fieldwork, Oneroad continued to be involved in church matters on the reservation. He was elected vice president of the Ptaya Owohdake or Dakota Missionary Society in 1914 and was an acting officer in the Itaya Owohdaka, a Santee

46. "Museum Notes," *American Museum Journal* 14 (1914): 119.

47. *American Museum Journal* 15 (1915): 272.

48. Laura L. Anderson interview with Edward Milton Red Owl, Michael I. Selvage, Sr., and John Eagle, January 5, 1994, Sisseton, S.Dak.; *Amos E. Oneroad*, 3.

fellowship. On April 19, 1916, the Dakota Presbytery accepted Amos Oneroad as a candidate for the ministry and ordained and licensed him as a Presbyterian minister on September 8, 1917, following his graduation from the seminary.[49]

In 1916 he joined Skinner in excavating an Indian village at Clason Point and at Throgs Neck in New York. He apparently became a staff member of the Museum of the American Indian, according to a Heye Foundation report.[50] Oneroad's friendship with Skinner, Harrington, and Parker continued to strengthen. From correspondence between them, it appears that it was Skinner who presented his friend Oneroad for membership in the Masonic lodge and that together they socialized in other New York circles as well.

When the United States entered World War I, Oneroad answered the call to serve. His daughters remembered that "with the outbreak of World War I, our father refused to neglect his traditional role and responsibility as an Akićita or warrior, and on June 10, 1918, he enlisted in the 20th Company Ninth Coast Defense Command, New York National Guard, and was honorably discharged on September 18, 1919, in New York City, fulfilling his obligation and duty to his country and people."[51]

While he was on a trip home from New York City, he married Etta R. Ortley on April 23, 1919. The Dakota Presbytery, anticipating his discharge from the service, ordained him to the Office of Evangelist on September 6, 1919, at Santee, Nebraska. In this position, he traveled to Fort Peck, Montana, to Greenwood, Flandreau, and Big Coulee, South

---

AMOS ONEROAD'S FAMILY

Amos Oneroad (Maȟpiyasna, Jingling Cloud) (1884–1937)
    m. Etta Ortley (1896–1922)
1. Wilbert Webster Oneroad (1920)
2. Joel Clinton Oneroad (1922)
    m. Emma Wantawa (1896–1952)
3. Cornelius Oneroad (1927–1973)
4. Arlene Oneroad (1929–)
5. Dorothy Oneroad Ackerman (1931–)
6. Amos Oneroad, Jr. (1934–)

---

49. *Amos E. Oneroad,* 3.
50. *Milwaukee Sentinel,* July 29, 1922.
51. *Amos E. Oneroad,* 3.

Dakota, and to Salt Lake City. Etta and Amos's first child, Wilber Webster, was born in 1920 but died soon after.[52]

At this point, Oneroad and Skinner commenced their project documenting the traditions of the Eastern Dakota. In their personal correspondence, Oneroad and Skinner referred to each other as "Tahaŋ" (brother-in-law).[53] Regarding the relationship, the family remembered:

> We always were told that Amos and his tiospaye (extended family) recognized that Amos had taken Alanson Skinner as his brother. While we do not know whether a special "hunka" or the "making of relatives ceremony was held" (at the time it would have been illegal to do so), as an extended family, we are positive that Amos took Skinner as his brother, and was considered as such, in a family way, by the entire extended family on the Lake Traverse Reservation ... and the name "Alanson" continues even today among the younger generation in our tiospaye.[54]

For the next five years, Oneroad split his time and energies between his employment as a Dakota preacher and his fieldwork with Skinner for the museum. In furthering the work of the Dakota Presbytery as an evangelist, Oneroad's Bible Institute colleagues coordinated with the Riggs family to set up a school to train native preachers. In October 1921 John Wright of the institute announced to Thomas Riggs that Amos Oneroad was at Santee Normal Training School where he would be an interpreter.[55]

---

52. *Amos E. Oneroad*, 3. Amos's cousin, Hazen P. Shepherd married Etta's sister Esther on May 9, 1909. Hazen Shepherd, son of Smiley Shepherd (Itohnakeduta, Red in the Face) and Sarah (Sada) Renville Shepherd and grandson of Gabriel Renville, was the first tribal chairman of the Sisseton-Wahpeton Sioux Tribe in 1946 under provisions of its first written constitution and bylaws. Wilber Webster Oneroad was named for Wilber Webster White, the founder of the Bible college Amos attended in New York City.

53. Correspondence with Amos Oneroad (1922–1926), MS 201, Box 1, Alanson Buck Skinner Collection, Braun Library, Los Angeles.

54. Edward Red Owl to Laura L. Anderson, February 15, 1994. The Oneroad and Skinner relationship is evident in the Oneroad family names. According to the Shepherd family tree transcribed by Edward Milton Red Owl, the grandson of Smiley Shepherd was Alanson Crissey Shepherd (b. 1921), who named his son, Alanson Frank Shepherd (b. 1954), and his daughter, Allyson Christine Shepherd (b. 1950). See also Melvin Gilmore, "The Dakota Ceremony of Hunka," *Indian Notes and Monographs* 16 (Jan. 1929): 75–79.

55. John Wright to Mr. and Mrs. T. L. Riggs from Santee Normal Training School, October 24, 1921, Thomas L. Riggs Papers, Incoming Correspondence, 1873–1940, box 5, South Dakota Conference United Church of Christ Archives, Center for Western

It was at this time that tragedy struck. Etta Oneroad died on May 4, 1922, giving birth to their second child, George (Joel) Clinton, who died later the same year.[56]

By July 1922, Amos Oneroad joined the staff of the Milwaukee Public Museum to assist Skinner, then the curator in the department of anthropology, in preparing a manuscript on the folklore and history of the Sioux Indians. Sometime in 1922, it was announced that Oneroad was appointed the pastor of Ohaihde or the Santee Pilgrim Congregational Church on the Santee Reservation in Nebraska. These were lean years for the Santee Normal Training School as enrollment was low. Wright's Bible Institute was still struggling in their effort to train preachers there, permitting Oneroad's temporary leave in Milwaukee to join Skinner—until Skinner's marriage.

Oneroad then returned to the Santee school as a native preacher. Fred Riggs, director of the school, mentioned that he discussed a Dakota missionary matter with Oneroad—specifically the corrections for the report forms for native preachers. He wrote, "I appreciate the liability of making liars of all these [Indian] preachers ... but if they carry out the requirement of reading this report every month to their church before they send it that will be some check-up on them." Riggs was condescendingly reflecting his concern that native ministers needed an incentive to exemplify moral behavior, in particular the avoidance of liquor and other vices. In the next paragraph he addressed the need to trim the staff and expressed the hope that the Indian part of their church would agree to

> not have an Indian preacher any more but to have the white man who is in charge of the Bible Department here be acting pastor of the church. This job ought not keep two men. It is extravagant and all out of reason. It looks to me as tho we could not afford to have Oneroad any longer than thru this school year. The people never have supported him and they are not satisfied because they do not get enough benefit from what the church contributes toward his

---

Studies, Augustana College, Sioux Falls, S.Dak.; Meyer, *Santee Sioux,* 312. Fred B. Riggs to Thomas A. Riggs, October 24, 1921, Riggs Family Papers. Stephen R. Riggs's sons were Thomas and Alfred; the latter was the founder of Santee Normal Training School and his son Fred was principal of the school.

56. George Clinton Oneroad was listed as an heir of his maternal grandfather, Henry Ortley, along with Amos Oneroad on June 15, 1922; Estate of Henry Ortley, Probate Court Records No. 9358, Department of the Interior, Washington, received by the Office of Indian Affairs May 29, 1922.

salary which is $30 a month during the eight months of the school
year and $55 during the summer months. That is far more than the
church [can] raise, and we came out this last season over a hundred
dollars behind, which the church is trying to make up now.[57]

For his teaching, correspondence school, and translation work,
Oneroad was paid seventy-five dollars a month for a full year. There
was not enough money coming in from Pilgrim Church and the
American Missionary Association to avoid going into debt in order to
pay his salary. Earlier Fred wrote to Thomas Riggs that he and Wright
had concluded that the Presbyterians did not have sufficient funds for
the Bible Institute and that the institute should cancel the training
program.[58]

The missionary effort was suffering from more than a lack of funds.
Native preachers felt that they were not regarded as equals by the
white missionaries. As one observer stated: "I confess it is a mystery to
me how you folks [the missionaries] can actually have given your lives
to the Indian and yet be constantly suspicious of him, not trust him,
and limit his possibilities by your attitude of pessimism."[59] Secretary
Brownlee of the Dakota Missionary Society suggested that the next
mission council should address the issue of race relations, specifically
superiority and inferiority complexes and the use of native leadership.

During this missionary debate, Oneroad continued a lively correspondence with his anthropologist friends. Writing Skinner from
Santee on March 20, 1924, Oneroad mentioned that he had a "nice letter from Geo Bird Grinnel." Grinnell had also sent his paper on the im-
migration of the Cheyennes, "which was good." In May he wrote that
he had finished reading two "good" books on the Dakota, one by
Samuel W. Pond and one by James W. Lynd, commenting that they
both "spoke like Dakotas."[60]

Oneroad also discussed his work with Skinner: "In reference to that
manuscript ["Traditions of the Wahpeton Dakota Indians," their Milwaukee collaboration] I would rather have you write the preface to
the paper, which counts a great deal for one who knows as much of Indian lore, but don't get mixed up with my Ihaŋktoŋwaŋ ancestor, part

57. Fred B. Riggs to Thomas L. Riggs, January 12, 1925, Riggs Family Papers.
58. Fred B. Riggs to Thomas L. Riggs, May 6, 1925, Riggs Family Papers.
59. Fred B. Riggs to Thomas L. Riggs, February 4, 1925, Riggs Family Papers.
60. Oneroad to Skinner, March 20 and May 24, 1924, Skinner Collection. See James
W. Lynd, "History of the Dakotas," *Minnesota Collections* (St. Paul: Minnesota Historical Society, 1889), 2:7–88; Pond, *Dakota or Sioux in Minnesota*.

Sisseton I suppose Wakaŋto [Blue Spirit], and Jingling Cloud [Maḣpi-yasna] is a Wahpetonwaŋ."[61] Of course, Skinner was conscious of the implications of linking these ancestors, and Oneroad was probably teasing Skinner.

Oneroad's letters were always good natured. He quipped that he wished he were out somewhere with Skinner digging up old heads again and finding some good relics. Then he joked that a friend's buffalo bull must have been a wiŋkta "so there is no calf yet."

At this time Oneroad clearly was on the lookout for a wife. He had previously told Skinner about Dr. Charles Frazier's daughter from Bazile church. Apparently the girl and her mother were willing that Oneroad court her, but her father objected.[62]

Oneroad wrote Skinner in July 1924 telling him of a trip home to Sisseton from Santee and reported on the events surrounding a reservation council held at Sisseton. Oneroad was to be one of the Sisseton-Wahpeton delegates to go to Washington to interview the commissioner of Indian affairs about moving the agency back to its former location and to see about the claims of the Sisseton and Wahpeton. He informed Skinner that when he came to Washington "I'll want you and [Arthur C.] Parker to be there to give me a few pointers."[63]

Skinner in responding to Oneroad's news also sent an article by Herbert S. Welsh, president of the Indian Rights Association, on the Pueblo Indian rites. "It is not as bad as many of the articles which have

61. Oneroad referred specifically to Skinner's publications on Native American folklore (1912, 1913, 1915 Menomini; 1914 Central Algonkin; 1916 Ojibway; 1916 Plains Cree) and reminded him that Maḣpiyasna's side of the family was Wahpetonwaŋ and that Wakaŋto was both Sisseton and Ihaŋktoŋwaŋ; Oneroad to Skinner, May 24, 1925, Skinner Collection.

62. Skinner ran afoul of Frazier by criticizing Bushnell's work, which Frazier advised, and through a journal quarrel with Truman Michelson on the reliability of information sources (Oneroad worked with Skinner and Frazier with Michelson).

63. Oneroad to Skinner, July 28, 1924, Skinner Collection. The old agency, about nine miles south of Sisseton, was the site chosen by the Dakota in 1869, rather than Brown's post at Lake Traverse or Sisseton or Fort Wadsworth (Sisseton). The agency was moved to Sisseton early in the 1920s. The Sisseton-Wahpeton based their claims on not having taken an active part in the 1862 war and therefore they should not have been deprived of their share of annuities according to the terms of the treaty of Traverse des Sioux (1851). The claims were settled in 1907 with payments to begin in 1909, but discussion on the issue continued. See Folwell, *History of Minnesota*, 2:418–37. Parker, the 1923 chairman of the Committee of One Hundred, advised Secretary of the Interior Hubert Work, who faced powerful criticism from the Indian rights movement.

been recently served to the public," wrote Skinner. He also enclosed the reply of "our Mr. [Frederick W.] Hodge. I suggest that you translate into Dakota . . . this article by Hodge, in full." Skinner had much to say on the topic.

> You probably know that there has been recently a very great deal of propaganda against the ancient rites of the Indian people, which has been promulgated by the Indian Bureau, and by various individuals connected with religious, semi-religious, and pseudo-religious organizations, one of the most violent traducers of the Indians being Miss Dabb of the Y.W.C.A. I do not know exactly your feeling with regard to the ancient rites, since you are of course interested in the propagation of Christianity, but I do know that, as a man and a Christian, you are interested in seeing that the Indian, both old and new, is not lied about in the public press. Only the other day a Mr. Edward A. Shields, field secretary of the Brotherhood of St. Andrew, was in to see me, having recently returned from Sisseton, and he had various things to say about the Dakotas whom he *professed* to admire. He tried to assure me that in the Indian dances the Dakota women took off their clothes and danced naked. This I consider a slur on Dakota womanhood, and know it to be absolutely false. Something simply must be done to counteract this sort of propaganda. The old-time Indian dances and ceremonies are rapidly disappearing, and many of them have no place in modern life, which the Indians realize, and, with the passing of the older generation, these ceremonies will naturally cease. On the other hand, many are beautiful and worthy of perpetuation, because they stimulate in the American Indian the pride of race which, for political reasons, has been almost taken from him by the Government. . . .
>
> Whatever may be one's feelings about these ancient ceremonies, no-one, whether or not in favor of them, can really approve of the systematic campaign of lying and defamation of character which is being carried on against the Indian throughout our country. It hurts the Indian in every way, and you know, and I know, that, from our own contact with the Indians, there are no immoral, obscene, nor degrading ceremonies practised by them in North America.[64]

Oneroad replied that he did not know who the clergy were or who Shields was or about the nude dances of Dakota women. He called the

---

64. Skinner to Oneroad, October 29, 1924, Skinner Collection. Fredrick W. Hodge edited the *Handbook of the North American Indians North of Mexico*, 2 vols., Smithsonian Institution, Bureau of American Ethnology Bulletin no. 30 (Washington, D.C.: GPO), 1907–10. Welsh was one of the founders of the Indian Rights Association in 1882.

accusation "absurd and ridiculous." He had once heard of one who came "almost naked," but she was under the influence of liquor, and Oneroad blamed the mniwakan or spirit water.

Oneroad's letters to Skinner in 1924, especially one of November 1, 1924, make it clear that he alone was collecting the "specimens" or Sisseton-Wahpeton artifacts for the Heye. He informed Skinner that several items were on the way, gave a detailed list of them, and stated from whom he received each one. He also put a price on each one. He believed he got them "pretty cheap" except for the weasel, which was seventy dollars, plus fifteen dollars for expenses. He remarked on the fact that he and Skinner had collected "so many Treedwellers." Furthermore, Oneroad suspected that the treedweller with a hat on was a fake, but the one from his grandmother, Hannah Shepherd, was genuine. Oneroad noted that the one from Huhazizi was really a mdoka.[65] He listed other items from Huhazizi: the treedweller, hawk, squirrel, loon, weasel ("are to act and scream in their own characteristics as known in the Grandmedicine dances"), fisher, and otter.

Oneroad and Skinner succeeded in bringing Oneroad's grandfather's traditional sacred religious objects to the Heye Museum to be stored and kept safe, rather than risk their being destroyed.[66] It was not just that the tiyospaye came to trust Skinner so that they willingly gave him what they ordinarily might have withheld. It was also that he respected Oneroad and became his facilitator. Skinner allowed Oneroad's voice to dominate the collection, adding only occasional commentary. Skinner put the artifacts he found in Oneroad's name, subverting the destruction of everything traditional by using the system in place— museums and anthropology.

While still working at Santee, Oneroad wrote Skinner of his recent encounter with anthropologist Melvin Gilmore. Oneroad was relieved that Gilmore had gone on to the Pawnee. He quipped to Skinner:

65. "The father of Huhazizi was a member of the medicine lodge and from him he learned and inherited all the mystical rites and ceremonies. . . . This one of Huhazizi's I am willing to take my hat off, because [it is] really a M DOKA [male animal] as you will see from its penis and testicals[.] I wish that Realred could have seen it and after that he won't think himself that he is not the only mdoka living, there are some real men left among the Wahpetonwan people." Oneroad indicated that these articles were used for the last time in 1894. Oneroad to Skinner, November 1, 1924, Skinner Collection.

66. The family maintains that the objects included his grandfather's sacred healing altar, pipe, and other related religious objects; *Amos E. Oneroad*, 2.

You said it he is a queer man maybe he belongs to the Redfox clan, he critised [criticised] words before I gave my explanations, we had an item for the Iapi Oaye sent in by John Roberts Iŋyaŋgmani about the old boundary. He wanted this item in English, it was very simple. it is understood by the old Indians what that boundary is, well he wanted to make something out of it that was not in Indian and I won't do it his way and we could not agree on it[.] he tried to make a stone of the first part of Iŋyaŋgmani. that got my goat. . . . I would like to come and work with you again. Do you really want me to come?[67]

Oneroad closed the letter by wishing he could visit Parker in Albany with Skinner or could join Harrington and his "Digger Indians" out in Nevada. He was anxious to hear what Skinner thought of the Wahpetoŋwaŋ medicine bags and was proud of the treedweller in particular. He ended a 1925 letter by telling Skinner he received a letter from Harrington and that he would like to be with him "breaking pots."

In contrast to Skinner who had great respect for Oneroad's knowledge, other anthropologists and the missionaries repeatedly expressed doubts about Oneroad's abilities. Oneroad not only had to contend with anthropological "authorities" like Gilmore, but also with missionaries like Fred Riggs. Riggs argued with Oneroad over correct translations and wrote to his uncle Thomas Riggs for a definitive decision. "Mr. Oneroad tells me a wording which I do not believe is at all right," wrote Fred. Then he asked Thomas if it was "Awaŋyakapi kiŋ" or "Awaŋyaŋka . . . with or without the 'kiŋ.'"[68]

On April 21, 1925, Fred Riggs wrote Thomas Riggs that the school at Santee was becoming a big burden. He was surprised on Sunday when Oneroad suddenly resigned from the Santee Normal Training School and left on Tuesday, April 14, after three years. "No reason given but that his family at Sisseton needed him. I think Oneroad came in on the sale of some land lately and he has a job in prospect with the American Museum next summer."[69] In fact, Oneroad's sudden decision was due to the death of his older brother Jack. Oneroad returned to Sisseton in order to replace Jack in caring for their aged

67. Oneroad to Skinner, November 1, 1924, Skinner Collection. Gilmore had segmented the morphemes of Iŋyaŋgmani incorrectly into Iŋyaŋ-g-mani, "stone-Ø-walker" instead of Iŋyaŋg-mani, "running-walker."

68. Fred Riggs to Thomas Riggs, December 29, 1924, Riggs Family Papers.

69. Fred Riggs to Thomas Riggs, April 21, 1925, Riggs Family Papers.

mother. At best, Fred's attitude toward Amos conveyed skepticism if not antipathy.[70]

In January 1925, Oneroad was part of a Ohnide okodakiciye or traveling ministerial fellowship. The *Iapi Oaye* reported on the sermons he delivered.[71] He filled in at Goodwill Church for his brother Charles.[72] He was elected president of the Santee Wayawa Ommiciye Itananpi kte or the Santee Alumni Association and served as an officer until the 1930s. By the fall of 1925 Oneroad expected to take a position in connection with the Museum of the American Indian, according to the *Iapi Oaye*.

In August 1925, Oneroad and Skinner took a trip to Devils Lake Reservation to research and secure items for the Heye Foundation. As Oneroad drove the Ford touring car along the muddy road near Tokio, North Dakota, it suddenly slipped over the edge of the grade, toppled over, and crashed down the embankment.[73] Oneroad crawled from the wreck and tried to free Skinner, who was pinned beneath the car. But Skinner's head was crushed, and he died instantly.

Members of Amos Oneroad's family reflected on the Oneroad-Skinner collaboration:

> At the time of Skinner and One Road's collecting, whether of artifacts or stories, our current understanding of these efforts is this: interests and motivations of the Heye Museum and others speaks for itself, however One Road was yet in training and school to be a minister and had to have a source of livelihood, hence his job was primarily financially motivated; however, being a true Dakota, he no doubt was fully aware of the official ban against possessing religious artifacts as well as promoting the stories and instructions from the former way of life, hence we posit that One Road collected and told the stories as a preservation effort.... although both church

70. *Word Carrier*, May-June 1925. Oneroad was replaced at Santee by Rev. Charles Frazier. Perhaps the conflict between Frazier and Skinner in anthropology influenced even Fred Riggs.

71. *Iapi Oaye*, February 1925.

72. Charles Wahacankato (Blue Shield) Oneroad (1867–1957) was the eldest of Amos's brothers. Arlene One Road, Amos's daughter, had no knowledge of Charles ever being a minister at Goodwill. She thought perhaps he was an elder of the church instead.

73. *Devils Lake* (Tokio, N.Dak.) *Daily Journal*, August 18, 1925, p. 1. Louis Garcia, historian for the Devils (Spirit) Lake Sioux Tribe, reported that "locals say he was fooling with the Wakanwacipi stuff and the spirits did him in"; Garcia to Laura L. Anderson, December 16, 1992.

and federal agency were in opposition to any action of preservation, since both active and controlling institutions on the reservation were committed to christianizing and civilizing the Sisseton and Wahpeton people. For those families who "sold" artifacts or stories to Skinner and One Road had a dilemma: either to hide their artifacts and suppress their stories, or give them to Skinner and One Road and receive payment for the artifacts and stories. The alternative definitely was one of eradicating the artifacts (considered as "heathen" idols preventing the christianization and civilization of the people) by the christian missionaries and this initiative was supported by the agents at Sisseton Agency. Any family at the time, faced with hard economic times, the memories of a lost way of life, and food to be purchased, understandably would agree to sell objects, since such objects if found in one's possession could be confiscated and destroyed by the Agent's Indian Police.[74]

After Alanson Skinner's death, going to the Heye was no longer an option for Oneroad. Skinner had been a manager for their agenda, a commentator on the collection, and a tutor, but the unpublished text was Oneroad's. Their eleven-year collaborative efforts—the manuscript drafted on the Eastern Dakota—fell into limbo. It is ironic, but logical, that, except for the 1919 piece, the only articles Skinner published on the Dakota were on the Sun Dance, the treedwellers, and the Medicine Dance. Skinner's topics were the ones that were the most sensitive and deemed "heathenish" by the white public. Yet these were the very ones most precious to the Dakota. According to the List of Indian Offenses, these were also the ones for which Oneroad would have been penalized for perpetuating during the years of repression on the reservations. But these were also the materials on "the vanishing race" the ethnologists urgently pursued for preservation.

In the light of Skinner's prolific publication record on other groups, this seems to have been their plan—to facilitate Oneroad in preserving what he revealed and to forestall repercussions and deflect further condemnation concerning the sensitive issues. It was not that the Dakota would not disclose their traditions to the earnest seeker. Instead it was that the fervor of white acculturation censured firsthand knowledge in order to disrupt the continued practice of native traditions. Yet ironically, it allowed for second- or third-person recounting of traditional tales if filtered through the world view of white society. Skinner and Oneroad worked to get around these restrictions.

74. Red Owl to Laura L. Anderson, February 15, 1994.

Unfortunately for Oneroad, Skinner's final will allowed S. A. Barrett, Mark Harrington, and Arthur Parker to divide his anthropological library equally. The Oneroad-Skinner manuscript ended up in Harrington's possession. Whether any of these men intended to complete the manuscript and failed or if they lost touch with Oneroad or if they ran out of time is not known. Regardless of the reason, the manuscript remained unfinished.

Turning his focus to his own life, Amos Oneroad married Emma Wantawa on January 15, 1926—his birthday.[75] Next, he accepted a call to Uno, Manitoba, to do missionary work among the Dakota people who were exiles from the United States. The *Iapi Oaye* printed letters between families anxious to renew ties disrupted by the 1862 war.[76] Oneroad's letters from Uno conveyed news of descendants and the deaths of some of the elders. His salary was raised to eighteen hundred dollars per year. He also received traveling expenses to minister to two other Manitoba stations, one at Pipestone and the other at Portage la Prairie.

In August 27, 1926, he wrote to Dorothy P. Skinner, Alanson's widow, in Oshkosh, Wisconsin, to invite her to visit. He mentioned he had not heard from Skinner's parents or Harrington, asked if she would "send those papers [the manuscript] on to me," and wondered if Harrington was in New York or out west. Oneroad still had back pain and trouble with his right ear as a result of the accident. He announced to Dorothy that he and his wife were expecting a baby and signed the letter, "your brother, Amos Oneroad." William Cornelius Guy Oneroad was born in 1927.[77]

By 1928 Oneroad had returned to South Dakota. His work finally settled around a congregation at Greenwood, South Dakota. A year later, he was appointed to the Yankton Agency church in Greenwood. Amos and Emma's first daughter, Arlene, was born there. On April 25, 1931, a second daughter, Dorothy Nancy, was born and named after Skinner's widow and his own mother.

At the Yankton Agency church, Oneroad seemed to resolve what had been reported as severe factional disputes. According to church

75. There is a four-year discrepancy between white documentation and the family's record of Amos Oneroad's age. The family records show Amos as being older; *Amos E. Oneroad* and information from Presbyterian Historical Society.

76. Peter Douglas Elias, *The Dakota of the Canadian Northwest: Lessons for Survival* (Winnipeg: University of Manitoba Press, 1988).

77. Oneroad to Dorothy Skinner, August 27, 1926, Skinner Collection.

records, "Congregational troubles were causing very serious friction in that flock, previous to this appointment of Rev. Oneroad. He has done fine work in this church. In May 1934, he was called to Flandreau, but Yankton Agency church succeeded in having him returned to them in October. This, in itself, is a good recommendation."[78] He soon became the pastor of Cedar and Hill churches, in addition to the church at Yankton Agency, and his territory ranged from Yankton to Wagner to Greenwood. At one time, he referred to Greenwood as "the remnant," presumably of his people after the scattering due to the 1862 conflict.

In September 1933, Oneroad began writing to John Collier, commissioner of Indian affairs, regarding the need of the Sisseton-Wahpeton bands to govern their own affairs as opposed to the federal domination of tribal business. "He drafted in both the Dakota and English languages documents for a Constitution and By Laws for the Tribe wherein authorities would be vested in the people," according to his daughters. "Such efforts met stiff resistance in the local Bureau of Indian Affairs Agency, yet undaunted he would petition intervention from Washington, D.C. Self-governance would not come to his people; however, his early efforts served as proto-type for later initiatives in self governance." He attended the Plains Congress of all the Sioux tribes held in Rapid City, South Dakota, on March 4, 1934. There he reviewed the Wheeler-Howard Act (Indian Reorganization Act), which he vehemently opposed.[79] The Sisseton and Crow Creek Reservations were the only Sioux reservations to reject the act. These two reservations eventually reorganized under approved tribal charters or constitutions.[80]

Throughout 1935, Amos Oneroad lobbied South Dakota Senator Peter Norbeck about obtaining congressional appropriations for the construction of Indian hospitals on the Yankton, Crow Creek, and Sisseton Reservations. Norbeck on occasion referred the composition of letters

78. Memo in the biographic file on Rev. Amos Oneroad, Greenwood, S.Dak., February 1935, provided by the Presbyterian Historical Society. A family photo of "Rev. and Mrs. Amos One Road, William Cornelius Guy, age 6, Arlene Helen, age 3, Dorothy Nancy, age 1, and adopted daughter Esther Nancy, niece of Mrs. Oneroad" was stapled to the letter.

79. *Amos E. Oneroad*, 4.

80. Nationally, 181 tribes voted to accept the IRA, and 77 voted against it. See Herbert S. Schell, *History of South Dakota* (Lincoln: University of Nebraska Press, 1968), 338.

to Oneroad as he had a high regard for Oneroad's level of education and verbal ability.[81] "He [Oneroad] often remarked to us that the government had prohibited by law and policy the practice of traditional religious healing practices among the Dakota people, yet the government would not provide medical nor health care facilities for his people. During his years in New York City, he had visited many hospitals and clinics and had been impressed with their operations, hence he felt that his people were entitled to the same quality care."[82] The government eventually built hospitals as a result of his efforts, and Arlene Oneroad, his daughter, worked at the hospital in Sisseton for more than thirty years.

Amos Enos Oneroad died on July 28, 1937, at the age of fifty-three. He was buried in Greenwood, South Dakota, at the request of his congregation rather than at home in Sisseton.[83] His daughters remember that "he tried very hard to meet the challenges of his times without fear, and in his associations with the rich and famous as well as the poorest of the poor, he did so in comfort and ease, having a special understanding for the human condition." His family said he was an Ikce Wićaśa or a common spiritual man. In one of his 1915 sermons entitled "Man Is Immortal," Amos said, "Truth is. Truth must be, will be discerned eventually, by everybody."[84]

ALANSON BUCK SKINNER

Alanson Buck Skinner was born in Buffalo, New York, on September 7, 1886, to Rachel Amelia Sumner Skinner and Frank Woodward Skinner, a civil engineer. He spent his childhood on Staten Island, New York. There he met William T. Davis, an archaeologist who taught him to find arrowheads and other traces of ancient Indian life. Davis became his lifelong friend and turned him toward the study of natural science, knowledge that greatly influenced his life.[85]

In pursuing this interest, Skinner sought out men associated with

81. Dorothy One Road Ackerman provided information on her father in a phone interview, December 9, 1993, and in a meeting, November 8, 1996, in Portland, Ore.
82. *Amos E. Oneroad*, 5.
83. Interview with Arlene One Road, January 4, 1994, in Sisseton, S.Dak.
84. *Amos E. Oneroad*, 5.
85. William T. Davis was an author and member of the National Science Association of Staten Island. Skinner cited his articles in "The Lenape Indians of Staten Island," *Anthropological Papers of the American Museum of Natural History* 3 (1909): 3–62.

the American Museum of Natural History. He listened to the advice of Professor Frederic Ward Putnam, head curator of anthropology at the museum, and became a friend of Harlan I. Smith and George H. Pepper.[86] During his teen years, he assisted Mark R. Harrington, then engaged in archaeological work in New York Bay. While on vacation from school in 1902, Skinner began working for the museum on a regular basis. He joined Arthur C. Parker and Harrington in the excavation of an ancient shell heap near Shinnecock Hills, Long Island. From then on, Parker and Skinner were friends.[87] Skinner accompanied Harrington on an archaeological excursion to western New York State in 1904 on behalf of the Peabody Museum at Harvard University. This trip was his introduction to ethnology; at Cattaraugus he visited his first Indian reservation, which was a Seneca settlement, and attended his first native ceremony.

After high school, Skinner tried a commercial position but ultimately returned to the work he had grown to love. He moved to Tompkinsville, New York, where he had unearthed Lanape Indian (Delaware Confederacy) excavation sites during his teens on an archaeological survey of Staten Island. Because of his intimate knowledge of the local problems and his excavation of many important sites, the museum brought the nineteen-year-old into the department of ethnology as a staff member in 1907; he stayed until 1916. He also contributed his series of specimens collected that year in Ontario, Livingston, and Erie Counties in New York from sites formerly occupied by the Seneca and Neutral Iroquoian Indians.[88]

86. Frederic W. Putnam had been the curator of the Peabody Museum of American Archeology and Ethnology at Harvard University. He organized the department for the World's Columbian Exposition held in Chicago in 1894 where he planned the United States' first public museum for anthropology, the American Museum of Natural History. His assistant was Franz Boas, whom he brought with him when he became part-time curator of anthropology at the museum. Ralph W. Dexter, "Non-Indian Biographies," in *Handbook of North American Indians*, 4:677; "Museum Notes," *American Museum Journal* 16 (1916): 74, 139.

87. Frederic Ward Putnam's students included Franz Boas, Roland Dixon, George A. Dorsey, Alice C. Fletcher, G. B. Gordon, Mark R. Harrington, Aleš Hrdlička, A. L. Kroeber, Charles W. Mead, Warren K. Moorhead, Arthur C. Parker, George H. Pepper, Harlan I. Smith, and Marshal H. Saville. See *American Museum Journal* 15 (1915): 315. Of these students, Boas and Saville worked with Skinner at Columbia, and Dixon worked with Skinner at Harvard. The others were colleagues at the museum and in the profession. Letters between Skinner and Parker are in the Skinner Collection.

88. "Museum Notes," *American Museum Journal* 7 (1907): 118.

In 1908 Skinner became a member of the New York branch of the American Folklore Society. Most ethnologists or anthropologists interested in Indians or indigenous peoples were members of the society. Robert Lowie and Roland Dixon served as presidents of the society, and Franz Boas was the editor of the *Journal of American Folklore.* Lowie was at the Museum of Natural History, Dixon at Harvard, and Boas at Columbia. To this preservationist group, folklore presented another way to collect artifacts of an indigenous society.

Skinner began his fieldwork for the museum in 1908, leading an expedition to Hudson Bay to study the Cree Indians. He also collected anthropological data and specimens in the James Bay region, particularly among the tribes of Labrador. A year later, he made a second trip to Hudson Bay and his first visits to sites in Wisconsin and on Manhattan Island. The museum department of anthropology installed an exhibit of specimens collected by Skinner during the summer of 1908 among the Winnebago, Ojibwe, and Cree Indians. On Christmas Day 1909, the museum sponsored a Skinner lecture on his study of the Naskapi, entitled "By Canoe to Hudson Bay." The journal ran a full account of the expedition.[89]

On his return to Wisconsin in 1910, he met John V. Satterlee, a "half-blood" Menomini, who informally adopted Skinner as his nephew. Not long thereafter, Judge Sabatis Perrote, a "full-blood," formally adopted Skinner into the Menomini under the Thunder-clan name of Sekosa or Little Weasel. Skinner later credited Satterlee's advice and teachings for his successful fieldwork with Indians.

Museums were moving toward a goal of public education and advancement of science and redirected their efforts toward an active program of collecting, research, scientific publication, and public education. Boas, as a professor at Columbia, turned the tide of developing anthropology from the theory of "evolutionary development" or society evolving from lower-undeveloped traits to higher-developed ones to a detailed study of customs in their relation to the total culture of the tribe practicing them. An investigation of the geographical distribution of customs among neighboring tribes aimed to detect historical causes that led to the development of the customs.

In a vast test of Boasian method and theory, Clark Wissler marshaled the ethnological resources of the American Museum of Natural History in an "effort to determine the origins and spread of the Sun

89. *American Museum Journal* 8 (1908): 78, 93; 9 (1909): 143, 259, 261.

Dance and military society complexes" among the Plains Indians. Thus Skinner went to the Dakota in Canada and the United States, Wallis to the Dakota in Canada, following Lowie to the Dakota in general, and Goddard to the Cree.[90] Skinner produced studies in rapid succession on the Menomini, Ojibwe, Oneida, Winnebago, Eastern Dakota, Bungi, Seminole, and Plains Cree.

At the same time Skinner continued his professional education. He enrolled at Columbia and studied under Boas and Marshal H. Saville, as well as Livingston Farrand and Aldoph Francis Alphonse Bandelier. He held a fellowship in anthropology from 1911 to 1912 at Harvard where he worked with Roland Dixon, another Putnam student, Alfred M. Tozzer, and D. Farabee. In 1911 Skinner published his comparative sketch of the Menomini in the *American Anthropologist* and an article on Menomini war customs.[91]

The American Museum of Natural History lent Skinner to the state of New Jersey for a few months in 1912 to be in charge of a statewide archaeological survey. That same year he was elected the honorary curator of anthropology of the Staten Island Association of Arts and Sciences.[92] On October 16, 1912, the executive committee appointed Skinner the assistant curator of the department of anthropology at the museum. The *American Anthropologist* published Skinner's article, "Traces of the Stone Age Among the Eastern and Northern Tribes." In this article Skinner pointed out that most archaeologists did not sufficiently realize that stone was not the only material worked by the aborigines of the stone age.[93]

90. E. Adamson Hoebel, "The Influence of Plains Ethnography on the Development of Anthropological Theory," in *Anthropology on the Great Plains,* Wood and Liberty, ed., 17–18. See Skinner, "A Sketch of Eastern Dakota Ethnology," *American Anthropologist,* n.s., 21 (1919): 164–74; "Sun Dance of the Sisseton Dakota," *Anthropological Papers of the American Museum of Natural History* 16 (1919): 383–85; "Medicine Ceremony of the Menomini, Iowa and Wahpeton Dakota," *Indian Notes and Monographs* 4 (1920): 262–305; and "Tree-dweller Bundle of the Wahpeton Dakota," *Indian Notes* 2 (1925): 66–73.

91. Skinner, "War Customs of the Menomini Indians," and "A Comparative Sketch of the Menomini," *American Anthropologist* 13 (1911): 299–312, 551–65. This was Skinner's first article with this journal, then edited by Swanton and Radin with Boas, Putnam, and Wissler on the editorial committee. Editors in the years following included Hodge, Lowie, Goddard, Speck, and Gifford. These relationship benefited Skinner's access to publication.

92. *American Museum Journal* 12 (1912): 217, 319.

93. *American Anthropologist* n.s., 14 (1912): 391–95.

At the American Anthropological Association council in 1913, Skinner and Herbert J. Spinden discussed the folklore of the Tewa and the Menomini. That year the museum reported that Skinner was making collections for the museum among the Western Ojibwe of Long Plains, Manitoba. After the four-month-long "collecting trip," he reported on his "study of the 'Bungi' in Manitoba . . . a name not heretofore appearing in ethnographical literature." He found out that several of the Bungi resided on the Turtle Mountain Reservation in North Dakota.[94]

Skinner's first article in the *Journal of American Folklore*, entitled "European Folk-Tales Collected among the Menominee Indians," appeared in 1913.[95] "Some Aspects of the Folk-lore of the Central Algonkin" followed the next year.[96] The same issue included articles by Boas and T. T. Waterman on myth and lore of the North American Indian. Waterman pointed out that no two tribes had been more important historically than the Sioux and the Iroquois and yet they were the least known, an observation Skinner no doubt noted, and emphasized the vitality of folklore that remained "in process of formation." He reported that only fourteen Dakota tales were recorded for such an important Plains tribe.[97] In other articles in this volume, Radin, Boas, and Goldenweiser quoted Skinner concerning folklore and the Menomini to support the "in process" claim. In 1914 Skinner published four articles on the Plains Cree, the Plains Objiwe, the Bungi, and the Algonkian.

An item in the "Museum Notes" section of the journal reported that it was Skinner's duty to give children's lectures, and he also spoke before the Linnean Society of New York on the Cree and Objibwe of Saskatchewan. Skinner worked amid the 1914 energy set in motion by Edward S. Curtis's "A Plea for Haste in Making Documentary Record of the American Indian" and Boas's presentation on Athabascan mythology.[98]

In this same year of hectic activity, Skinner and Lowie discovered Amos Oneroad, who was on a visit to the museum. Both men "found it profitable to take down from his dictation notes on many subjects of ethnological interest such as war customs, terms of relationship, social

94. *American Museum Journal* 13 (1913): 152, 240, 288; *American Anthropologist* n.s., 15 (1913): 63–77, 689.

95. *Journal of American Folklore* 26 (1913): 64–80.

96. *Journal of American Folklore* 27 (1914): 97–100.

97. *Journal of American Folklore* 27 (1914): 1–54, 374–410.

98. *American Museum Journal* 14 (1914): 47, 78, 107, 137, 163, 189.

usages and ceremonials."[99] Shortly after that, Skinner and Oneroad made a field trip to Sisseton, staying with Oneroad's family.

In 1915, Skinner, now rising in the fields of archaeology, ethnology, and folklore, joined members of the Museum of the American Indian, Heye Foundation, taking charge of an archaeological expedition to Costa Rica. He also maintained a frantic publishing pace. The next year Lowie and Skinner completed five publication reports on their fieldwork among the Indians. Lowie concentrated on the Ute and Shoshone, while Skinner worked on aspects of the Iowa, Kansa, and Ponca tribes. These pieces appeared in a special volume of the *Anthropological Papers*, "treating the societies and social organizations of the Plains Indians in an exhaustive manner."

In addition to these publications, Skinner reviewed four authors for the *American Anthropologist*. In the review of Louis Spence's *Myths of the North American Indians*, Skinner concluded that the author's comments were sometimes erroneous, open to objection, misused standard terms, and omitted standard authorities. Second, he reviewed the British scholars Barbara Freire-Marreco and John Linton Myres and discovered that they were unaware of such sources as Dorsey, Wissler, and Dixon. Skinner further pointed out that they had "preconceived ideas of what the ethnology of the 'Red Indian' should be," which biased their selection of sources. This essay echoed Boas's distrust of armchair anthropology. Third, Skinner reviewed Arthur Parker's book on the Seneca prophet, saying he found it partly misleading and lacking conclusions but it was well researched and good overall. That Skinner was reviewing works by prominent anthropologists indicated the level of professional status he had achieved. In this same volume, Leslie Spier reviewed Skinner's work on the Indians of greater New York, calling it "concise," "clearing," "an excellent account," "invaluable," "unified," and "consistent." This year had been Skinner's most visible in the journals. He was publishing articles, reviewing peers, and having his activities reported in the museum, anthropology, and folklore journals.[100]

His relationships and his record brought Skinner into the politics of the profession in 1915. He was elected assistant secretary of the American Folklore Society under the leadership of Pliny I. Goddard, George Lyman Kittredge, Jesse Walter Fewkes, and Charles Peabody.

99. *American Museum Journal* 14 (1914): 119.

100. *American Anthropologist* n.s., 17 (1915): 577–81, 341, 180–84, 185–87, 581; *American Museum Journal* 15 (1915): 85, 86, 88, 262, 272, 315.

That year the *Journal of American Folklore* published his article on the Menomini word "Hawatuk." The next year Skinner published an article on European tales from the Plains Ojibwe and another on tales of the Plains Cree.[101]

During these years, journal debates were brewing concerning theory and method. Lowie "protested against the acceptance of oral traditions as historical records."[102] Also, members of the profession reevaluated the focus on origin, type, and dissemination and proposed new goals. Simultaneously, the research focus turned more to the folklore of the borderland countries of the United States and of Europe, coincident with World War I.

Skinner presented his final paper at the Museum of Natural History on "Chronological Relations of Coastal Algonkian Culture" in 1916. That same year he resigned his position to accept a similar one at the Museum of the American Indian, Heye Foundation.

The museum community had provided Skinner with a multidisciplinary environment, and ethnology became an intrinsic part of his work. Harrington later said Skinner believed the study of archaeology necessitated an understanding of the living Indians, and, in consequence, he acquired the field techniques of the ethnologist. It was as an ethnologist, Harrington believed, that he would best be remembered.[103]

The Heye Foundation, in conjunction with the Hispanic Society of America, sponsored concentrated studies in South America. Skinner, along with S. K. Lothrop and former mentor Marshall H. Saville, was sent south. His new job took him to eastern Costa Rica, where he investigated deep tombs in the region of Las Mercedes, and to the Talamanca frontier of Panama.[104]

Skinner's work in journals reveals his concerns with data accuracy and collection methods in the changing and growing field of anthropology. For the *American Anthropologist* in 1916, Skinner reviewed Max Schrabisch's work on Indian habitation in Sussex County, New Jersey, as interesting but lacking the measurement and data of Spier and Harrington's archaeology. J. P. B. de Josselin de Jong praised Skinner in the same issue for not "normalizing his spelling" of representational native language material. However, de Jong claimed Skinner was uninformed on the methodology of using an informant and urged Skinner

101. *Journal of American Folklore* 28 (1915) :258–61, 417; 29 (1916): 330–40, 341–67.
102. *Journal of American Folklore* 30 (1917): 161–67.
103. *American Museum Journal* 26 (1926): 101.
104. *American Anthropologist* n.s., 18 (1916): 619.

to record the informant and provide the transcription. The Dutch reviewer also asked whether statements made were based on information from the informant or on experiences of the author himself. Methods of research and presentation of results were being revised and were subject to new criticisms. European linguists had a longer history of informant research and methodology. Skinner made strides to improve his methods. The year after de Jong's review, Skinner obtained a set of phonograph records of songs and rituals of the Menomini medicine dance.[105]

Skinner's rate of publication slowed markedly between 1916 and 1919, a decline that Harrington attributed to the death of his first wife. Skinner had married Gladys MacCrae in 1916. Within two short years he lost both his wife and child as a result of a difficult pregnancy.

Skinner spent 1918 at an excavation at Throgs Neck and Clason Point, both New York archaeology sites. Oneroad as a Heye staff member joined Skinner in the excavation of the Indian village at Clason Point.[106] Skinner and Oneroad's friendship continued to strengthen.

When World War I broke out, Skinner made numerous attempts to enlist but was rejected each time due to physical defects. The New York Coast Guard finally accepted him, and he served with the Ninth Coast Artillery, a unit in which Oneroad also served.[107]

Skinner resumed publishing in 1919 with his concise article on the "Dakota Ethnology" and one on the Sun Dance of the Sisseton, which was included in Lowie's edition on the Sun Dance. Next, Skinner published his Plains Ojibwe tales in the *Journal of American Folklore* along with articles by Sapir and Kroeber. As the focus of ethnologists turned abroad, folklore studies of the American Indian tapered off.[108]

On December 29, 1919, Skinner married Esther Allen. The following year he accepted the position of curator of anthropology in the Public Museum of the City of Milwaukee. And he resumed a hectic publish-

105. *American Anthropologist* n.s., 18 (1916): 118–20, 120–27.

106. *Milwaukee Sentinel*, July 29, 1922. Clason Point's first inhabitants were Siwanoys, whose village, Snakapin, was one of the largest Indian villages along the shoreline of the Bronx.

107. *Indian Notes and Monographs* 2 (1924): 247–57.

108. *American Anthropologist* n.s., 21 (1919): 164–74; *Anthropological Papers of the American Museum of Natural History* 11 (1919): 383–84; *Journal of American Folklore* 32 (1919): 280–305, 346–55. The only exceptions for the next five years were a few articles in the *Journal of American Folklore*: Grinnell and Gladys A. Reichard in 1921 (34: 269–334), Frank G. Speck in 1923 (36: 273–80, 298–99), and Lowie in 1924 (37: 1–242).

ing pace. He reviewed Arthur Parker's excavation work on a prehistoric Iroquoian archaeological site. The *American Museum Journal* of 1920 noted that Skinner had resumed fieldwork with the Menomini. His friends at the Museum of Natural History kept track of his endeavors, and they brought out a third edition of his "The Indians of Manhattan Island and Vicinity." For Robert Lowie, editor of the *American Anthropologist,* Skinner reviewed David I. Bushnell's 1920 work on native ceremonies and burial as "ignorant," superficial, with "a mass of misinformation and obsolete data." Bushnell, Skinner surmised, ignored the sources. However, the extent to which Oneroad and Skinner discussed these subjects on the Dakota is unknown. Skinner's first fieldwork specifically for the Milwaukee museum took him to the Shawano, Wisconsin, mounds and to the Green Bay archaeological site with J. P. Schumacher.[109]

Skinner succeeded Samuel A. Barrett as head of the anthropology department at the Milwaukee museum. Barrett had worked for the Heye before coming to Milwaukee, but Skinner was more "imbued than Barret with Heye's almost ruthless determination to collect even at the expense of rapport with the people whose artifacts he sought." Skinner admitted that the Menomini named him "Little Weasel" for his persistence in making them reveal what treasures they had hidden away and wearing them down to get them to part with them. Harrington's comments reflected a more lenient view of Skinner's collecting. Harrington claimed that due to Skinner's love and admiration for the American Indian, their ideals, point of view, outlook on life, achievements, and his sympathetic understanding of their problems, they loved him and gave to him freely what they might withhold from others.[110]

While Skinner was at the Milwaukee museum, his second wife died in childbirth in 1921 but was survived by their daughter, Esther Mary Allen Skinner. Again his publication record suffered, and Oneroad came to be with him. Now, with a daughter to care for, Skinner married a third time, less than twenty months after the death of his second

109. *American Anthropologist* n.s., 22 (1920): 78–79; 23 (1921): 255, 366–70. See David Ives Bushnell, Jr., *Burials of the Algonquian, Siouan and Caddoan Tribes West of the Mississippi,* Smithsonian Institution, Bureau of American Ethnology bulletin 83 (Washington, D.C.: GPO, 1927).

110. Nancy O. Lurie, *A Special Style: The Milwaukee Public Museum, 1882–1981* (Milwaukee: Milwaukee Public Museum, 1983), 59; *American Anthropologist* n.s., 28 (1926): 276.

wife. His new wife, Dorothy Preston, was a Wyandotte. The Wyandotte conferred on him the Deer clan name of Tronyetas or Round the Sky. Nevertheless, Skinner preferred to be called Sekosa, his Menomini honorific. The Bald Eagle clan of the Pottawattamie adopted his daughter and gave her the name Mekisekwa, the Eagle Woman, when she was twenty months old.[111]

By 1922 Skinner was back in the field collecting, this time in Oklahoma among the Sauk and Iowa. There he acquired an entire series of gens peace pipe bundles and war bundles. Swanton and Lowie had him writing reviews for the 1923 issue of the *American Anthropologist.* Skinner called attention to Sapir's mistakes in his work on Sarcee pottery, again praised Arthur Parker's archaeology of the Iroquois, and pointed to two distinct culture types and origins in Warren Moorhead's Maine archaeology. Skinner published only one paper in 1923, on the material culture of the Iowa Indians.[112] The next year he published four.

During his brief stay at Milwaukee, Skinner added significantly to Barrett's Menominee materials and brought in extensive collections from the various tribes in Oklahoma, obtaining especially fine Iowa objects. He resigned in 1924 and returned to the Museum of the American Indian, a move that must have spurred his enthusiasm for work as his list of publications surpassed its earlier peak. He received his first merciless review when Truman Michelson criticized his ethnology of the Sauk. Michelson berated him at length for believing his Indian informant without cross-checking the informant's information with historically correct documents, thereby missing the obvious contradictions. Michelson assaulted Skinner's assumptions, his reliance on Harrington, and his preoccupation with "gens." Then he called the article valuable "raw material."[113]

In reply, Skinner pointed out that Michelson himself fell blindly into the same informant bias. Michelson also had accepted the information of his own Dakota informant, Dr. Frazier, without cross-checking the documentation. This put Michelson's informant in as much conflict with the record as Skinner's informant, only on different aspects of the same episode. Beyond that paradox, Skinner insisted that Michelson missed the point of informant information. Skinner

111. Dorthy Preston, who belonged to the Porcupine clan, was named Peiintrawl (Can't Find Her); "Indians Adopt White Children," *Milwaukee Journal,* June 5, 1923.

112. *American Anthropologist* n.s., 25 (1923): 428, 94, 269, 286.

113 Lurie, *Milwaukee Public Museum,* 59; *American Anthropologist* n.s., 26 (1924): 293.

pointed out that recollection or depiction of events often did not co-
incide with historical records. These contradictions were tools of cultural information, not mere misrepresentations of fact.[114] This echoed
the earlier Lowie and Goddard argument on oral history and represented a unique and somewhat farsighted observation on the nature
of "fact" and the interpretation of events.

In 1925 Skinner was among the Seneca of Allegheny making ac-
quisitions for the Heye Foundation. He published three articles about
that trip. In all he published approximately twenty-four articles that
year. Skinner's last review for the *American Anthropologist* was on
Arthur Parker's work on the Algonkin Flint Mines. He again praised
Parker.[115]

Skinner's last article in the *Journal of American Folklore*, entitled
"Traditions of the Iowa Indians," appeared in 1925.[116] There were presentational changes in this work that reflect the evolution of ethnological methods. Skinner noted motifs, made comparisons to other
folklore traditions, cited comparative sources, named informants, and
recorded collection methods, all considered progressive changes in anthropological method. He concluded that the Iowa were associated
with the Central Algonkin, exhibited a strong influence from the
Plains, and had a special similarity to the Eastern Dakota, especially in
their tales.

In the last two years of his life, Skinner also began to write fiction,
vivid Indian stories that appeared in various magazines, especially
Adventure and *Frontier.* He wrote several poems as well. "Slaves of
the Lamp Called Science" was one poem that attracted considerable
attention.[117]

Skinner's career was cut short on a research trip with Amos Oneroad to the Devils Lake Reservation. Oneroad was driving when the
car skidded off the slippery country road near Tokio, North Dakota,
on August 17, 1925. Skinner was killed instantly. He was survived by
his wife, his four-year-old daughter, and his parents. In an obituary,
Harrington wrote that Alanson Skinner was a "sympathetic and ap-
preciative friend of the Indian race, learned student of Ancient America, prolific author of scientific works on Indian subjects, lecturer, fiction writer, poet." Harrington continued, "gone forever was that

114. *American Anthropologist* n.s., 27 (1925): 340–43.
115. *American Anthropologist* n.s., 27 (1925): 601; 28 (1926): 286.
116. *Journal of American Folklore* 38 (1925): 425–506.
117. Information from inventory sheet, MS 201, Boxes 2, 3, 4, Skinner Collection.

wonderful memory, that bubbling humor, that active mind, that ra-
diant, cheerful personality."[118]

In 1922 Amos Oneroad joined Alanson Skinner in Milwaukee at the
Museum of Natural History to work on portions of a joint manuscript.
It was then that they assembled the first renditions of the tales. To this
they added some tales that they had collected on their 1914 field trip to
Sisseton. It is this manuscript, which has three parts, that is in the Skinner Collection in the Braun Research Library, in addition to other
Skinner papers. The manuscript was typed, with handwritten notes in
the margins and interlineated. It is clear from the documents at the library that Skinner planned to publish the ethnology and the tales.

"Eastern Dakota Ethnology" is eighty-one pages long. It is presented
here in the order it was found, but because it was most likely a work in
progress, it does not contain all the parts listed in the accompanying
"Outline for a Monograph" (see appendix). "Traditions of the Wahpeton Dakota Indians" is a 113-page collection of folk tales. It seems to be
a final draft and has only a few handwritten corrections and notes. It
corresponds to its table of contents, but one page is missing from the
original manuscript. This page ended the tale "Iktomi has Revenge
upon the Buzzard" and began the tale "Iktomi and the Ducks." "Wahpeton Dakota Folklore" is twenty-seven pages long. It repeats eight of
the tales found in "Traditions of the Wahpeton Dakota Indians" and
some tales that embellish the ethnology. Therefore, it is not included
here. The manuscript has very few footnotes and even fewer citations
of other sources or literature in the field. The comparisons made were
primarily to other tribes rather than to the work of other scholars or
documents, except in the ethnology on the matter of "gens."

It seems clear that Skinner had prepared the manuscript with a
larger work in mind, as indicated by the "Outline for a Monograph."
The final manuscript was to include: introduction; customs of pregnancy and childbirth and customs connected with infancy from the section on the life of the individual; religious concepts; hunting and fish-

118. Obituary by M. R. Harrington, *Indian Notes and Monographs* 2 (1925): 247–253.
See also *American Museum Journal* 26 (1926): 101–2; *American Anthropolgist* n.s., 28
(1926): 275–76. Samuel A. Barrett, Harrington, and Parker were bequeathed Skinner's
anthropological library. In the event of Skinner's parents' deaths, Barrett or Harrington was awarded guardianship and custody of his daughter. See MS.201.1: Last
Will and Testament, Skinner Collection.

ing, agriculture, foods and their preparation, and miscellaneous customs from the material culture section. The section on material culture was also supposed to have subsections on: manufactures, processes, etc.; weapons; musical instruments; ceremonial paraphernalia; and art. There was no section labeled "conclusions" or any summation.

Skinner had published an article on weapons, musical instruments, and art in 1919 in the *American Anthropologist* and may have planned to include that piece in the final monograph. Skinner and Oneroad also intended to cover other topics on which they had published—the Sun Dance, the Tree-Dweller, the Medicine Dance, and a sketch of Dakota ethnology.

The Braun manuscript has a different style from Skinner's journal articles. It is full of anecdotes and embellishments and is presented in a less formal tone. This account reads like Oneroad's personal narrative. Skinner's voice is apparent in the comments in the margins of the narrative. In the text, Oneroad is identified as Jingling Cloud (Maḣpiyasna), leading to minor confusion since his grandfather had the same name. It would have been clearer to refer to the elder as Jingling Cloud and the younger as Amos Oneroad. Either Skinner and Oneroad did not give a thought to the dilemma, or they used the insinuation of the ancestor's voice as a subtle validation of the collection and placement within the Sisseton-Wahpeton community, a common rhetorical device.

On the Eastern Dakota, Oneroad had the major role in the collection of information and artifacts and in drafting the text. Some of the recollections of "old lifeways" and "long time ago" tales are on four-by-five-inch loose-leaf notebook paper; others are on handwritten or typed eight-by-eleven-inch letter paper. Skinner also took down "notes on many subjects."[119] Oneroad contacted many of his relatives and friends, who provided information and gave specimens to both men. Many of the passages included in the ethnology and Skinner's journal articles were direct quotes from Oneroad's letters or the notes that accompanied the specimens sent to Skinner.

Skinner then arranged the material for presentation and had Oneroad review and approve the manuscripts and Skinner's comments. Skinner kept the manuscript-in-progress with his papers. However, he apparently refrained from publishing on topics that would be taboo for Oneroad to write about as a Sisseton-Wahpeton and a native pastor. Most likely the entire monograph-in-progress would have been

119. *American Museum Journal* 14 (1914): 119.

published as a joint effort, Skinner recognizing Amos E. Oneroad as
the major contributor with himself as the director and facilitator of the
publication. In fact, the title page of the manuscript listed Amos's
name first and Alanson's second.

In accordance with the methods of the times, very little attention
was paid directly to individuals, to the dynamics of the community, to
the political economy, or to the continuum of the past with the present. That was perceived as introducing bias to the material and data.
However, it was not entirely rooted out. The presentation of the material was left to the narrator's discretion. Where the speaker was suc-
cinct, as if answering a direct question, it was left brief. Where the
speaker indulged in following the topic to a story that came to mind,
it remained. The tradition bearers recalled, retained, and passed on
what was familiar. They wove in their own personalities, points of
view, concepts of society, and ideas of their community. This text
shows that "relics of the past" and recollections of "everything given
up pertaining to the old Indian way of life" were not that far removed
from individuals or their community. Skinner exercised interpretive
restraint and let the individuals' recollections, their descriptions and
explanations, speak for and represent the Dakota community instead
of interpreting, explaining, or theorizing. The ethnology comple-
ments the folklore as it informs readers of the lifeways of the Eastern
Dakota.

Folklorists and Euro-Americans still struggle with English labels to
define the Dakota tales. The question arises whether to call them folklore, legends, stories, tales, or oral history. All the labels skirt the judgment of truth or fiction and impose the segregation of the secular and
the spiritual. The Dakota feel that their oral tradition encodes more
than just a fictitious yarn; it carries their beliefs, bits of their ancestors,
themselves, and reality.

The tales map the traditional Sisseton-Wahpeton setting as the territory surrounding the head of Coteau des Prairies. The tales speak of
the mounds near Enemy Swim Lake, the catlinite pipestone quarry,
the practice of the Grass Dance, and the legend of Hoop Ravine. The
other people named (Gros Ventres, Hidatsa, Mandan, Objibwe, Oglala,
Yankton, Cheyenne, Crow, Kiowa) contested the Sisseton-Wahpeton's
perceived borders and further suggest the parameters of their experience. Features mentioned (lakes, bogs, woodlands, prairies, trees, the
types of wood, the food gathered, and the animals encountered) define
the terrain in the Dakota experience. The various tools, food utensils,

domiciles, pastimes, lifeways, and attire described by the narrator suggest the Dakota use of the environment. The descriptions in the ethnology of the material objects acquaint one with that which was familiar, add definition to the characters of the tales, and pinpoint the features within the society's folklore.

The tales include hunting and daily activities more frequently than war and refer to ordinary routine more than the unique. They demonstrate social roles, particularly the role of a young man and what he should know about his world. The tales also define the role of a woman, the function of the lodge, social organization, and honorific customs. They point out and indirectly explain the herald, the messenger, the wiŋkta, the wakaŋ boy, the witch, the shaman, and the heyoka. How one is to perform in response to the routine is given considerable emphasis: how to be a good host or a good guest, how to hunt or butcher and prepare the food, how to honor the dead, the folly of immoral acts, the importance of spiritual respect, and the risk of not being astute and aware.

Motif symbols are identifiable: the four directions, the six directions, repetitions of four, origins and Uŋktehi, the ancestor song, the dream fast, the medicine dance. The tales invoked these motifs in seriousness and obligation. Those regarded as affecting one's life are Waziya, thunder, witches, wiŋktas, and heyoka. The tales suggest various concepts concerning the physical effects of beliefs, reincarnation, transformation, and conception. The symbols allude to associations denoted by that category. As one example, the circle is associated with the lodge, the encampment, the womb, the bay, the water, transformation, and reincarnation.

The Oneroad-Skinner collection includes nineteen tales about Iktomi, the Dakota spider character. The tales concentrate on the adolescent stage of life. They appeal to humor through absurdity and the conflict of the norm in society and activity. "The Adventures of Iktomi" is the serial of a maturing male who due to his character leaves home and travels. He exposes the follies of one who thinks he has answers for everything, the craziness of trickster pranks, and the recklessness of immoral and unsocial acts. Iktomi finally settles within a society, but even tricks his own family.

The white population of Oneroad's day may not have appreciated the humorous absurdity in Iktomi tales. In fact they considered them obscene. In comparison, it seems that Ella Deloria did not collect any potentially obscene or offensive tales. She mentioned the reluctance

of her informants to repeat any vulgarities to her. Oneroad-Skinner included these tales but substituted euphemisms for any term a publisher of the 1920s might have considered offensive.[120]

Most cultures and societies use grotesque images, irreverent language, and lower body stratum images in some of their repertoires.
Such images are part of Iktomi's character—flatulence, buttock and
genital preoccupation, uncontrolled sexual urges and intrigue,
homosexual encounters, and breaking conventions. Through humorous absurdity in ignoring the culturally defined limits and boundaries,
Iktomi hypothetically tests those boundaries. The tales amuse, validate
the culture, educate, impart morals, and provide social approval to
those who conform and ensure continuity. At the same time that the
tales reinforce the stability of the norm, they prevent direct attack on
the social norms by providing an accepted form of release and boundary testing.

In collecting these Iktomi stories, Amos Oneroad and Alanson Skinner
challenged the dictates of the dominant culture. But their collaboration
itself also ignored many conventional models of behavior. Their part-
nership was based upon trust, respect, and a broad and liberal compre-
hension of culture. The fine work they produced, reflecting this unusual closeness, is a belated bequest to people of both cultures.

120. Ella Deloria, published eight tales on Iktomi; see *Dakota Texts*, Publications
of the American Ethnological Society, vol. 14 (New York: G. E. Stechert & Co, 1932), ix.
Among American Indians the trickster took a human appearance with the Winneba-
gos' Wakdjunkaga, the Kiowas' Saynday, the Blackfeets' Old Man, the Poncas' Ish-
tinike, the Arapahos' Wiho. Animal tricksters include the Ojibwes' Hare, the Pawnees'
Coyote, and the Raven of Northwest tribes. See Alan R. Velie, *American Indian Literature* (Norman: University of Oklahoma Press, 1991), 44–45; Paul Radin, *The Trickster:
A Study in American Indian Mythology* (New York: Greenwood Press, 1969), 181.

A NOTE ON EDITORIAL PROCEDURES

The following text is an annotated transcription of the original typescript with the holograph comments. The footnote numbers refer to the present editor's annotations and are not part of the original work unless specifically identified as such. The present manuscript has headings inserted for clarity and organization. The headings were selected from the "Outline for a Monograph on the Ethnology of the Eastern Dakota Indians" (see Appendix) found with manuscripts in the Skinner Collection and are enclosed in square brackets. Curly brackets indicate handwritten additions and corrections to the original typewritten copy that were probably made by Oneroad or Skinner. Skinner's notes are in curly brackets in the footnotes. Any editorial corrections or additions to the text are set off in square brackets. Readers will note certain inconsistencies within these pages. Amos Oneroad spelled his surname as one word, but many family members prefer to spell the name as two words.

For information on Dakota diacritical marks, see page 6.

Nancy Shepherd Oneroad, Hannah Shepherd,
and Joseph S. Shepherd, about 1890

Amos (left) wearing his grandfather's traditional attire and Mr. Grey Earth

Amos in Coast Guard uniform

Amos Oneroad wore traditional regalia when he gave lectures in New York. The Oneroad family said that they found the picture amusing.

Amos in the uniform of a Boy Scout leader

Lena Longie, Raymond Finley, Peter Oneroad, and Nancy Shepherd Oneroad (front row), unidentified woman, Hattie Dumarce Oneroad, Amos Oneroad, Jacob Oneroad, John Oneroad, and Charles Oneroad (back row), about 1915

Amos attended the Society of American Indians banquet, May 14, 1914;
he is seated in front of the pillar. Alanson is next to him (with his hand
raised to his chin). Charles Eastman and Arthur Parker are at the head table.

Sisseton and Wahpeton
Traditions and Customs

{Eastern Dakota Ethnology}

SOCIAL ORGANIZATION [CIVIL AND MILITARY ORGANIZATION]
[**Tribal Divisions**]. Simon Ćekpâ, a Sisseton, sixty-seven years old, gave the following list of gentes [tiospaye] for his group and also the Wahpeton and Santee [Sioux].[11] He said that these groups had paternal decent and were exogamous.[2]

Sisseton

1 Amdowapuskiya, Clothes-dry-on-their-backs {Riggs, Ashley}
2 Basdecesni, Do-not-slice-meat {Riggs, Ashley (1884)}[3]
3 Ohdihe, Counts-like-a-robe {Riggs, Ashley}
4 Itokak tina, South-dwellers {Ashley}
5 Pabaks Ihyanktowana, Cut-head-Yankton
   a Pabaksa {Dorsey & Riggs give Yuches [?] as a division of Yanktoni (p. 185)}
   b Yankton

    1. Simon Ćekpa (One of Twins), identified himself as a Sisseton of the Itokak-tina or "South-dweller" gens. He said he was the first drum owner of the Sisseton Omaha Society and Grass Dance and provided information on the gentes, on dress, and on the mounds. Ćekpa lived on the east side of Pickerel Lake or Du-Lynn Coteau Beach, Day County, South Dakota, with his wife Minyopewiŋ.
    2. James Owen Dorsey states that in Dakota "gens is o-tshe'-ti [oćeti], 'fire-place'; hence one of the names which the Dakotas have given themselves, O-tshe'-ti sha'-ko-win, 'seven fire-places,' comprising the seven original gentes, now tribes.... The sub-gens is ti-o-shpa-ye, 'a group of those who camp by themselves'"; see Dorsey, "'Gens' and 'Sub-Gens' as Expressed in Four Siouan Languages," *American Anthropologist* o.s., 3 (1890): 320. Dorsey (1891:257). He also also wrote that the tribes belonging to the Siouan linguistic family were still divided into gentes, each gens consisting of consanguine, who reckon descent in the male line. Where descent was in the female line, the name "clan" was used instead of "gens." Several of the tribes were divided into half-tribes, and others were composed of phratries, each half-tribe or phratry being divided into gentes. In several of the tribes, each gens was composed of sub-gentes; Dorsey, "The Social Organization of Siouan Tribes," *Journal of American Folklore* 4 (1891): 257–63.
    3. Stephen Return Riggs, a missionary, wrote a Dakota ethnography, text, and grammar in 1893 and compiled a Dakota grammar and dictionary in 1852. Dr. Edward Ashley was the U.S. Indian agent at Winnebago in the late 1800s and at the Standing Rock mission by 1925. Ashley edited and published *Ampaokin.* His death announcement in *Iapi Oaye* identified him as Episcopalian and having served in Yankton, at Sisseton Agency, and at Crow Creek, S.Dak., and in Fairbault, Minn. Riggs footnoted Ashley's gentes; *Dakota Grammar, Texts, and Ethnography* (Washington, D.C.: GPO, 1893), 158–59. Handwritten notes from Skinner and Oneroad show that they were trying to solve the confusion surrounding various gentes.

6 Pte Yutesni, Do-not-eat-buffaloes
7 Kap'oja, Light-lodges {Ashley}
8 Cankute, Shoots-the-tree {Ashley}
9 Manintina, Live-by-themselves {Ashley}[4]
{ Added Bands: (7 of 9 with Ashley; 3 of 9 with Riggs)
10 Riggs, Dorsey, Ashley 5 lodges[5]
11 " "   " In Danger
12 " "   " —— Woodlens place
13 Ashley North Island Dweller Band
14   "   Village at the Bend
15   "   Barbed [?] Fishhook}[6]

The following explanations are given for the names of the gentes [tiyospaye]. In the case of the Clothes-dry-on-their-backs, it is said that when they had fresh meat and were in a hurry to travel they simply packed it on their backs even though it wet their clothes and let it dry there. The Do-not-slice-meats are said to have earned their name because they were too stingy to cut meat for others. The South-dwellers to which band my informant [Simon Ćekpâ] belongs, as their name implies, were the southernmost members of the Sisseton. Each band has its place in the Sisseton camp circle and this band always camped on the south side. The Pabaksa were known as nomads and roamers. No explanation of their name could be obtained. The Pabaksa and Yankton were about the time of the outbreak.[7] The Yankton are said to be true Yankton but not connected with those of the prairie. The Do-not-eat-buffalo gens got their name because they were very poor

4. Skinner, "Sketch of Eastern Dakota Ethnology," 172, lists nine groups as Sisseton.

5. James Owen Dorsey, ethnologist, member of the Bureau of American Ethnology, and an Episcopal missionary to the Pawnee, published "The Places of Gentes in Siouan Camping Circles," *American Anthropologist* o.s., 2 (1889): 375–79. He also edited Riggs's Dakota dictionary of 1889 for the Smithsonian Institution, Bureau of Ethnology, and Riggs, *Dakota Grammar, Texts, and Ethnography*, for the Department of Interior.

6. James H. Howard, *The Canadian Sioux* (Lincoln: University of Nebraska Press, 1984), 15–21, lists Tizaptaŋa as "Five Lodges (10)" and Okopeya as "In Danger (11)" and Ḣeyatatuŋwe as "Back Villagers (14)" from Riggs, *Dakota Grammar, Texts, and Ethnography*, 158–59, 185, and Dorsey, "Social Organization of Siouan Tribes," 259. Number 12 could be Riggs's and Dorsey's "Little Place Bare of Wood." Number 13 could be Ashley's North Island Dwellers, number 14 his Village at the Bend, and number 15 his Barbed as a Fishhook.

7. "The outbreak" may refer to the Dakota War of 1862, which continued through the late 1800s plains wars.

and had no running horses so they were unable to get any tender buffalo cows but were obliged to feed upon tough old bulls. This title is an
nickname and has no reference to any taboo. The Light-lodges got
their name because they always ate any meat which they obtained on
the spot instead of jerking it and put it up in packages to be left behind
in a underground cache or carried with them. Consequently, they always traveled light. The Shoots-the-trees are said to have been very
fond of target practice in the evening. The Live-by-themselves gens is
said to have kept out of the camp circle as though ashamed when all
the others were together.

Each band had its own sacred pipe and each family man had a pipe
which he kept to offer visitors.

There were individual names in each band which were handed
down from father to son or at least from generation to generation but
apparently these names were not gens names like those of the Iowa
and other Southern-Siouan tribes, but were considered honorable because of glory which former warriors had shed upon them and were
not connected with any eponymous animal.

The rule of exogamy was sometimes abrogated in the case of a
young man wishing to marry in his own gens. The matter would be
discussed by the elders and if there was no actual blood relationship
between the young couple, the marriage ceremony was not performed, but the couple was given a tipi and food and they were from
that time considered married. Such a ceremony, however, was rare.

In former times it is said that the Sisseton were called Skiskita'a-
toŋwaŋ, or "water-shed village" and that the name Sisseton was a corruption of this.[8] The locality where they dwelt near Lake Traverse was
also called Ptaŋsinte, otter tail. {Hoasinsinatowan (Fish slime is the root
of the word Sisseton.)}[9]

8. H. S. Morris in a letter to his uncle, June 5, 1936, stated that Reverend Thor
Make, a Sisseton of the Standing Buffalo clan born at Browns Valley, "says that 'Sisseton' has nothing to do with -fish- but that the band or village was called Skistita en
tipi—Dwellers at the isthmus because of the isthmus dividing Lakes Traverse & Big
Stone and that the whites like Irarelites [Israelites] of old 'could not frame to pro-
nounce it aright' but said Sissitowan instead of Skisks'tonwan – interesting." Morris
Papers, Carnegie Library, Sisseton, S.Dak., letter provided by Mary Torness.

9. This paragraph was on page 11 of the manuscript and was followed by the
subtitles "Bear Custom," "Sacred arrow," and "Tatonka okodakicikya"—buffalo society. This appeared to be a page of miscellaneous notes; therefore the first paragraph
is appended to the preceding text on the Sisseton and the other three paragraphs at
the end of "Civil and Military Organization."

Wahpetonwan

Unlike most of the Sisseton, whose gentes were nicknamed from one parcularity [sic], the Wahpetonwan, who were considered more sedentary got their names from the localities in which they lived, they were:

1. Witotina, Islanders. {Island at South end of Big Stone Lake}
2. B'deiyena, River-extending-into-a-lake (Lac Qui Parle)
3. Ḣaḣa atonwan, Falls-dwellers (At the Falls near Granite Falls).
4. Utapahipine, Acorn-pickers, so called because they dwelt in the oak forest.
5. Wiyakaotina, Sand-dwellers.
6. Hiŋtahaŋkpanyan, Basswood-latchets.[10]
{7. Inyan ceyaka - Little-rapids.}
{8. Cankaga otina - Log dwellars}

With regard to the last-named division [6. Hiŋtahaŋkpanyan, Basswood-latchets], the following story is told:

A very handsome young girl from this gens rode with a youth from another village. She had no latchets on her moccasins so she procured basswood shreds for the purpose. When her husband brought her to his people they laughed at her.

There seems to be no doubt but that these gentes formerly occupied separate territories. Isaŋti, the so-called Santee division was made up of gentes who were known by the names of their chiefs for the most part. This band was originally known as the Mdewankantonwan to the Santee, one of their subdivisions who derived their name, as some say from Knife Lake where they dwelt and others because they obtained knives in exchange from traders, became more important and better known to the whites because they resided nearer to them.[11]

Isanti

{These were originally Mdewakanton and Wahpekute}
1. Śakpe (six)
2. Taoyateduta, His Scarlet people, also known as Little-crow's band. These were the true original Mdewakanton.
3. Huśaśa, Red Legs. These were the original Wahpekute.
4. Tipi, Lodge

10. Skinner in "A Sketch of Eastern Dakota Ethnology" recognized six groups. Here he was trying to reconstruct the gentes according to Ashley, Dorsey, and Riggs; see Riggs, *Dakota Grammar, Texts, and Ethnography*, 156–94.

11. This Knife Lake is east of the Mississippi River and southeast of Mille Lacs in Kanabec County, Minnesota.

5. Wabaśa, Red Banner or Standard {Wapahasa}

6. Isaŋti (Isaŋati), Knife Lake

{Some grounds for claims advanced in T. M. Riggs p. 159 that Mde-wakantons were the only Santees originally in native opinion.}[12]

[Oceti Śakowin—Seven Council Fires].

The Hunkpati are the people now dwelling at Crow Creek.

It will be noticed that in the seven fires several subdivisions of the Eastern Dakota are given what would seem to be undue prominence, being placed on a level with the main divisions. This is due to the varying fortunes and vicissitudes of the tribe. The Waȟpekute died out and coalesced with the Mdewankanton who in turn were overshadowed by the Isanti. The name Isanti was also generally applied to the Mdewakanton but all of these changes did not effect the structure of the Eastern Dakota as given elsewhere.

The original seven fires of the Sioux are supposed to have been separate divisions or important bodies of the tribe who were independent of each other until they met the French who suggested that they form an offensive and defensive alliance.

The Oceti Śakowin or seven council fires of the Sioux were:

1. Mdewakanto[n]wan or spirit lake dwellers.
2. Waȟpekute, Shooters among the deciduous leaves.
3. Waȟpetonwan, leaf dwellers.
4. Sisito[n]wan, village among the fisheries, {also called Hoasinsin or Skissitaatonwan}
5. Ihankto[n]wan, dwellers at the end village.
6. Ihankto[n]wanna, little dwellers at the end village.
7. Titonwan, dwellers on the prairies.

[or]

Oceti - Sakowin or Seven Council Fires.[13]

1. Mde-Wakantonwan - Spirit Lake Dwellers or Mysterious Lake Village

12. The source here is not clear. However, Riggs, *Dakota Grammar, Texts, and Ethnography,* 159n3, explained that the Mdewakantonwan, removed from Minnesota to Santee Agency, Nebraska, were the Santees, but white men on the Missouri, with utter disregard of the facts (the original meaning was more limited and specific), called all the Minnesota Dakota "Santees." See also *Word Carrier,* January 1888.

13. See Dorsey, "'Gens' and 'Sub-Gens,'" 320, and "Social Organization of Siouan Tribes," 257; Riggs, *Dakota Grammar, Texts, and Ethnography,* 156; James R. Walker, *Lakota Society,* Raymond J. De Mallie, ed. (Lincoln: University of Nebraska Press, 1992), 15; Howard, *Canadian Sioux,* 3; Royal B. Hassrick, *The Sioux* (Norman: University of Oklahoma Press, 1964), 3, 6.

2 . Wahpe-Kute - Shoot among deciduous leaves
3 . Wahpe-Tonwan - Village among deciduous leaves
4 . Sisinyun-Tonwan - Village among Fishey Scales
5 . Ihanktonwan - Dwellers of End Village
6 . Ihanktonwannna - Little End Village
7 . Titon-wan - Dwellers of the Prairie

Divisions of the Teton:[14]

Tetonwan, prairie people
Oglala
Sicanghu (burnt thighs)
{Kunwi?a}(lower people, lower {Brule})[15]
Itazipcona (without bows, sans arcs)
Hunkpati {opposite end of village in the circle}
Hunkpapai {Near or Next} in the circle
Oohenonpa (two boiling)
Minikonwaju (water spring {planter})

Skinner.[16]	Riggs and Dorsey.
Sisseton	
1. Clothes-Dry-On-Their-Backs	4. Dryers-On-The-Shoulder
2. Do-Not-Slice-Meat	5. Native name given, not translated
3. Counts-Like-A-Robe	7. " " " "
4. South-Dwellers	
5. Cut-Head –Yankton	
6. Do-Not-Eat-Buffalo	
7. Light-Lodges	6. " " " "
8. Shoots-The-Tree	
9. Live-By-Themselves	
	1. Five-Lodges
	2. Okopeya
	3. Little-Place-Bare-Of-Wood

14. See Walker, *Lakota Society*, 1 9; Hassrick, *The Sioux*, 3, 6.
15. "Keda wi cache" is crossed out.
16. It is impossible to determine if Skinner or someone else typed and inserted the following outline and paragraph on the Sisseton and Wahpeton in the manuscript. There are no script corrections as there are on others so handwriting comparison is not possible. However, the typeface is larger on this page than on the others. Someone else probably inserted this page, perhaps a scholar in later comment.

Wahpeton
1. Islanders
2. River-Extending-Into-A-Lake
3. Falls-dwellers
4. Acorn Pickers
5. Sand-Dwellers
6. Basswood-Latchets
{7. Little Rapids}
{8. Log Dwellers}

1. Dwellers-In-The-Leaves
2. Ball-Players
3. Thicket-Dwellers

Isanti
1. Sakpe (Six)
2. His-Scarlet-People {Taoyateduta}(Mdewakanton)
3. Red Legs {Huśaśa} (Wahpekute)
4. Lodge
5. Red Standard {Wapahaśa}
6. Isanti (Knife-Lake)

In Skinner's account we seem to have a mixture of Wahpekute and Mdewakanton bands, evidently resulting from the confusion following the banishment of the Sioux from Minnesota. The names given by R. [Riggs] and D. [Dorsey] for the bands of these divisions do not at all correspond with Skinner's list.

Each gens had its own place in the camp circle of the band. The drawing shown in Fig. oo [not included in the collection] gives the position of the Sisseton gentes. Each gens had its own group of councilors or wakiconza consisting of twenty men.[17] The councilors' tent was placed in the circle in front of the spot where the gens was camped. The councilors of all gentes got together for a grand congress when matters of trival importance came up. A herald was chosen to go about the camp and announce its movements. The councilor's duty was to watch and guard the people, to help them in moving, to take care of poor people, and have their loads carried for them. On buffalo hunts they collected beef for the poor but never hunted themselves. The akicita were responsible to them and carried out their orders. There

17. Dorsey, "Social Organization of Siouan Tribes," 259, has a drawing showing the place of "gentes" for the Sisseton-Wahpeton camping together and the Sisseton camping alone. Riggs, *A Dakota-English Dictionary* (Washington, D.C.: GPO, 1889), defines "wakiĉoŋza" as "one who determines or decides; to purpose or determine for one" and "wakiĉoŋze" as "a leader or chief; or one who decides," in accord with the Teton dialect. See Walker, *Lakota Society*, 60–61, concerning the Oglala Lakota and Hassrick, *The Sioux*, 172–73, using "Wakincuzas" for the Teton Lakota.

were no leaders among the councilors, all having equal authority. In the tribal council twenty men of each gens voted as a unit after deciding among themselves. Decisions were announced as final by the herald. The title wakiconza means "executor."

[Officers, Government, Warriors, and War Customs]
Chiefs
The chieftainship among the Santee, Sisseton, and Wahpeton was hereditary. The chief was called wicasta yatapi. This is now generally translated as "He eats the man," but this is a folk etymology according to the well-informed Dakota and the word is really derived from wicasta itancan or yatanpi an expression meaning "honored man" and is a corruption of that term.[18] The chief had no authority whatever in the tents of the wakiconza or executioner who are elected by the people except when there is a grand tribal council when he has absolute control. Ordinarily, the thinkers act as councilors and over rule him. The head chief has a soldier under him who acts as his special agent. For other occasions akicita or police are selected from among the braves. From what the old men said I gather that sometimes the akicita were selected from among the braves of some special society but this was certainly not always the case.[19]

Making of Chiefs
The chief's office was handed down from father to oldest son. Anciently, the chief might be a medicineman or might be a man who had worked up from a lowly origin or a warrior who had attained great honor. It became customary when these early chiefs died to confer the office upon their sons and thus the position became hereditary.

Wakiconza or Councilors.
When on the move, one half of the councilors marched ahead of the village and the other half in the rear. Their duty was to watch and

18. See Hassrick, *The Sioux*, 26, 28–30, on "Wicasa Itacans and Wicasa Yatapikas (Supreme Owners)."

19. See Robert H. Lowie, "Dance Associations of the Eastern Dakota," *Anthropological Papers of the American Museum of Natural History* 11 (1913): 132–37. Little Fish identified wiŋtcacta yatapi as a single man with power to make treaties; four ministers known as akitcita; waiyutaŋ, "food-distributor," and ten judges, waŋyatco, with authority during the chase. Tawatcihe-homini said the Wahpeton were divided into three local groups presided over by a single chief.

guard the people. If two bands met on the prairie the people stopped right there at some distance from each other and dressed in their best clothes. This act was called omaha kiyotag kapi (Omaha setting). They would then line up beside each other and advance in two long lines, singing and giving presents. Then they would mingle and enjoy themselves.[20]

{War Honors}

The following war honors with their rewards were recognized by the Eastern Dakota.

First, to touch a living enemy. This was the highest honor and for it the warrior received the right to wear a single eagle feather, standing upright on the back of his head.[21]

To be one of the next three to touch the enemy also brought the same reward but the honor was considered not so great as to be the first coup striker.

Taking a scalp. This was next in value to counting coup. It was only necessary to take a single lock from the head where the hair radiates. This would only count for a man who had no opportunity to strike a coup at the same time. Coup strikers received no additional honor for taking a scalp. A scalper had the right to wear a bear's paw on his right foot.

To be wounded. A man who was wounded in battle marks a red spot on a eagle feather at the point where the black tip joins the white. If a wounded man takes and counts coup upon an uninjured enemy he is entitled to wear a prairie wolf's tail on his left foot when he dances. When a man is wounded by a wounded enemy he may wear a whole fox skin around his neck or a black eagle feather from an eagle's tail, stripped on both sides, the shaft standing upright between.

For stealing a horse, a man has the right to carry a whip on his wrist during the dance.

Saving a comrade is looked upon as the bravest of deeds. A man who has done this has the right to reenact the performance when dancing.

A man who has gone to war in a canoe attaches a little paddle to the

20. Skinner in "A Sketch of Eastern Dakota Ethnology" stated that each gens group of twenty "wakicun" or councilors had a tent of its own.

21. Also see Wilson D. Wallis, "The Canadian Dakota," *Anthropological Papers of the American Museum of Natural History* 41 (1947): 18, on feather war honors.

eagle feather which he wears in his hair.[22] If he went on horseback he might paint horse tracks in white on the rear of his breechclout.

An enemy going alone into a Sioux camp and getting inside the camp circle was never injured by the Dakota. He was looked upon as no longer a foe but was taken into the chief's lodge where he was kept and cared for and all shook hands with him and those who did so had the right to wear an eagle feather. Among the Dakota a young man of their own people getting into the enemy's camp in this way had the right to wear a war-bonnet; the eagle feathers in it represented the enemies who wounded him. The prisoner in the Dakota camp when he has achieved this feat was finally released with gifts of horses.

An interesting case of Yankton war symbols occurs in a pair of moccasins obtained from Peter One-road. These moccasins are beaded and quilled on the soles as well as on the upper surface and were intended to be worn when the owner was on horseback. In 1874, One-road and a party of Sioux were attacked by the Ponca near the mouth of the Niobrara River. The Ponca were led by two of their chiefs, Charging-wolf, and Returning-bear, both of whom carried repeating rifles, but One-road with an old fashioned smooth bore, shot and killed Returning-bear and mortally wounded Charging-wolf. He also counted first coup on both of these men. For this reason he has attached to one moccasin a tail of a wolf and to the other the foot of a bear to show all the world that he had vanquished Charging-wolf and Returning-bear.

Among the Dakota, women had the right to receive eagle feathers for acts of bravery, but, like the Plains-Ojibway they might not wear them. Instead, they generally gave the feathers to their male relatives.[23] It is highly annoying to the Sioux to see representations of Indian women or pictures of white women dressed as Indians showing them wearing eagle feathers. Their first question is, "When did that woman kill an enemy and who gave her the right to wear the feather?"

22. Skinner in "A Sketch of Eastern Dakota Ethnology" discussed canoes and his discovery that dugout canoes were still used by all three peoples—Isanti, Wahpeton, and Sisseton. He also stated that the latter two formerly had many bark canoes.

23. Wallis, "Canadian Dakota," 18, said that a Wahpeton woman might not touch an eagle feather nor any part of the body of an eagle as the bird is "wakaŋ" and that eagle feathers not worn were usually hung in the tepee in full view.

War Honors Accorded to Horses

The Dakota thought a great deal of their chargers. Horses that had been wounded in battle had eagle feathers tied to their tails or manes and red cloth hung around their necks. A man about to go into battle would say to his steed, "Now, my horse, you shall wear an eagle feather and be painted with red or blue paint and I shall give you red cloth if you are brave in this battle and come through with speed." Steeds that are not even "running horses" are greatly encouraged by such promises, the Indians say. During ceremonies the war horses were led around and acted in a very proud manner. Some of them had buffalo masks with horns put over their heads. The Santee division is said not to have done these things and to have derided the others and the Tetons because they rode to war, while as the Santee went on foot. In later times, however, the Eastern Dakota did the same thing.

"Challengering"

When a man or a society of young men is given a feast, it is very often that there are few present who have any war counts and some of the braves may come in and walk off with a kettle of food which they have provided. This is called "akicita taking."

Sometimes a man who has himself given a great many feasts of this type but who has not been invited to the one in question will come in, tell of his generosity, and remove the kettle. On the other hand, when all the old great warriors were giving a feast some young fellow might enter and tell of the greatest coup of all, claiming that he had struck his first enemy before he had ever spoken to a girl. This was said to have been very rare, for almost everyone had fallen in love before he went to war. Then the young man would take the kettle away from the akicita and give it to some old people but he himself could never partake. An akicita at a dance, observing some youth or girl to be bashful would catch the diffident one and dance with him or her and keep it up until a relative came forward, told a brave deed, and gave a present to the captor in ransom. The akicita were supposed to kill dogs that wandered into the dance. When an enemy wandered into the camp circle and was considered safe, they went around to collect goods to present to him when he was released. Among the Dakota, the Akicita did not hold office for life, only for short periods when as individuals they were appointed for camp duty. This was not true, however, of the akicita who formed the body guard of the chief.

They were appointed for life and were always known as so-and-so's head soldiers. An akicita of this sort talked for the chief, executed his orders, etc.[24]

War Challenge

A man's brother-in-law who had done a brave deed is likely to taunt him by taking off his breechclout and shake it in his face. The other has no redress even if this is done in public although it would be a deadly insult coming from anyone else. Meanwhile, the women will cry "di di di di" in praise of the warrior. The insulted man will wait for the first opportunity to go on the warpath. If he is successful he will rub his member on the dead foe and he will return early in the morning with wolf yells. The herald will announce that So-and-so was insulted by his brother-in-law and said he would kill and copulate an enemy and he has done so. The warrior will now approach his brother-in-law and say, "I will do the same thing to you that I did to the warrior if you ever insult me again."

Soldier Killing

When a man disobeyed the rules and hunted the buffalo ahead of his party, the akicita would visit him in a body after the hunt was over. As they approached his tipi, one of their number would call out, "What are you!" and the culprit would reply that he was Hidatsa, Gros Ventre, Mandan, or some other hostile tribe. The leader of the akicita would recite his coups and the akicita would crawl towards him as though he were an enemy. Suddenly, the leader would give the charging yell, the so-called "war whoop" and each one of the soldiers would strike the culprit in the same manner and with the same weapon that he had struck an enemy. The offender might be very seriously hurt in this way as they did not scruple to strike him down with a gun butt or tomahawk. If the offender had a brother-in-law among the akicita, who had taken a scalp, the brother-in-law would come and cut off a

24. Skinner in "A Sketch of Eastern Dakota Ethnology" (p. 173) mentioned that the "akicita," known as "soldiers" or "police," occasionally may have been selected for bravery among the Sisseton. He concluded that the Eastern Dakota more nearly resembled the Algonkian and Southern Siouan than the Teton in this respect. Thus "the akicita performed the typical acts of soldier killing, had their separate tipi, and their challenging contests, etc., in regular Plains style." Lowie, "Dance Associations," said the Wahpeton choose akicita for bravery.

lock of his hair which meant that the akicita must give the culprit a horse. If the culprit fought or acted in an aggressive manner he was likely to be very roughly handled and maybe even killed. If he escaped with his life, he was despised by all the people who told him that he might as well put on a shirt. Some time later one of the akicita was likely to recount his coup and then give the culprit a horse if he had behaved himself well. When the soldiers are back in the tiyotipi arrangements were made to restore any of his property which they might have destroyed.[25]

{Place in Tiyotipi}

In the soldiers' lodge there was a bundle of painted sticks striped red, blue, or painted solid black. Red stood for those who had counts on a foe, black, warriors who had been wounded, and blue for wealthy men in the tribe. {A white stick stood for a common man.} The akicita would take some of these sticks and stick them in the ground before the different lodges.[26]

For a wounded man in each case they would fire a gun and stand before the tipi singing. Then the lodge owner was obliged to give them a present such as a bag of buffalo meat, moccasins, or clothing. He might then pull out the stick and return it to the akicita.

In this way they would make the rounds of the whole camp and return with a great load of presents some of which were put to one side. The culprit was then called in and was set beside the door like an honored man. The presents and then a horse in addition were then given him and he was feasted. After this the councilors made a speech: a sort of sermon in which he was told that he was brave and that the had been treated after the manner of their ancestors and that he must stand his punishment like a man.

25. The Riggs dictionary defines "tiyotipi" as a "soldiers' lodge" established for the purpose of making laws and providing for their execution. The object is generally to regulate the buffalo chase. Wissler (1947:16) said it was located in the center of the camp and was a meeting place for older men with two young men in constant attendance, cooking and performing services for the old men.

26. Wallis, "Canadian Dakota,"17, said that if the stick fell over it was thought to indicate the shortening of one's life-span.

Akicita Wicaktepi—Soldier Punishment[27]

If a man who has been a great warrior and braver than any of the akicita in camp has done something out of the way he can defy the akicita when they are sent to punish him. If for instance, he had killed a wounded enemy who was armed and able to do him damage he could hold the soldiers after they had counted their coups and tell them his deeds saying, "If any of you have done this then you are the only ones who are entitled to strike me." It is said that no war honors are counted on the United States soldiers since they were hired to fight and were therefore looked upon with contempt by the Dakota.

Warriors Test

Braves were accustomed to swallowing small live snapping turtles to make them very courageous. It is claimed that there are bones in the turtle resembling spears and knives. This swallowing of live tortoises is similar to the Menomini and Omaha custom.

Oaths

If two warriors disputed concerning war honors they would not be allowed to argue. Old warriors would say, "Whatever your mouth says will come back again." It was thought that people who argued about these things were likely to be killed. If a man wished to take his oath upon any matter he would raise both hands aloft to wakan tanka and say, "The great spirit hears all and sees all.[28] He knows that this is so." But this was never done in connection with war counts.

War Medicines

Certain men had the ability to prophesy about war even as much as half a year ahead. Sometimes a man would dream that he had to go to war. Then he would sing about spirits and those he was going to kill. He would be shown the country of the enemy; perhaps he would see an Ojibway in his bark canoe with his wife and two or three children. Then he would see his own party preparing to shoot them and see

27. "Akicita Wicaktepi" literally translates as "soldier killing." The verb "akici-takte" translates as "to punish officially," "to punish for the violation of a law"; Riggs said that this was done by those who had attained the status of "brave" and consists in the killing of a horse or dog, cutting up tents and blankets, and breaking guns. If the latter verb were used, the affixing of the pronouns "wica- . . . -pi" would translate "them . . . they."

28. "Wakaŋ taŋka" translates as "great spirit."

them later go up and count the coups. Or, if the Ojibway escaped or were wounded or his own people wounded, all would be made clear to him. Then he would sing and get out his medicines. He would make a sweat house and smoke until the time for the war party to go had arrived.

The night before starting to war he would call the party to come to a secret lodge where they rehearsed their war songs. They held filled pipes straight before their faces while they sang. Medicines were opened and spread out before them on a carpet of white down. Each warrior had his own wotawe.[29] Some were connected with the bear or other powerful animals and some with birds. The war prophet was usually the possessor of a little stone, takuśkanśkan, the spirit in which could go off as an invisible scout to see the foe.[30] While the spirit stone was scouting, the others would all shut their eyes and the leader would sing. At last he would talk to the spirit stone saying, "Hai hai." Then the others would know the stone was back. Pipes were then offered to the six directions, lighted and smoked. Then they would feast, make their moccasins ready, and prepare to start before dawn. The old men of the camp would sing in honor of the youths and their relatives would wail for fear they should never see them again.

War Charms

The nearest approach to the war bundle which can be found among the Eastern Dakota is the wotawe. They are charms made by people who have dreamed of thunder, panther, eagle, wolf, fox, elk, or loon, beaver, muskrat, and diver. The last four being important because they were on the raft when the world was made and dived to get the earth for its crust.[31]

---

29. The Riggs dictionary defines "wotawe" as "armor, weapons consecrated by religious ceremonies; whatever is relied upon in war."

30. The Riggs dictionary lists "Taku'śkaŋskaŋ" as one of the Dakota gods, the moving god or god of motion. Dorsey said that the moving deity lived in the four winds, and the four black spirits of night did his bidding. The consecrated spear and tomahawk were its weapons. The buzzard, raven, fox, wolf, and other animals were its lieutenants, to produce disease and death; James Owen Dorsey, "A Study of Siouan Cults" in Smithsonian Institution Bureau of American Ethnology, *Eleventh Annual Report* (Washington, D.C.: GPO, 1894), 445. Wallis purchased hunting and fighting stones from three men and put them in the National Museum in Ottawa; Wallis, "Canadian Dakota," 80.

31. See the version of the "Earth Diver" tale called "The Origin of the Medicine Dance," page 188, below.

The warrior who dreams of one of these, makes a war club, a spear, or an arrow, a horn or a gun.[32] This is manufactured inside a medicine lodge and it is consecrated and pointed to the four winds, to zenith, and nadir. The skins of the sacred animals mentioned are also used. These are wrapped up together and there are many songs for the medicines, which are usually in groups of four, and which are further subdivided into four parts. The wotawe is hung up on the poles in the center of the lodge or outside. It is never allowed to touch the ground, for if this happens, the owner might as well be dead.

Whistles are placed in these bundles and when ceremonies are held for them only those who have dreamed of the same spirit that appeared to the owner may come. Sometimes a man may have several dream guardians and may go to any of them. If a warrior wants vengeance on the enemy he hires an old man to be his herald. The old man goes through the camp calling for a certain group of dreamers, say perhaps the fox (presumably the tokana society as these are very important[33]) to help him out. Meanwhile the warrior hangs brave clothes on a horizontal bar and prepares to feast. Those who have received the invitation, join him and volunteer and go to war with him. They usually get others from the tribe at large to join them.

Whenever one would be added to the party his women would weep because it was supposed that he was about to die. All stood in a circle and the newcomers were placed in the center where even elders would approach and give them fine horses to ride into battle. The host then arose, made a speech, and told the assemblage why he had done this. Then all procured extra moccasins and that night all the braves would dance with their wotawe and smudge them with the sacred incense.

32. Skinner in "A Sketch of Eastern Dakota Ethnology" (p. 167) stated that bows, often quite long, and arrows tipped with stone, antler, or bone, and rawhide shields were common weapons. Skinner found the war club was either ball-headed or flat and shaped like a gun butt. He determined that stone-headed clubs, like those of the prairie Sioux, were probably not used to any extent, unless by the Sisseton. Ashley related that among the Sisseton and Wahpeton Dakota the warrior was forbidden to eat the tongue, head, or heart of many beasts. There were other animals of which the heads might be eaten, but not the tongues. A warrior about to go on the war path could not have intercourse with women but must go through the purification of the inipi or sweat bath, which lasted four days. A married warrior could not touch his own weapons until he had thus purified himself; Rev. E. Ashley to Dorsey, March 24, 1884, in Dorsey, "Study of Siouan Cults," 444.

33. The "Tokana" society was a social association rather than a religious one according to Skinner; see page 76, below.

They would leave before dawn and when a mile away from the camp of the enemy would imitate whatever animal was their dream guardian.

On their return, when a short distance from their people they would wait until early in the morning, cry like their guardians, and as soon as this was heard in the camp a party was made up to go out to meet them. If they had killed foes, they would all be painted black. An old man was taken from the village as a herald who would announce to the villagers as they approached, which members had shot enemies, who had been struck, who wounded, who took scalps, and who killed. Each brave sang his own song, telling of his deeds and describing his enemy, how he was dressed, how he acted, etc. Scalps taken were fastened on hoops and suspended from long poles. These were given to the family or relatives of those who had been slain. The women received them and sang victory songs telling of their revenge when they at last reached the inside of the camp circle while the women stood back and held up the scalps while they danced by themselves.[34] The songs repeated the names of the successful warriors and recounted their deeds. The dance was kept up all day and the relatives of the successful braves gave horses to the poor people. After a war party had returned for sometime in the morning and evening the warriors could be heard singing about their deeds in different places. For four months at least, once a month, the scalps were repainted and danced. At the end of this time each man who took a scalp adorned it with ribbons and beads and buried it. The bodies of slain foemen were cut and their heads gashed, but Jingling-cloud had never heard of their hearts being eaten although some of the others mentioned this.[35] Captives were always well treated. A man on his first war party carried the extra moccasins of the other braves and cooked for them.[36] After a war party, all the warriors who took part were obliged to use sticks when they wish to scratch their heads until the scalps were buried.

After the first four scalp dances warriors were washed with sweetgrass and water and given pipes. When on the warpath the braves would touch a buffalo intestine and tell whether or not they had ever

34. Howard, *Canadian Sioux,* 53, 170, called the scalp dance Iwakici Wacipi. See also Walker, *Lakota Society,* 66.

35. Here it is not clear if Skinner is speaking of Jingling Cloud the elder or of Amos Oneroad. Two paragraphs later, he is definitely speaking of the elder man and not the younger.

36. See "A Boy Joker," page 192, below.

been familiar with a winkta.[37] This ceremony was called witansnaon okiye, "those who court the virgin." If a winkta was present on the warpath he mentioned the names of all his lovers. The intestine was prepared by a man who had never been to war, who put red down upon it. Winktas were encouraged to join war parties because they were thought to bring good luck and were prophets. Sometimes a man would approach a winkta and ask him to prophesy that he was to do a brave deed. The berdache would then set up a stick, make a little shield, or a bow and arrow, or a club, and indicate on the stick the way in which the deed was to be performed by the warrior, telling him at the same time where the sun would be when he would do this thing. The berdache says, "So will you do when the time comes and that is the way it will happen."

Prisoners who were brought inside of the camp circle were always spared by the Eastern Dakota. Once an Ojibway was brought in and a young man of the Sisseton camp wanted to kill him. Maȟpiyasna [Jingling-cloud] volunteered, if the council so decreed, to shoot the Sisseton rather than have him violate this custom. The council agreed and so he did. Though he had no grudge against the warrior and afterwards, Jingling-cloud, the elder, supplied that family of this man with food when he returned from his hunt in order to show his good will. The Ojibway was afterwards taken 1½ days journey into the woods towards his own country and released. The following spring a letter written on birchbark was found. On the bark was scratched the figure of a man taking long steps with footprints that showed he was running.[38] This referred to Iyangmani [Iŋyaŋgmani] or Running-walker, the Wahpeton chief. The other side showed a man with clouds over his head and crooked lines running from them. This referred to Jingling-cloud and the whole meant that the Ojibway were coming to

37. Riggs defined a "wiŋkta" as a "hermaphrodite" or a bisexual. Skinner alternated this Dakota term with the term "berdache." Walker, *Lakota Society,* 127,147, includes Deloria's comments on wiŋktas bestowing obscene or scatological nicknames that became commonly used.

38. Skinner in "A Sketch of Eastern Dakota Ethnology" (p. 167) and "Medicine Ceremony of the . . . Wahpeton Dakota" (p. 262–305) has sections on "picture writing" that describe writing on flat bark slabs and on birch bark. He stated this was common particularly in connection with hunting charms and the medicine dance. He said he collected five Wahpeton examples but that several more Sisseton examples were in the Museum of the American Indian. The latter article had pictures of three song boards.

make peace with the Dakota through these two warriors. The Dakota prepared to receive them and in a few days, Ojibway scouts came in with their candipaȟta (tobacco bundle) composed of little bags of tobacco and the Dakota sent some back by them. Then the Ojibway approached and peace was made.

When they drew near those of the Wahpeton who had horses circled back and forth between their own people and the Algonkin and both sides sang. The Sioux dedicated their songs to Running-walker and Jingling-cloud. When the two lines were near they stopped facing each other and the head chief on each side approached with tobacco and the hunka song dedicated to the four winds was sung concluding with the words: "Long live Iyangmani and Maȟpiyasna. As long as you two warriors live, no one will dare to run over us."[39] Meanwhile, the chief brought out a pipe which he offered to wakan tanka and the directions. When he had done this he gave it to the opposing chief and all the Ojibway took a whiff. Then the Ojibway prepared their pipe in their own way. After this everybody approached and shook hands. The Ojibway chief gave his best horse to Running-Walker and a lot of mococs of rice and maple sugar.[40] Then the Sioux and Ojibway mingled giving presents and the Ojibway were brought into camp where they were told where to pitch their tents. That evening, Running-walker invited all the Ojibway to his lodge while Jingling-cloud singed a deer whole and made the "chief dish" for them. The Ojibway thanked him and told him that from that time forward they looked upon him {Jingling-cloud} as being half Ojibway.[41]

39. Riggs translated "huŋka" literarily as "ancestor or parent." See Melvin R. Gilmore, "The Dakota Ceremony of Huŋka," *Indian Notes* 6 (1929): 75–79. Gilmore agreed with Riggs's definition but added that any person who had become elevated in the people's esteem might be given this title, and those so called constituted a social aristocracy within an essentially democratic community. Gilmore credited Charles Frazier for the information on the huŋka. See also William K. Powers, *Oglala Religion* (Lincoln: University of Nebraska Press, 1975), 100, on the Huŋka ritual "to create a bond between two people which is stronger than a kinship tie." Walker, *Lakota Society*, 49, 52, 63, 105, called it an adoption.

40. A "mococ" is a container, usually made of birch bark; the word is Ojibwe. Skinner collected a Menomini birch-bark "makuk" used to store maple sugar; see Robert E. Ritzenthaler and Pat Ritzenthaler, *The Woodland Indians of the Western Great Lakes* (Garden City, N.Y.: Natural History Press, 1970), 14, 16, 68–69, 155.

41. See "A War Story," page 196, below. It is the same anecdote with a few presentational differences.

Bear Custom

Among the Santee and Wahpeton it was customary when a warrior or warriors had killed a bear for them to whoop before they entered the camp on their return.[42] This sign was known by all the people. They always buried the bones of the bears which they used for food and never allowed a dog to touch them.

Sacred Arrows

The sacred arrows, waŋwakaŋ, constituted a sort of a war bundle and were known to the Sisseton as well as to the Teton. They were carried to war and the man who bore them on his back could not turn back but had to go forward. A pipe was taken with them.

Tatonka Okodakiciya—Buffalo Society

[This] was a group of warriors which formerly existed and it had among its regal a shield and straight spear and the no-flight idea was in vogue among the officer.[43]

[SOCIAL LIFE AND ORGANIZATIONS][44]
[Societies and Ceremonies]
Tokana Wacipi[45]

This society was looked upon as being not at all a religious but a social association. It is said that the founder had a vision in which he went into a village where the kit-foxes dwelt. They talked, acted, and looked just like people. While he was there, one of them showed him their own and only dance. He learned it and its songs, and when he came to himself he gathered a crowd of youths and taught it to them. The real foxes as well as the kit-foxes are known to have these same songs and

42. Wallis in "Canadian Dakota" (p. 121) said the warrior gave four whoops.

43. At this point in the original manuscript, there is a change from a small (about 10 point) type to a larger and sharper type (about 12 point), showing a change in typewriters.

44. Skinner in "A Sketch of Eastern Dakota Ethnology" (p. 171) referred readers to the writings of Wissler and Lowie and the *Anthropological Papers of the American Museum of Natural History*, vol. 11 (1913). Here Skinner listed the military societies of the Plains type as: Tonkana, No-Flight, Mawatani, Raven Owners, Badgers, Owl Feather Wearers; he also listed social societies of the Plains type: Omaha; and social societies and dances of the Central Algonkian type: Buffalo Dance, Medicine Dance. Robert Lowie in "Dance Associations" (p. 102–42) described the Kit-Fox Dance, the No-Flight Dance, the Buffalo Dance, and the Raw-Fish-Eaters' Dance in detail, had less information on the Dance of the Thunder Dreamers, but included other Sisseton and Wahpeton dance descriptions from Fort Totten, N.Dak. Lowie also did not say much

dances, but no one has ever been able to obtain songs from the coyotes or wolves. The officers of the society were as follows: Four leaders, called *tokana itaŋcaŋ* who carried straight spears wrapped with otter fur and bearing pendant feathers. These men were pledged never to flee in battle. They were required to shave the head, leaving a roach, which was maintained during their incumbency which lasted for four years, at the end of which time new officers were elected.

One herald, whose business was to announce for the leaders and to tell the people who had been chosen to feast and entertain the society.

    2 wayutanpi or waiters[46]
    4 ħoka or singers[47]
    4 chorus women
    40 to 50 members.

The four leaders had charge of everything. Whenever they were ready to dance, the society members stripped to the gee string and wore long quilled fringes something like those often seen attached to the bottom of pipe bags. They paraded around the camp. They painted their faces only as they wished but put no paint on their bodies. They wore quilled garters on their legs below the knees and all wore long beads made from the bones of rabbit's legs as earrings.

The Tokana did not seem to have the custom of stealing wives from the members of the Mawatani society nor was the spirit of rivalry [word?] Iowa, apparent from anything to be learned from the Eastern Dakota.[48] If one of the members had his wife stolen by any other individual in the tribe, all his fellow Tokana would join him in taking away the woman from the offender whom they whipped severely.

---

about the medicine dance, which he considered outside his scope. Wissler addressed the Oglala divisions of the Teton Dakota. Wallis (in "Canadian Dakota") in 1914 described the Wahpeton Holy [Medicine] Dance, the War Dance, the Young Men's Dance, No-Flight Dance, Buffalo Dance, White Buffalo Dance, Elk Dance, Bear Dance, Raw Fish Eaters Dance, and Raw Dog Eaters Dance from Portage La Prairie, Manitoba, Canada.

45. A tokana is a small gray fox or kit-fox. Riggs said it was "tokala" in the Teton dialect or "tokandaŋ" and that "wacipi" was "dance." The information on this dance was given by Simon Ćekpa. Lowie (in "Dance Associations," 105–6) related that the Sisseton "Little Fish" declared that young men not belonging to the napeśni danced the tokana, they roached their hair, and Ciptoduta (Red Beads) saw the dance once.

46. Riggs translated "wayutaŋpi" as "servants; ones who pass food around."

47. "Ħoka" translates as "the badger," whereas singers would be a variant of "dowaŋpi."

48. The manuscript ends at this point on page 32 and begins again on page 33; Skinner may have intended to insert an explanation of some sort.

Mawatani Wacipi[49]

Like the Tokana, this was also a social society which started from a dream. There were no leaders except the organizer and there were eight male and eight female singers, a herald, and two waiters. The members were forty in number, twenty of whom painted black and twenty red. Those who painted red wore feather headdresses made of scarlet and dyed owl feathers. When they wore eagle feathers they attached a little scarlet feather to the tip of each. Those who painted black wore raven feathers with a black weasel skin fastened to the tip of each. It is said that this dance was called after the Mandans, Mawatani, because the founder was a member of that tribe. They were originally called the Red Owl Feathers (hihaŋśunwapaha).[50] When the Sioux first learned that the Mandana "owned" the same dance and had had it before them they changed the name of their performance in honor of the other tribe. No young men were allowed to take part in this ceremony, only men who were heads of families and had respectable standing.

Omaha or Grass Dance. Pezimi hnaŋka.[51]

This society and its dance were brought to the Dakota by Peter One-road, the father of Jingling-cloud, and another young man in 1868. The date is well remembered by all the Yankton and Eastern Dakota in the neighborhood of Sisseton because there was an eclipse of the moon at that time. As a matter of fact, the songs were brought by the two Dakota the spring preceding the formal starting of the dance which took

49. Simon Ćekpa provided this information. Wallis (in "Canadian Dakota," 53–58) said that some thought the dance was the name of a band of Chippewa. He was informed that the society was introduced to the Wahpeton by a Sisseton named "Sweetgrass" or PezickuiA [Peźiskuya], who originated the dance for success of the buffalo hunt. A revival of the dance by another leader was attempted about 1857, which Peźiskuya neither opposed nor supported.

50. According to the Riggs dictionary, "hiŋhaŋ" means "owl," "hiŋhaŋśa" is "the red owl," and "śuŋ" is "the large feathers of a bird." "Wahpaha" can mean a hat or a bonnet or a standard, shaft, or pole on which feathers are tied and used in the Dakota dances. Lowie (in "Dance Associations," 110–12) attributed the origin of this dance to the Mandan but says it also bore the name of a Dakota band. "Mawatadaŋ" is the word for the Mandan Indians in the Riggs dictionary. Lowie said the Sisseton dance came from "Little Fish," who claimed Ptahana (Otter Skin) originated the dance, and the Wahpeton one came from Tawatcihe-homini.

51. The Riggs dictionary gives "peźi" as meaning "grass" and "mihnaka" as meaning "to put in under the girdle as a knife or hatchet; to wear round the loins." See Howard, Canadian Sioux, 146–71, on Canadian Dakota grass dances.

place in the fall, but no interest was aroused until autumn. Later, local lodges were established at Enemy Swim Lake, Brown's Valley, and other places in the neighborhood. Simon Cekpaw, a Sisseton, and the writer's informant for this and the Mawatani and Tokana dances, was the first drum owner of the Omaha society. According to him the society originated with the Omaha.

Two Omaha dressed like clowns (Heyoka), were tied together and went around the village singing songs.[52] No one paid much attention to them until they began to sing about the braves. This aroused public interest and the society was founded. Among the Dakota the original clown songs are completely forgotten, but the warrior, victory, and coup songs are preserved. The ceremony finally became known as the Grass Dance because those who went to war in winter had the right to carry grass in their belts because in winter grass was carried by members of a war party for use in starting fires and to put in their moccasins to keep their feet warm.

The officers are as follows:

1 drum keeper (originally the founder)

8 leaders

4 singers, called icapa yuha, or Drumstick Owners[53]

4 women singers selected by the four male singers as a chorus

2 pail dancers (cehtakpea, pail charger)[54]

2 waiters

1 whip bearer (icapsinte yuha)[55]

2 serving stick bearers (canwiyuze yuha)[56]

1 food dipper (wiyohnakiya)[57]

Another Dakota name for this society is the *Okadakiciye Owasin* or "All Friends." It corresponds with the name Heyuska which they say also means "all friends."[58]

52. Howard, *Canadian Sioux*, 173, quoted Sam Buffalo on the role of "playing Heyoka" or "Heyok'a Kaġa" in connection with "pail charging" and the Grass Dance.

53. The Riggs dictionary has "icabu" for drumstick and "yuha" for owner.

54. According to Riggs, "ceh" is a contraction of "Ćega" meaning "kettle" or "pail" and "takpe" means "to attack." See Howard, *Canadian Sioux*, 164, for a translation of "charging of the kettle."

55. The Riggs dictionary has "icapsinte" for "whip."

56. In the Riggs dictionary, "ćanwiyute" is a "wooden measurer," and "wiyuźaźa" is a "basket; colander."

57. Riggs dictionary lists "iyohnakiya" as "to give to eat." The "w-" prefix changes the verb to an adjective.

58. See Howard, *Canadian Sioux*, 146, 160, 165.

In former times the Dakota made a large square log house, supposed to represent an Omaha earth lodge, to shelter the society.

The "Pail Chargers" are braves, and during the feast they take the pail of dog meat or other food and reenact their coups, striking the pail before it is turned over to the waiters to distribute the food. The food dipper feeds the leaders from a spoon, beginning with the drum owner.

The dances are entirely of a social nature and there is no religious function whatever connected with them. It is the only dance which is still kept up by the Dakota in the neighborhood of Sisseton. As among other tribes presents are freely given and received during the performance. Many features are extremely modern and innovations are constantly being adopted. Hoops are carried by the dancers who writhe their bodies through them as they perform. These they say were directly copied from acts that they saw in traveling circuses. Juggling with oranges instead of clay balls and dancing on the tight rope are now features of the society.

Dance of the Thunder Dreamers[59]

A man who had dreamed of the thunder would erect a pole about thirty feet high to the top of which he hung an image of a thunderbird.[60] Around the base of the pole he made a circle of green branches looped over. This was to represent a nest and a raw fish was placed in it. The dreamer then sat at the foot of the pole on the south side in a hole which had been dug for him. He wore a grass headdress drawn

59. Thunder Dreamers are identified as Heyoka. See James R.Walker, *Lakota Belief and Ritual,* Raymond J. De Mallie and Elaine A. Jahner, ed. (Lincoln: University of Nebraska Press, 1 980), 1 55–57; Howard, *Canadian Sioux,* 48, 1 71 –73; Wallis, "Canadian Dakota," 1 11 –2 23; Lowie, "Dance Associations," 1 1 3–1 7. Skinner in "A Sketch of Eastern Dakota Ethnology" (p. 1 72) listed a number of cults and dances decidedly original in his view, with a few found among both Eastern and Western Sioux but among no other peoples. These societies and dances were: Elk Ear, Thunder, Elk, Double Women, Bear, Raw Fish Eaters, Yumini Watcipi, Mocking Dance. Skinner said the Bear Dance resembled the Central Algonkian ceremony only in the title of that ceremony.

60. See Skinner, "The Algonkin and the Thunderbird," *American Museum Journal* 1 4 (1 91 4): 71 –72, for general significance of the thunderbird. Dorsey in "A Study of Siouan Cults," (p. 441 –43) quoted Riggs (*American Antiquity,* 2 :2 67) on the circle dance with a similar description of a great bird image cut from bark, suspended atop a pole, and shot to pieces. Howard (*Canadian Sioux,* 1 05–6) called the Thunderbird Wajiŋyaŋ. Sweetgrass or waćaŋǧa was used to appease this god and make thunderstorms less violent. Those who dreamed of the Thunderbird must join the Heyoka society.

down over his shoulders and this was twisted and tied in a point straight over his forehead. His head was covered with down. He had a drum which he beat and he sang while others danced around bearing drums, and at intervals they would bite and eat the raw fish. At a certain peculiar stroke of the drum the dancers knew that he was signaling that he had seen a vision of the enemy and they all shot at the thunderbird image until the string was broken and it fell. Then each rushed to it trying to be the first to snatch it. The dreamer prophesied when the enemy would be seen and the first person to touch the thunderbird would be the one to count the first coup.

Girls' Purity Ceremony

Girls sometimes gave a certain ceremony for virgins. A round stone was set up and the girls used to come forward one by one to touch it and swear as to their purity. If any lied, the stone toppled over. If any young man heard a girl swear and knew to the contrary, he accused her and dragged her out of the crowd, and she was subjected to all manner of ridicule. If there was any question about the matter the young man had to take oath by the arrow test. If he lied and the test proved it, he would be hurt on the next warpath and in addition he was thoroughly thrashed by the Akicita. This is a Sisseton ceremony and it is also found among the Wahpeton and Santee.

Raw Fish Enters [Eaters] Society[61]

This ceremony was partaken of by those who had as their guardians, the bird called the hontka, (cormorant), loons, divers, otters, and mink.[62] Big wooden bowls of the largest kind were filled with raw fish

61. Wallis in "Canadian Dakota" (p. 65–67) said the dancers went around the circular ceremonial ground, which had an opening in the east; when they arrived at the opening they went out and took a bite of the fish but did not touch the fish with their hands and that a war party invariably followed this dance. Also see Edward Duffield Neill, "Dakota Land and Dakota Life," *Minnesota Collections* (St. Paul: Minnesota Historical Society, 1872), 1:283, Pond, *Dakota or Sioux in Minnesota,* 415–16, and Mary Eastman, *Dahcotah: Life and Legends of the Sioux* (1849; Minneapolis: Ross and Haines, 1962), 77–79. Howard (*Canadian Sioux,* 13) identified this society as "a distinctively Santee dancing society, imitating the cormorant." See also Lowie, "Dance Associations," 123–24.

62. The Riggs dictionary lists "huŋtka" as the cormorant, or a large water-fowl, rather than "hontka." Wallis ("Canadian Dakota," 65) called the dance "osa'k Awutapi watci'pi," which may be from "żożoka," a fish-hawk; "yuta," to eat; and "wacipi," they dance.

which the host dipped out. Some of the grass was pulled away from a patch of ground and upon the bare earth was laid red or blue paint with red and white down and all their medicines were exposed there. The host would tell why he gave this feast, saying it was done to prepare the spirits of those who ate raw fish and had directed it to be done at this time. Then he would order certain of those present to sing, and while this was going on the braves fell to on the raw fish, giving the cries of the animals which they had as guardians. Some were able to eat so fast that they were finished at the end of the first song and just gave the medicine yell, "E ho ho ho ho." Those who could not finish by the end of all the songs had to give some present to the host.

Buffalo Dance[63]

This society was sometimes called the *Nigetankin Kinyan* or big stomachs.[64] Members painted their faces longitudinally half and half, blue and white. Most of the members had to have buffalo power but some who had not were admitted in order to increase the membership. The leaders acted like buffaloes, bellowing and pawing, and all wore buffalo masks over their heads.

The society was "owned" by a man who possessed the drum. This was a large instrument made out of a cottonwood log and covered with buffalo hide, painted half blue and half white. On the upper side was a buffalo head painted in the center with a line drawn through it. The drum sticks were four in number and given to four youths or braves who kept them until time to use them. The drum was never set on the ground; it was carried around even during the dancing.[65] After the cer-

63. Lowie ("Dance Associations," 120) reported that his information came from David Whale and Little Fish, who credited Standing Buffalo, the Sisseton leader, with reviving the Buffalo Dance when he was young. They said the paint differed with each individual. Lowie's article has descriptions of the Buffalo hunt. Wallis ("Canadian Dakota," 58–64) related several personal tales concerning the Buffalo Dance (and HidowAi'nAkA [Hdaiŋyaŋka], "Jingling Runner"; and Susu'wanitci, "Without Testicles"). Also see Howard, *Canadian Sioux*, 171.

64. "Nigetankin Kinyan" or "niǵetaŋka kiŋyaŋ" literally means "stomach-big-to-fly."

65. This monograph does not contain the section on musical instruments; it is found in Skinner, "A Sketch of Eastern Dakota Ethnology" (p. 169). Skinner declared that the deep water drum, which was characteristic of the medicine lodge elsewhere, may have been used in the "wakaŋ watcipi," but ordinarily the tambourine or deeper kettle drum, with one or two heads, was most common. He said ceremonial rattles were usually made of sticks strung with deer hooves or of deer hooves cut in fancy

emony a feast dances and songs were very fast; the performers would bellow like buffalo and running into the crowd would pursue the people. Some put buffalo heads on their horses, leaving eye holes so that the horse could see.

Medicine Eating Feast[66]

This feast, which is perhaps connected with the *Wakan wacipi*, was one of the "Eat All" type so frequently mentioned by the early travelers and missionaries among the Central tribes.[67] Everything had to be eaten by the guest, and presents were given to those who finished first. A box of eagle feathers, ten in number, was obtained by a Wahpeton woman, and we were told that these were gifts for successful contestants. The first person to finish received two feathers which he later exchanged with his host for presents. The next four to finish also received two feathers which they could redeem later on. Sometimes a penalty was

shapes and strung to wear about the neck or over one shoulder in dancing. He continued that the rattles used in the medicine dance were gourds. Flageolets, often carved with loons' heads, were used for courting, and bone whistles for war purposes and the sun dance. Metallic jinglers were probably the successors of deer hooves and used on clothes and bags as rattles.

66. Skinner in "A Sketch of Eastern Dakota Ethnology" (p. 172) stated that the Medicine Dance deserved more than a passing mention. He claimed it resembled the Ojibwe and Central Algonkian Midewiwin, but its organization and ritual were of a very different order; he placed it with the Iowa, Oto, and Winnebago—perhaps intermediate between the Omaha and Ponca and Central Algonkian types. Finally, he said that the coyote dance resembled the Winnebago woman's dance and that heyoka clowns are found among many Plains tribes. See also Skinner "Medicine Ceremony of the ... Wahpeton Dakota," 262–305.

67. Riggs (*Dakota Grammar, Texts, and Ethnography*, 227–29) called the Wakaŋ wacipi the Mystery Dance and said it was confined to the Eastern Dakota and was a secret organization entered through mysterious death and resurrection. The badge of the order was the wakaŋ sack, which should contain four kinds of medicine and represent fowls, quadrupeds, herbs, and trees. A necessary adjunct was the Wakaŋwohaŋpi or Sacred Feast, of the "eat all" kind. The Dakota claim this was communicated to them by the great Uŋkteȟi or god of the water. Dorsey ("Study of Siouan Cults," 440) described punishment of those who violated their obligations as members. Wallis ("Canadian Dakota," 42, 69–77) in 1914 was told by a seventy-year-old man that his grandfather's great-grandfather was a child when the Wahpeton first saw white men and then they possessed only one dance, the wakaŋ watcipi, and other dances were introduced subsequently. It is the most honorable society. It was said the words of the songs are unintelligible to the members and may have been borrowed from the Fox or Sauk; see Gideon H. Pond, "Dakota Superstitions," *Minnesota Collections* (St. Paul: Minnesota Historical Society, 1889), 2:222–28.

inflicted upon those who did not succeed in finishing their portion, for example, we have heard of an old woman who had several dresses taken away from her because she failed to win. Our informant, Mrs. Gray-shawl, was once given a deer's head, neck, and lungs to eat all by herself. She finished first, won the prize, and was making a pipe ceremony while the others were still eating. She denied that this ceremony had anything to do with the Medicine Dance, but other informants contradicted her statement.[68]

Wapiya or Medicineman[69]

A Medicineman when called to attend a sick person first causes a sweat house to be built. The patient is brought there and permitted to enter. Then the medicineman calls his familiar spirits to the spot. He has a little "moving spirit stone" (takuśkanśkan). This stone has the power to stop and bring back to the human body the spirits or souls already on their road to the hereafter or, in other words, to restore the sick to consciousness.[70] It can also find lost horses, etc., or game. When the pa-

68. Skinner discussed the "Medicine Ceremony of the . . . Wahpeton Dakota," 262–305, and included sections on the origin myth, the initiation ceremony, the ten rules of life, the ceremony itself, and funeral customs for society members. The Medicine Dance and the Sun Dance were not included in the monograph found in the Braun Research Library. However, it is likely that he intended to include the material on them because his monograph outline indicates sections for them. See Skinner, "Sun Dance of the Sisseton Dakota," 383–85. See also Pond, *Dakota or Sioux in Minnesota;* Pond, "Dakota Superstitions," 222–28; Riggs, *Tah-koo Wah-kan,* 90–92; Eastman, *Dahcotah,* 74; Neill, "Dakota Land and Dakota Life," 269–71. See Wilson D. Wallis, "The Sun Dance of the Canadian Dakota," *Anthropological Papers of the American Museum of Natural History* 16 (1919): 317–80, and James H. Howard, "Notes on Two Dakota 'Holy Dance' Medicines and Their Uses," *American Anthropologist* 55 (1953): 608–9, and *Canadian Sioux,* 127–38, for Canadian Dakota comparison.

69. Wallis ("Canadian Dakota," 78–79) noted that medicine men could converse with wakaŋ things, locate stolen or lost property by singing songs, make predictions about the near or distant future, perform wonders and transformations, engage in magical contests with other medicine men, and heal the ailing. Wallis provided anecdotes on medicine men and names WakiAsuA [Wakiŋyasuśa] (Thunders Roaring) and Pa'cha [Paśda] (No Scalp) as medicine women. Neill ("Dakota Land and Dakota Life," 269–71) said that those who wished to become medicine men must be initiated through the medicine dance.

70. Wallis ("Canadian Dakota," 82) reported that Wakaŋ taŋka told the Thunders to teach the medicine men to use a large stone, powdery and white within but sparking on the outside, when all other medicines failed, as there are only a few such stones. Pond ("Dakota Superstitions," 238) called Takuśkaŋskaŋ the "four winds."

tients and doctor are together in a sweat lodge the doctor narrates the stories of his fasts and his supernatural dream guardians and what aid they have promised him. Then he weeps, sends the spiritstone off, and the waiting people outside all stand.

All this time the doctor has been sweating his patient, sprinkling the hot stones in the lodge with water which he shakes upon them from a bunch of straw. This is repeated four times and he also talks to the spiritstone, sometimes advising the patient what to do in the future to be cured. Sometimes the doctor learns from his spirit aid that the patient has been shot by a witch arrow (a claw, a bunch of hair, a bead, or a bit of cloth) which has been mysteriously driven into his body near the heart, or in the throat. Then he would sweat his patient again and then return to the people outside. The wapiya [conjurer] then brings in another medicineman to help him with his songs. Then the two medicinemen take the patients again into the lodge, clean a place which they cover with down, and provide tobacco, medicines, and a little bowl of water. He again tells the story of his vision and then begins to act like one of the animals whom he relies upon as a guardian. He goes to the place where the arrow has been shot into the patient's body, bites it, and sucks at the supposed wound until he falls over, while companion cries "e ho ho ho." Then the second doctor blows medicine on the first until he recovers, sings again, and tries once more. At the fourth trial the wapiya is exhausted and four other medicinemen must be called to come and suck at his mouth, while others sing to the accompaniment of gourd rattles. The first three men usually fail, giving the task and uttering the medicine cry, but the fourth man succeeds in bringing out the witch arrow from the mouth of the first medicine man who sucked it from the patient. This is thrown into a bowl of water so all can see it and the patient is pronounced cured. The head medicineman is then paid by the relatives of the patient. He keeps the medicine arrow, or sometimes sent [sic] it back against the witch. An arrow returned in this way is certain to kill the witch who shot it in the first place. It is said that the Teton Sioux also have these practices.

Some of my informants said that if a medicine arrow is extracted from a sick person and not sent back, the witch is obliged to pay a heavy indemnity, such as a horse, to the doctor.[71] A few medicinemen were said to be so powerful they could bring out a witch arrow from a patient at the first trial. Some doctors had the power to plunge their

71. See Howard, *Canadian Sioux*, 134–35, on the "medicine arrow."

hands in hot water or walk on fire in their bare feet between attempts to draw forth the medicine.

Hunting Medicines

Little charms were used for the capture of such animals as the beaver, otter, fisher, mink, bear, wildcat, buffalo, deer, and eagle. They were made of objects usually "received" in dreams, such as roots and herbs pulverized and tied in little buckskin bags which were kept by their owners, often being carried around in their pouches.[72] They were never kept in the tipi, however, but often left quite a long way off. When a man wanted to get any of the animals mentioned, he would give a feast, make an altar by scratching off the surface of the ground for some distance, to form a rectangle, set up four sticks, and place his medicine in the center. Sweetgrass was burned and songs sung. When he was through he and his companions would feast. If the man had a gun he would smudge it in the fumes made from the medicine. The medicine was thought to fly mysteriously through the air and attack the hearts and nerves of the game so that they could not escape.

Jingling-cloud's great-grandfather, who bore the same name, had a very sacred medicine for hunting deer. With it went a little birchbark scroll having a deer drawn on it, showing the heart and the nerves down to each hoof. When the old man wished to kill deer he took a bit of medicine on a stick and touched it to the heart of the deer figure. Then he smudged the bark drawing over a fire in which he had put a little of the medicine, put the scroll in his pouch, took his gun, and started off singing his sacred song in which he referred to deer as the "four-legged animal," saying "Four-legged animal, I have made you walk off your trail." If he shot at a deer in a herd, he would not raise the barrel of his gun after firing, but drop the muzzle forward. This he thought would frighten them and so he often killed a whole herd, one after another. When he got home his people would dress the animals for him. Sometimes he would singe the top of the deer's nose, skin it, and send a herald to call his neighbors in to eat it. Most of these hunting ideas are also characteristic of this [the] Ojibway, Menomini, and other Central Angonkian tribes.

A hunting medicine obtained by the writer consists of a small woven

72. Wallis ("Canadian Dakota," 82) stated that all medicines and all medicine bundles were the result of dreams.

bag, said to be of Ojibway origin, with beads on some of the strands, a little nag [bag] of medicine, and two flat sticks carved on both sides with mnemonic song devices. These figures represent animals which the owner desires to kill. The heart and nerves which he hopes to numb by his medicine songs are carved on the figures. The medicine itself like the woven bag, is said to be an Ojibway hunting charm, but the wooden song records were made by a Wahpeton Dakota.

The first song is for the otter. Incense is burned which attracts the otters who come directly to the hunter. The incense is kept in a thimble until it is used. The song, which is supposed to be in Ojibway, can also be used for hunting deer. It is: ake ki wan daiyaa manetu. Another song is: kunimedukan.

Buffalo Tail Medicine
This consists of a buffalo tail which apparently was once painted red on the inside. In hunting buffalo the tail was suspended outside the lodge, the proper song was sung, and as the wind blew the tail, the herds were constrained to come to the hunters.

Medicines for Healing the Sick
In common with all the Central Algonkian tribes, the Eastern Dakota were and are acquainted with an infinitude of root, bark, and herb medicines. The late Mrs. Grey-shawl once took the writer into the attic of a deserted house and there showed me a medicine which she had secured. It was a tall plant with broadly lanceolate green leaves and had green berries. This she had suspended from the rafters after plentifully befurbishing it with scarlet down at intervals along the stem. The plant was called "Serpent Root" and was supposed to grow with the head of the serpent-like root facing east and the tail to the west.[73] It was a potent medicine plant for some special ailment that I could not ascertain, and had its own special song in the Wakan Wacipi or Medicine Dance.

Magic Medicines for good luck and for love are carried in thimbles on the persons of many of the older Indians. There is a regular good luck medicine of the typical Algonkian type used to bring friendship and good will.

73. Possibly snake root, which is a stimulant that is used to increase perspiration and as a pain reliever, anti-spasmodic, tonic, and for bilious conditions; see Joseph Kadans, *Encyclopedia of Medicinal Herbs* (New York: Arco Publishing Co., 1973), 184.

Berdaches[74]

A boy was once very sick and a winkta learned of it and said it could cure him. The boy objected violently to having anything to do with the winkta. He was overruled by his parents and did indeed get well. He was then obliged to marry the winkta as a reward. When the berdache married him it was given new clothes by the boy's parents and then went off to collect gifts for them. While it was gone the boy died and the winkta hearing of it cut its hair and returned in mourning with horses for the parents. They gave it gifts to cease its mourning and accept its presents. If they had had another son then they would have been obliged to give him to it. If a winkta nicknames any person then that person must tell the name or be very ill.

The story is told of some girls who teased a winkta and were accordingly nicknamed by it. One of the women never mentioned it until she was sick years afterwards when it occurred to her to confess it and she became well.

[LIFE OF THE INDIVIDUAL]
Dakota Naming Customs

Among the Eastern Dakota the custom of Ordinal names to the children as they are born, is found. Thus the first born, if a boy, is called Caske, the second Hepanna, the third Hepina, the fourth Catanna, and the fifth Hakedan. No names occur for more than five, and the last name, Hakedan, as I understand it, means "The Last" with an inference of pity about the title, so that it really means "The Pitiful Last."

With girls the first born is given the name of Winona, the second Hapanna, the third Hapstinna, the fourth Wanske, the fifth Wihake.

Sometimes these ordinal names are born throughout life by the individual. For example the writer was once acquainted with a middleaged Wahpeton who had no other name than Caske. However, this is not often the case, for young men who had distinguished themselves in battle in former years, or in modern times who had displayed conspicuous generosity, were entitled to take new names, especially those of distinguished ancestors now dead. I am also told that men who had had great misfortunes sometimes discarded their names as unlucky and took new ones.

---

74. Skinner retold this story, entitled "A Berdache Story," page 1 95, below. Dorsey ("A Study of Siouan Cults," 467) pointed out that the term for sodomy was "wiŋktapi," and therefore berdaches should not be called hermaphrodites.

In olden times it was customary for the successful warrior to change his name at the Iwakicipi or Victory Scalp Dance, when he "threw away" the old name and took the new one, at the same time giving a horse to some poor person while his relatives also gave gifts broadcast, that the people might remember the new title.[75] This is still done, but I believe on the occasion of the Grass Dance or one of the Warrior Society ceremonies.

Aside from these changes which were made in later life, the baby is usually given a name other than the ordinal name in the following manner. The father or grandmother of a child can name it for some of his deeds done in battle or after a famous ancestor. A few guests are invited to the lodge, or to a dance or a great feast where presents are given and the name announced. The father or mother holds up the child and asks some old man to tell the people what its name is. He cries, "Hear ye, So-and-so says that hereafter this child shall be called after his grandfather" (or some other relative, provided that relative is deceased). After this the presents which are kept nearby, are brought forth and given. It is said that when the child is first brought in to the place where the ceremony is held the women give the "woman's cheer" and when the herald has finished they cheer again and sing when the goods are given away. In the song, the child's name is repeated and the women yell whenever it is mentioned.

Types of Names

Having no clan or gens system the Eastern Dakota do not possess the clan, and gentile names found among the Southern Siouan and Central Algonkian tribes for example. From his own data and that of Riggs and Dorsey, the writer presents the following types.[76]

1. Ordinal names, as mentioned above, such as Caske and Winona.
2. Names consisting of a single noun as: Maḣpiya, Cloud; Hoksidan, Boy; Wowancinyan, Faith.
3. Names consisting of a single adjective, as Śakpe, Six.
4. Names formed by a noun with a modifying adjective, the commonest type of all: Mato-maza, Iron Bear, Two Star, Oneroad.
5. Two nouns may be used, as Mato-tatanka, Bull Bear;

75. See "War Charms," page 71, above. See also Howard, *Canadian Sioux,* 53, 170.

76. The Dakota language transcription system in the manuscript is inconsistent and was in the process of being corrected, obvious in all the handwritten notes and corrections on this page. I chose to use the last form noted by hand on the manuscript.

Maȟpiya-wicasta, Cloud man. (The adjective follows the noun, in Dakota, and the second noun in this case should be first translated. Thus Mato-Tatanka is literally Bear-bull, but Bull-bear is the correct translation).

6. A possessive pronoun may be prefixed to the name, as: Taoyate-duta, His Scarlet People; Tapetatanka, His Great Fire.

7. They may consist of verbs in the intransitive form as: Wakute, Shoote; Wanapeya, One Who Causes Flight.

8. They may be compounded of a verb and an adverb, as Stands Fast.

9. They may be made up of an intransitive verb and an adverb, as Iyanymani, Running Walker.

10. They may be made up of a noun modified by an adverb, as: Maȟpiya-sna, Jingling Cloud; Ȟeȟaka-mani, Walking Elk; Tatanka-najin, Standing Buffalo.

Puberty, Fasting, and Dreaming [77]

Among the Wahpeton, unlike their Algonkin neighbors, boys only are required to observe the puberty dreamfast, and the age at which the ordeal takes place is from sixteen to eighteen, later than is usually the case among the forest tribes. In anticipation of the great event during childhood the youths are taught certain prayers and formulae for appeal to the Great Powers.

Maȟpiyasna was taken by his grandmother with the other children of his family, to the shore of Drywood Lake and there caused to cast red down into the water with a prayer to Unkteȟi of which he remembered the following:[78]

> Uncina maka kin den mahen
> Grandma earth the this inside

77. This section was repeated in the folklore manuscript as "Notes on Puberty Fasting and Dreaming" (it is included here and deleted there). Howard (*Canadian Sioux,* 125–27) called this rite Hamdeciya; Riggs listed "haŋmde" as "to fast and dream, to have intercourse with the spiritual world."

78. "Uŋkteȟi" is listed in the Riggs dictionary as the Dakota god of the water. Dorsey ("Study of Siouan Cults," 438–40) stated that these gods have the power to send from their bodies a wakan influence or "toŋwaŋ," which is irresistible even by the superior gods. This power was common to all Taku Wakaŋ and was infused into each mystery sack that was used in the mystery dance. The mystery feast and the mystery dance were received from these gods. The Uŋkteȟi were thought to feed on the spirits of human beings. The offerings required by them were swan's down reddened with vermilion, deer skins, dogs, mystery feasts, and mystery dances.

nonge   hdubdaya   non kapi   kta kehapi
the ears to spread out you be there will you have told me
qon akantu wakanheja om wahi
but upon   children with I came
nawajin   onsihanyan   wahinyajice
standing mercifully down
duta waśte yadaka   unocupi
red well you have loved we give
anpetu kin de ska qa waśte
day the this clear and good

"Grandma inside this earth! You have promised me that you would prick up your ears. I have come and stand upon (this earth) with these children. We mercifully give you this red down which you love so well. (Let) this (day) be clear and good."

At the conclusion of this invocation, the children, who stood on stones near the brink, cast their down into the water.

When undergoing their fast, the youths would retire to the top of a hill and wailed there all night. Some had their hands tied behind their backs to keep them from running away. In many instances four stakes were set up and the faster was tied between them and left there all night. They do not blacken their faces, this is only done for mourning, or on return from a war party.[79]

Jingling Cloud gave the following anecdote to illustrate this procedure. At Fort Totten a youth intending to fast went with his chum up on a high hill called "The Devil's Heart."[80] The chum dug four deep holes and set the stakes in very firmly. The faster loosened his hair and stripped his pipe and tobacco pouch, for his partner was to help him to smoke at intervals during the night.

When all was in readiness the chum went away, leaving the faster wailing "Hee-u! Hee-u! Hee-uuu!" Just about dark he sneaked back with his face whitened to resemble a ghost. The faster, in terror tried to break away, but could not. Four times the joker approached, and on the last trip he washed his face and offered the pipe to his chum, saying,

79. Skinner in "A Sketch of Eastern Dakota Ethnology" commented that the Central Algonkian blackened their faces, and both sexes fasted. Skinner also observed that among the central tribes dreams were generally about some great fundamental mythic power of the universe, the sun, morning star, thunder, moon, horned snake, or underworld bear or panther.

80. This is near Devils Lake, N.Dak.

"How are you?" His chum was very angry but could not help himself. Towards morning the Morning Star appeared, and then the faster saw a hill to the north of him rise up and come down to the lake, like a monster with a huge mouth ready to grab him. This was too much for the faster, who, with a desperate wrench broke away from his moorings and fled without having his vision.

The Beings who most frequently have mercy on fasters are the bear, buffalo, elk, Unktehi, and Tree Dweller or Canotina.[81] Men who dream of the Wiŋyaŋ Nunpapi, or double women must become berdashes.[82]

The Dakota dreamer must take whatever dream comes to him. Unlike the Menomini he may not try again.[83] The "spirit" may appear to him in its true shape as an animal, or it may come as a man, interview him and go away as an animal.

Dreams of this nature are not to be discussed in public. The most common occasion for referring to them by doctors is before taking charge of a patient. Then the healer recites his dream and enumerates his powers.

Jingling Cloud's great grand father, Iron Bear, had the grizzly bear as his guardian. He was often wounded but recovered through its aid. On one occasion a party of Gros Ventres and Mandans drove some Dakota into a hollow and shot down on them. Although the Sioux killed the Mandan chief, whom Iron Bear (the hero) would not allow to be scalped, the others prevailed, and all the Dakota were slain except Iron Bear, who was wounded. When the allies gained possession of the field

81. "A little dwarf who has great power for hunting. He can make people come to him, and then gives them valuable information. After this he rattles off the names of his visitor relatives, winding up with 'Will you give me this?' The bewildered visitor always agrees. He is then told that he must make a feast four times a year, is taught the proper songs, and dismissed. When he gets home he finds that some or all of his relatives, whom he has been hoodwinked into giving to the dwarf, are dead, but he ever afterwards has great powers"; Skinner's note on a Tree Dweller or Ćaŋotiŋa in "Tree-dweller Bundle of the Wahpeton Dakota," 66–73. See also Howard, *Canadian Sioux*, 108–9; Dorsey, "Study of Siouan Cults," 475; Stephen R. Riggs, *Mary and I: Forty Years among the Sioux* (Boston: Congregational Sunday-School and Publishing Society, 1880), 71. Riggs dictionary gives "Caŋotidaŋ" as Dakota god of the woods. The suffix "-na" and "-daŋ" are both diminutives, but "-na" was most frequently used in the Sisseton dialect.

82. Howard (*Canadian Sioux*, 107) quoted Robert Good Voice, Sam Buffalo (Round Plain), and Kenneth Eastman (Oak Lake) as stating that those who dreamed of Double Woman usually became good craftworkers.

83. Skinner in "A Sketch of Eastern Dakota Ethnology" (p. 171) stated that the Central Algonkian could reject a dream three times.

and saw that their chief was unscalped, they merely counted all four coups on Iron Bear and released him. They left him lying on the field, but were astonished to find, on the following day, that he had escaped, and the tracks of a grizzly lead [sic] away from where he had lain. They trailed the animal to a thicket, where they found a wounded bear lying groaning. Later, when Iron Bear did not return, the Sioux heard of what had happened from the Mandan, and found his skeleton in the bushes where the bear had been.

The Thunder is an important dream guardian. He appears to dreamers as a man with his hair cut just below the ears as though he were in mourning.[84] He carries a gun. The Thunder always prefaces his statements by saying that he has heard a cry and has come in answer. He can give war powers, prophesying the number of scalps and coups, etc., the recipient shall get. The faster must cause four ceremonial sweat houses to be built, use each in turn, and must sing certain sacred songs while sweating. If a war leader does not keep his obligations to the thunder he may lose some of his warriors.[85]

The following peculiar ideas are held concerning the reason why certain animals appear to some individuals, and, although they might perhaps be just as well classified under beliefs connected with the transmigration of souls, they will be noted here.

A man may know his personal guardian before he is born, and such a person makes this fact public as soon as he is old enough to speak. This fact will lead him to pray to this pre-natal guardian when he undergoes his puberty fast. The Powers who are connected with this phenomenon, which, by the way, resembles the Menomini idea concerning the thunder, are the Unktehi, buffalo, elk, coyote horse, thunder, and bear.[86] The person who claims previous knowledge of these powers usually maintains that he has led a previous existence, but was killed in war, after which his spirit wandered about, visiting various Indian bands and tribes until it found someone who pleased it.

84. Hair cut just below the ears was a sign of mourning. This image was hard to dispel when white society insisted that Indians cutting their hair was a sign of acculturation and civilization.

85. Wallis ("Canadian Dakota," 83, 86) was told Thunder taught medicine men and granted powers prior to birth that remained in the individual's possession throughout life; in addition, powers were acquired during the individual's lifetime by encounters with specific wakan beings, such as Stone, Spider, Buffalo, Gull, Dog, Turtle, and Clown.

86. {See Anthropological Papers of the American Museum of Natural History, Vol. XIII, p. 00"} [Skinner's note].

These wandering ghosts are often very hungry and wretched, so it is customary for Dakota who are charitable to offer food to the wayfaring spirits and pray before eating, saying: "Spirits partake of this food, bless it that this day may be bright. This day may we be provided with a four-footed animal (as food) and be satisfied."[87] Couples who habitually do this are apt to be rewarded by having some passing spirit enter the body of the woman and be born as their child.

The story that a reborn person tells of his relation with the Powers is of this order. Having left the corpse the ghost wanders around until it sees a man standing on a high bank or hill who calls to it and invites it into his lodge. When its draws near, the hill turns out to be a magic home, with a door facing the east or the southwest. As the spirit enters the man it becomes an animal. The spirit guest sees the tracks of other human beings going in and coming out, as it enters. Once inside it the anthropomorphic host reveals his secrets and medicines to the ghost, forecasts its future life, and takes care of it for some time, when it is dismissed. The ghost then visits the Indian villages and peeps into the tents until it strikes a family it fancies, then it goes in and is born. The things that the ghost hears as it enters the tent are its last recollections of the spirit life. When next the spirit comes to it will be in the body of a child, probably about four years old, having been in a trance from the moment of entering its mother's womb.

The child, on realizing who it is, is bewildered, he no longer recognizes its parents knowing that its real first parents were others. The phenomenon usually comes to light when the children are playing. Some child will ask the little one what its name is, and the *wakan* boy will reply giving his former title instead of the one he is now known by. The children, astonished, tell their parents who inform those of the wakan boy, who then realize he is *en rapport* with the Powers. It is not always necessary for such a child to fast like the others as he already knows the proper things to do, the feasts and sacrifices to make for his guardian, and when he performs rites his patron appears again and instructs him.

Jingling Cloud has often heard people tell of their experiences of this sort. A Kiowa young man in Oklahoma invited some Yankton to visit him and told them that in a former existence he had been a Dakota. He told them his name, where he lived, who his relatives were. All these details were later investigated and found to be correct.

87. {This custom also has a Menomini parallel} [Skinner's note].

One of Jingling Cloud's uncles claims to have been reborn three times. The first time he was a whiteman and a blacksmith in the east. As evidence of this he is an excellent gunmaker and repairer today, although without instruction. His second existence was as a Hidatsa in a village located on a branch of the Missouri. He and some other Hidatsa were in a rifle pit and were surrounded by Dakota. There was a trench running from the rifle pit to the river he tried to flee down this with his bow and arrows but was met by a foe wearing a buffalo horn headdress, who struck him over the head with a sword and killed him.

When he came to, it was as a spirit detached from his body, and he was a spectator of the Sioux scalping his own corpse along with those of his comrades. Then he became cold and miserable. He was apparently still clad in his blood soaked clothes, so he determined to go back to his wife and son. He traveled along a few feet above the earth, but unable to tread upon it. The gusts of wind blew him back for he had no substance so could not make headway against them.

At last he reached the village, but the wind prevented him from entering. He could see his wife and child inside his lodge, and tried to call to them to ask for dry clothes, but they did not hear him. People passed back and forth very near him, but only the dogs saw him and barked furiously. He could see the lodge poles, and the contents of the tipis, but the lodge covers were transparent and invisible.

In some of the tents people were eating corn cakes baked in the ashes. He was very hungry and wished that they would invite him to eat, but they did not, so he wandered on forlorn. Here and there, as he traveled, he met various animals who saw him, greeted him, and gave him shelter and comfort and told him their secrets.

At last he came to a village where he saw a lodge in which sat a young and lovely girl working hard at porcupine quill embroidery. He went in and sat down, but the girl took no notice of him, and, though famishing, he was ashamed to speak to her there alone. Finally the girl said: "I'm going out," and suiting her actions to her words, she got up and left. He waited a long time for her to return, and at last he got up, went to the door of the lodge, stepped out, and was born. The busy woman was his twin sister, who came into the world nearly twenty-four hours before he did; the lodge where he sat was his mother's womb. The midwives thought his mother would die, for it seemed as if he would never come forth. He was able to recall everything up to the moment of his birth, just as soon as he was able to talk.

It is said that sometimes female twins are reincarnated "Double

Women" or *Wiŋyaŋ Nonpapi*, exceedingly *wakan* and important, or if the twins are male and female, that they were formerly man and wife, but in this case the man's story and statement that he never saw the girl who was born with him before he entered the lodge that turned out to be his mother's womb, and proves her to be his sister.

[Courtship, Marriage, Polygamy, and Divorce]
Marriage Ceremony

The Dakota watched their daughters very closely but they contrived to meet the young men at dances. The boys would edge up as close as they could and talk to the girls. After they had met several times and found that they cared for each other, the parents of the boy try to arrange a *wohanpi* or ceremonial marriage.[88] The boy's father or an old man hired by him would take a pipe of tobacco to the girl's parents and ask for her. If accepted the old man raises his hands palms downward, facing the girl, and say, "Hai." Then the older people smoked and the girl is dressed and taken over to the groom's lodge. Two red spots are painted, one on each cheek, and she was given her parents' best running horse to ride over upon. When all was ready, the girl's male relatives took the lead, carrying their guns, and a close relation led the horse upon which the girl was mounted. Meanwhile, the other family prepared a great feast and six of the groom's relatives, brothers or cousins, went out to meet the girl. If the groom had neither brothers nor cousins, then his uncles went forth. They carried with them a red blanket and lifting the girl from her horse they would put her in the blanket and the girl with hanging head was carried into the groom's lodge, where the girl's relatives gave her away, challenging any other warrior present to do likewise if he was brave enough. The girl's male relatives fired their guns, refused the feast offered them, and went back, leaving the groom's relatives to eat the feast. After this, the groom's family went to the girl's parents carrying hides and garments to give to the sisters or cousins of the girl. The groom's relatives then re-dress the bride in fine clothes, re-braid her hair and re-paint her face. Now, all is ready for the groom's relatives to go to the girl's family where they are received and feasted. Then presents are given by all parties concerned to the poor and many presents are given to the girl's relatives.

Sometimes the proceedings are reversed and the girl's family buy the groom for her, particularly if he is an industrious fellow. Some-

---

88. The Riggs dictionary translation of "wohaŋpi" is "a boiling; a feast."

times when a young man wants a girl badly he tells some old female relative to take the guns and blankets and visit the male relations of the girl with the proposition. They talk the matter over and, if agreed, they divide the presents and bring the girl to him. If she is poor, of course, she has to walk. Four young men are sent over to bring her in, in the blanket. All these proceedings are reversed if the girl makes the overtures for the man.

Another method of marriage is this: A youth who is attracted by a girl may come to her lodge at night and stay outside. He signals to her with a flute, when she goes for water. He meets her and talks to her, or after the others have gone to sleep he may enter the lodge and talk and sit by her head. Finally, they may run away together to another band. Later, they would invite the girl's parents to visit them and give them presents.

Adultery

This crime was punished by whipping as a rule, but sometimes a guilty wife had her hair cut off by her husband. It was rarely that the nose was forfeited. Their clothes were also torn. If a member of the Napeśni dance learns that his wife is being courted by another, it is considered a disgrace for him to remonstrate or to resist as he is supposed to be brave. If he takes any notice of the offense he will be kicked out of the society and have his clothes torn by the akicita.[89]

Divorce

Divorce among the Eastern Dakota was very simple. If a man found out that his wife was unfaithful to him, he simply called upon her lover and forced him to take the woman.

Giving away Wives

This custom which was very much like that practiced by the Ponca and some other tribes during the Heyuska was sometimes known among the Eastern Dakota.[90] Once, Bawling-bull during a dance had the her-

---

89. According to the Riggs dictionary, in the "napeśnikaǵapi" or "make-no-flight" dance and feasts connected with it, one makes a covenant not to flee in battle. See Lowie, "Dance Associations," 107–8, on the No-Flight Dance; the Sisseton Little Fish and Red Beads had been members in their youth; the Wahpeton Hepana said the dance originated in a Thunder revelation.

90. Heyuska could be translated either as horns or hills, cleansing or whitening. Skinner used it here to signify the grass dance, "all friends," or Omaha dance.

ald announce that he would give a horse to the first old woman who cared to claim it and added that the first man to enter his lodge might have his wife. Some of his brothers-in-law were angry and got there first and refused to allow anyone else to enter. They took back his wife but Bawling-bull with great show of contempt took his son to his sister's lodge until he married again. Not infrequently dancers gave away their wives in this fashion just to show how brave they were.

Plural Marriage

A man who married the older sister usually married the others, as they became of age, so they would not be separated. The oldest became the head wife or *teyakicyapi*.[91] This title is only used by visitors.

[Mortuary Customs and the Hereafter]
Funeral Services

It was supposed that everybody had two spirits.[92] Of the two spirits which my informant knew one was called *wanagi* or soul, this is the spirit which goes to the hereafter; and *wacanagiwuhapi,* the ghost, which stays in the mourning bundle with the lock of hair. This idea of two spirits, one of which remains behind and the other going to the hereafter, is also found among the Menomini and Plains-Cree.

When a person dies, a lock of hair was cut from the head of the deceased and wrapped up in a bundle and kept very carefully. The bundle is decorated and hung up and it is thought that the ghost stays in it or near it. Sometimes the relatives who have charge of the bundle, hear a voice or a whistle or may even see a person nearby. It is always kept in the back of the lodge in the center behind the fire. Food is offered it from time to time and it is thought that the ghost partakes of it in spirit. After the ghost has used it anyone may eat the food.

The bundle is kept for a long time. Finally, a feast is given for the ghost. When the feast is prepared, the bundle is hung up on a pole with presents nearby. Someone is selected to eat what is left when the spirit has partaken of the feast in essence and he receives the presents which are placed with the bundle. It is always necessary that the person who eats the feast be of the same sex as the deceased. When this is all over,

91. Riggs said that when a man had more than one wife, one called the other "teya." Riggs gave the definition of "teyakiciyapi" as those who stand in the relation of "teya" to each other.

92. {Some earlier writers claim that there was confusion in the minds of the Dakota as to the number of spirits that a person had, some Indians claiming as many as four. See Minnesota Historical Society Collections, p. } [Skinner's note].

the relatives wail for the last time. When the lock of hair is buried the spirit is then thought to leave. This is quite separate from the feast of the societies for the dead and was done for everyone. If a person belonged to any of the societies, say the Kit-fox, or the No-flight, then his organization would come to his lodge and stand outside in a circle singing their songs.[93] Finally, a man would take a knife and cut a hole in the left arm of each member to show that they too took part in the mourning for the dead with the relatives. All the time they continued singing. Finally, they take the body and bury it.

In this connection it should be noted that the Eastern Dakota, unlike their Algonkian neighbors, do not have the custom of removing the corpse of the deceased through the back of the lodge but always carried it through the door. From two to three years after the society has conducted the funeral, the relatives of the deceased get up a feast and invite the organization there at which time they give them presents which they have collected. This ends the mourning of the family. Among the Dakota there is no counting of coups at the funeral as is found among the Menomini and Winnebago. Women formerly cut their arms and legs. The father of the young man always punched a hole through his arm. The society brothers of a dead man always felt in duty bound to mutilate themselves in the same way as the chief mourners had done.

Of recent years the Wahpeton and Santee bury the bodies of their dead in the ground, but it is said that the Sisseton used to use a scaffold erected on four poles, and also that before 1851 the Wahpeton and Santee also used to put the bodies of their dead on trees or less commonly, placed on a scaffold.[94] Some of the old people objected to throwing earth over the dead when they were buried in the ground.

It was customary to make the grave shallow and to lay the body in

93. "They had a great day for Private Hoarce Borse [Amos Oneroad's cousin] killed in action in France. . . . They had a real Military Escort from Waubay to the little Indian Episcopal Church in the shores of Enemy Swim Lake[,] name very appropriating for a hero. I think the three countries came to pay its last homage and respects and śungi [Fox] was laid to rest. . . . The song of the Kit-foxes Society once more rang out as in olden days after the return of the warriors—and probably John will sing the song when if you get to stop here in Sisseton"; Oneroad to Skinner, March 28, 1922, Skinner Collection.

94. One could speculate on the significance of this date. The major treaties with the Dakota setting up the early reservations were the Treaty of Mendota and the Treaty of Traverse des Sioux, both signed in 1851. This date may have evolved to represent the impact of acculturation, which was a divisive factor among Iŋyaŋgmani's people.

it as though the deceased were asleep. Then sticks were placed over it and the earth heaped upon them. Then a split log house was put over the grave. This form of burial was called *Canotihnakapi* (sleep inside).[95]

According to Jingling-cloud, the body of the deceased among the Wahpeton was dressed in its best and then wrapped in a buffalo hide. If the Indians were dwelling in the forest it was placed on a branch of a tree; if on the plains, on a platform or scaffold on top of a hill. Sometimes it was buried in the ground, the grave being dug with a digging stick. Occasionally, the body would be left in a tipi and the tipi deserted.[96]

When a man was dying the mourners made a great wailing as he drew his last breath, and again when the body was being carried out from the door of the lodge. The chief mourning came, however, when the body was laid in the ground when the relatives cut their hair, gashed their arms. They would kill the man's favorite horse and dog at the grave and put his guns in or leave them on a platform.[97]

Jingling-cloud thought that there was only one soul which resided in the heart.[98]

If a Wahpeton man, who was well known, died, the widow cropped her hair below the ears, put on a wretched dress and wore a buffalo robe with the stripes of porcupine work on it torn off, and the tails, jinglers, and red feathers removed. All the clothing and goods of the deceased were given to the poor, except her tent and blanket. She did not appear in public places, but stayed at home doing needle work and wailing in the morning and evening. She was not supposed to smile or laugh. The period of mourning was supposed to last four years, but could last longer if desired. Very young girls were sometimes permitted to remarry after two years. When the period of mourning was over, relatives combed her hair and put deer tallow in it and braided it before the multitude and feasted with her. Then she donned new clothes and her relatives give her presents. Orphans receive gifts of clothes

95. The literal translation for "caŋotihnakapi" is "wood-dwelling-dead persons laid away."

96. Ella Deloria said that this was an indication of honor. See "A Boy Joker," page 192, below.

97. Skinner in "A Sketch of Eastern Dakota Ethnology" (p. 170) stated that a characteristic among the Eastern Dakota was the custom of having the society of the deceased, Kit-Fox, No-Flight, or whatever it might be, mourn for him.

98. Here again it is not clear if Skinner is speaking of Amos Oneroad or his great-grandfather.

and horses from others. At the end of the mourning, clothes were given to orphans or poor people. This was done by an old man who was paid for his trouble.

Hereafter

The Wahpeton believe that the soul goes to a round house on high where the great spirit lives. First, the soul travels to the west and then up. It crosses a river flowing from the west. Then departed ancestors are found who dwell on both sides of the river, and there are guards along the road to tell the village herald when a new soul approaches. The herald first questions the newcomer as he approaches the village. He then announces through the camp that so-and-so has come. The relatives then take the newcomer into their lodge and offer him food. Sometimes spirits come back and they are always hungry. The people therefore offer food to ghosts. Sometimes they place it on or near the grave. This is a double act of charity for the living poor will devour the food after the spirits have taken the essence.

When a man dies, a lock of his hair is taken and put in a bundle of clothes. The bundle is called *wapahta* as "the spirit of the departed brave."[99] It is kept one year and from time to time tobacco is put on it. At the end of that time there is a feast and the hair is buried.

Some of the Eastern Dakota claim they have learned of the hereafter from people who have gone into trances or have apparently died who have come to life again. Sometimes such persons have remained as many as four days in a trance, and are able therefore to tell very well of the other world. There is a long road of the dead traversing the earth, which the souls must follow until finally they reach a river, before crossing which they hear voices trying to scare them back. However, if they see anyone passing on ahead, they follow the crowd and cross. On the other side of the stream they meet deceased relatives who cry and give them food. People who dream of crossing usually die soon afterwards, even if they come to life later.[100] Some of those they find on

99. This is not a translation of "wapahta." Riggs defined "wapahta" as "a bundle, a pack"; or "pahta," "to tie in bundles."

100. {But those who do not eat the food offered them by the souls will live. The writer had a peculiar dream of this nature during an illness just preceding his visit to Sisseton, in which he refused to partake of a dog feast. This, all his Dakota friends regarded, as the only reason for his recovery, and he received several visits from survivors of the families of those he dreamt of meeting, to inquire about the appearance and welfare of their dead} [Skinner's note].

the other side were still alive but these too soon die. Those who do not cross the river, live to a normal age. Some are unable to find any way of getting over the water. Others find footprints. There is no bridge.[101] Tradition states that the milky way is the path that the warriors tread, but no returning dead person has ever spoken of having gone on it.

Mounds.[102]

Simon Cekpaw, a Sisseton insists that all the old people account for the mounds by saying that anciently there were very numerous people dwelling in the country where they now live. These people were war-like and though they had no bows and arrows, were well-provided with warclubs of stone covered with rawhide. In their hand-to-hand combat many were slain and with shovels made from flattened bark by means of stone axes, earth was scraped up and the bodies, which were first laid on the surface of the prairie, were covered with earth. Wolves would dig in the mounds and the relatives would fill in the holes and place more earth on them until the mounds grew very large. Even in more recent times people who died out on the prairie were sometimes covered with rawhide and earth heaped on them. Sometimes they threw on more earth in later years. It is said that Victor Renville opened a mound and found a skeleton which showed that one of the legs had been broken and then healed again.[103] A deer horn lay beside it. Most mounds occur near Brown's Valley and near Enemy Swim Lake.

[MATERIAL CULTURE]
[Houses, Costumes, etc.]
Dress
The Sisseton, Santee, and Wahpeton used to dress differently. The Sisseton men parted their hair in the middle and wore it in two braids wrapped with strips of otterskin. They had legging and shirts of buckskin which were garnished with extremely long fringes mixed with the scalplocks of enemies which they either took or bought from others.

101. Skinner in "A Sketch of Eastern Dakota Ethnology" (p. 169) stated that the souls were not supposed to have to cross a bridge.
102. According to another section entitled "Mounds," which was on a miscellaneous sheet and crossed off, "the Eastern Dakota used to bury their dead intrusively in mounds even as late as eighty or ninety years ago but never made them."
103. Victor Renville, the son of Gabriel Renville, was a scout. He was also an ordained Episcopal priest and served many churches on and near the Sisseton Reservation. See Anderson and Woolworth, eds., *Through Dakota Eyes*, 105.

They also used twisted strips of weasel skin on their leggings particularly, and long leg strips of porcupine quills. They used breechclouts of leather and wore buffalo robe blankets.

The women wore buckskin leggings and a one-piece garment of the Plains type.[104] However, the dress of Waanaton's wife in New York Historical Society is of Ojibway type with separate sleeves.[105] The Wahpeton and Santee dressed rather similarly. The men banged their hair in front and back and dressed it in four little braids, two hanging over the forehead and two in the rear. They also wrapped their hair with bright-colored cloth, rather than with otterskin. Their shirts, which were of buckskin, are said to have been fringeless; their leggings were like a trouser leg with the seam in front and small at the ankle with a large flap at each side of the foot. A narrow strip, about half an inch long, was cut in fine fringe and sewed into the seam in front. The tops of the leggings were large with double strings to fasten to the belt.

None of the men, according to Simon Cekpa, one of my informants, roached the hair, except officers of the Tokana who wore their hair this way during the four years of their incumbency. Jingling-cloud, however, gives some contradictory evidence on this point, saying that in very ancient times, the roach hair dress was known.

The women of the Santee and Wahpeton wore blouse-like shirts in cloth at least in recent years, and skirts made of a square piece of buckskin wrapped around the waist in true Central Algonkin style. Of recent years, the shirts were of calico and the skirts were ornamented with silk ribbon applique. A calico shirt adorned with native-made silver brooches was obtained from Mrs. Gray-shawl, a Wahpeton.

Headdresses All the divisions of the Sioux seem to have worn the eagle feather war-bonnet and the deer's hair roach. Simon Cekpa once made a close fitting skull cap covered with white weasel skins and adorned with a pair of split buffalo horns. Buffalo horns were sometimes added to ordinary war-bonnets and eagle feather bonnets with long trailers were donned by horsemen.

Woven sashes were also worn around the head. Eagle feathers were assumed by those who had earned the right to wear them.[106]

104. Skinner in "A Sketch of Eastern Dakota Ethnology" (p. 164) said women wore Central Algonkian dress but included no details.

105. This was probably the wife of Wanata (the Charger).

106. Skinner in "A Sketch of Eastern Dakota Ethnology" (p. 164) said warriors who had entered the camp circle of the enemy and escaped alive were entitled to wear the war bonnet.

Necklaces Necklaces were made of wampum of trade beads, and of deer's hoofs cut into divers[e] shapes and strung on buckskin thongs. Grizzly bear claw necklaces of the Sauk and Fox type wound with otter fur were formerly worn. The writer collected a bear's paw necklace made from the entire skin of a paw slit so that it would go over the head of the wearer.

Sashes These were worn by the Eastern Dakota about the head, over the shoulder, or around the waist, and differ in no particular [way] from those used by the Central Algonkin.

Beaded Garters These garters are said only to have been worn by the Santee. Like those of the Central Algonkian they were worn outside the legging below the knee and were articles of adornment for men only.

Moccasins Anciently, the Wahpeton and Santee wore moccasins with large ankle flaps of the Sauk and Fox type. Then they took up moccasins of the Ojibway style, soft-soled like the former, seamed over the instep, and with extension uppers that came over the ankles and with hardly more than a notch for flaps. This style still persists among all the bands of Eastern Sioux. The Sisseton are said to have been more addicted to wearing the hard-soled type of the Plains.

[Dwellings]

Bark House—Titonka[107] According to my Wahpeton informants, long poles are taken and thrust into the ground and arched over across each other to form the framework of this type of lodge. If the poles are not long enough two are lashed together with basswood string. Cross pieces are tied with bark to the main poles about two feet apart. The outer covering, which is tied on, is of birchbark in the Minnesota country and of cottonwood farther west. The bark roof is begun at the bottom and succeeding layers are made to overlap the preceding ones at the top. A smoke hole is left at the apex and a little round bark flap is made to pull over it when it rains. This is placed slantingly so it will slide over on the west side, as the rain in the Eastern Dakota country usually comes from the west. As this type of lodge is usually used in winter, dirt or straw, or both are piled up around the outside. Sometimes, the lodges were entirely covered with earth. Clay or straw was used to chink up the cracks on the inside. All the lodges of this description which the writer saw among the Eastern Dakota were of tem-

107. If this were "titaŋka," it would translate as "big or great dwelling."

porary construction for summer use, and closely resembled those of the Iowa, Kansa, Winnebago, Ojibway, and Menomini, being round in groundplan and semi-globular or round roofed. Sometimes large beams were used in building these lodges in ancient times making them more like the earth houses of the Omaha and Mandan. The doors of these were covered with hide, canvas, or bark and were square in shape. Two sticks were set up outside the entrance to form door posts and the bark door slid open and shut between them. None of the lodges which came under my observation had benches built around the walls inside, as among the Algonkians, Jingling-cloud thinks that they were never used, but this is doubtful in my opinion. Instead of the benches, it is said, that willow brush was banked along the wall. Willow hoops were set up very close to each other and overlapped around the fireplace and straw or hay was packed on the floor between this boundary and the bush seats. Buffalo robes were flung over the piles of brush next to the wall.

The cooking utensils were kept on each side of the door. It was a rule that no one should step over the fireplace or lift a coal with the blade of a knife. The grandmothers, if there were any in the family, had their place next to the door. If there was only one grandmother, she sat on the left of the father. Mother and children sat on the right or vice versa. The guest's place (*catku*, or front) was directly in the rear opposite the door and behind the fireplace.

Square Bark House The square bark house, called *tanpawokaya* (Birchbark tent), was the summer lodge and was made of a pole foundation with square sides and angular roof exactly like those of the Menomini and other Central Algonkian.[108] This type of lodge has long been obsolete. It had benches around the wall inside and the door was at one end or at the side. It was easily taken down and put up.

Conical birchbark tents like those of the Ojibway are said never to have been used.[109]

Tipi The Waḣpeton skin tipi is made of fifteen poles with a three-pole foundation. One pole forms one side of the door, the other two the back. In setting up the poles the builder works back from the door post to the center then returns and works the other way. Then another pole is used to raise the tent cover which is tied to it making four

108. "Taŋpa" means "white birch bark."
109. Skinner in "A Sketch of Eastern Dakota Ethnology" (p. 165) said the Wahpeton and Isaŋti used the square bark house in the summer and the round or hemispherical lodge in the winter. The latter were sometimes heavily built and earth covered.

for its foundation. This pole falls in the rear of the lodge. A rope is thrown about the top of the tipi poles and is then tightened by means of this tying pole. Then the front of the lodge cover is pinned down, and the cover stretched a little further. Holes are dug with a digging-stick for the poles. Care is taken to keep the hide cover about five inches from the ground so the poles can fit in. Tent pins are put in, two at the door, and two half way around, to stretch the cover. Then the others are driven in to hold it down. The anchor rope is then thrown inside the lodge and pegged down to the ground just as the writer has observed it among the Plains-Cree. The poles are then stuck in the sockets of the ears. A long stick is hung horizontally on the bottom of the door flap to hold it down.

The Eastern Dakota, in general, use the three-pole foundation. The three poles are first tied together at one end and then set up in a tripod. One goes at the door and the other two at the rear. The other poles are cleverly interlocked and the rope brought around them twice to hold them, and then anchored to a tree or a peg in the ground. Three or four other poles are then slipped under the tie to make it firmer and the cover, which is made of from seven to nine hides, is raised on a single pole and put over the frame. The front is then fastened with pins and the bottom pegged down. Two other poles are used to regulate the ears. They fit into sockets in the ears, and according to the way the wind blows, one of the poles is shifted to raise or lower the ear and regulate the draft. In two lodges which the writer observed, the main framework was made up of nine poles. Just before the bottom of the tent is pegged down, holes are dug for the poles to slip in. Cedar wood is preferred for the poles.

The buffalo hide tipis, which by the way, were more common among the Sisseton division, were formerly ornamented with disks of quill or beadwork with horsehair hanging from the center and porcupine quill pendants with metal jinglers were hung along the front. The top of the lodge was often painted red, black, or blue. The fire was built in the center of the tipi and directly behind it was the *catku* or "back center" where guests were always seated. Sacred objects were kept there or placed in the rear directly behind the spot hanging on a tripod. The three foundation poles are called *iticiyakaske* or "uniting poles," the other poles were known as *tosu.*

[Household Utensils]

Pottery-making In making pottery, my Wahpeton informants declare a stiff tenacious clay was taken and pounded. Then dark blue flint of the type used to make axes was secured and burned over and over in a hot fire until it crumbled. It was then pounded on a flat stone with a heavy grooved stone bone-crusher until it was pulverized, after which it was mixed with the clay for tempering, and the whole was pounded again until it was elastic like gum.

Then the potter made a flat bottom and built up the sides of the vessel, the coil process not being employed. At the top two little curved lugs or ears were made on opposite sides. Buffalo sinew, taken from the neck, and the hoofs of the same animal were boiled to make glue which was smeared over the inside. Then a wooden paddle with figures carved on it was used to stamp the sides while they were yet moist. The vessels were then burned, but no one remembered definitely whether this was a separate step or whether the burning was done while the vessel was in use. The Indians were of the latter opinion which the writer believes to be erroneous. When finished, the outside was of a reddish color and rought [*sic*] with the tempering showing, the inside was smooth.[110] Pottery making was entirely the work of the women and Dakota pottery is said to have been inferior to that made by the Mandan, which the Sioux well remember.

Arrow Points and Other Stone Implements In spite of the widespread Dakota tradition to the effect that arrowheads of stone now found are not the work of human beings but of the spider Inktomi, some old Wahpeton declare that flint was used for knives, scrapers, and arrow points. The knives are said to have been very large. Grooved bone crushers, hammers, and axes were made of stone. The axes were exceedingly dull as compared with those of metal. In hafting these objects wood was twisted about the groove and made secure with green rawhide which dried with an iron grip. A few grooved bone crushers still exist in the possession of the Indians.

In cutting wood with a stone ax, the work was done by placing a stone under the wood and then hammering the wood until it was crushed and could be broken with the hands. For finer work, flint axes of stone and a bluish color were used to chop with some success. Riggs and Dorsey observe that the French in 1680 found the Dakota killing

110. Amos wrote that he had picked up some more pottery and a small arrow point in the garden, which he put away with his collection; Oneroad to Skinner, July 28, 1924, Skinner Collection.

buffalo with stone arrows and cutting meat with stone knives etc. (184) flint was obtained at Knife Lake.[111] According to some Wahpeton informants, flint arrows and spears were used until relatively recent times, stone arrow points being used up to within fifty years ago, especially among the Oglala. Some were used in the Minnesota outbreak as late as 1862, but as above mentioned, folklore has it that those found on the ground are said to have been made by black spiders. I have seen some bone arrow-heads made by Sisseton individuals exactly in the shape of the metal arrow points used today by the Oglala and other western divisions.

Berry Crushers Round stones were used to crush berry pits on a flat metate. Cherries were also cured in the sun after having been pounded in this manner and were put in buffalo tripe mixed with buffalo fat marrow and meat and packed away in parfleches. Huge grooved stone mauls were used to crack buffalo bones which were later boiled to extract the oil.

Cooking in a Buffalo Skin When on the hunt, if without cooking utensils, the hunters would procure four pegs which they set up and then stretched over them a square piece of green buffalo hide with the hair outside. A flat stone was laid on the bottom to open out the receptacle and hold it down and water was poured in. Then stones were heated in the fire and carried over to the improvised kettle by means of a long green stick with a crook on the end. They were then dropped into the water until their heat made it boil. Sliced meat was thrown in, and when the skin receptacle had shrunken until it was too small to hold more, the cooking was said to have been completed. It was from this manner of cooking that the Assiniboine (Ojibway-Stone Sioux) derived their name. Animal stomachs were used as kettles in the same way, but are said to have burned more readily. For these a hole was dug in the ground and the stomach opened and pegged down around the mouth of the hole. Bark vessels were never used to cook with as among several woodland tribes, although they had their place as household utensils.

Household Utensils It could not be learned definitely that mats of reeds or bulrushes had been made within recent years, but at an earlier date they are said to have been abundant among the Santee tribes and the Wahpeton.

Mats A mat made of braided corn husks built up in circular fashion and sewed together was obtained by the writer from a Wahpeton

---

111. Skinner was not explicit about this source.

woman. This type of mat is known among the Iroquois and Delaware, but I have not seen any specimens from any of the other tribes of the Eastern Woodlands, although they may well occur.[112]

Bowls Bowls for eating and gaming were made of the knots of trees by burning and scraping [and] were abundant. These were usually plain and circular except in the case of those used in the Medicine Dance. The latter were always furnished with animal head handles. This is also true of the spoons used by the Eastern Dakota for the Medicine Dance. Wooden spoons with loons or duck's heads on the handles were consecrated to the "Raw Fish Eaters." Spoons were made of wood or of buffalo horn. The Yankton utilized the horn of the mountain sheep, but such spoons were rarely seen among the Eastern Dakota, who had no access to the habitat of the Big Horn.[113]

Fire Making For making fire, a wooden hearth was prepared and a small shallow hole bored in it. Tiny flint chips were dropped in the orifice and then a stick, held between the palms of the hands, was twirled in the depression. When the fire started to smoke, a little punk was added. The bowdrill was not known.

Buffalo Hide Shields Buffalo hide shields, while used by all the Eastern Dakota, were naturally more common among the Sisseton. They were made of thick hide from the bull's neck, first boiled, and then shrunk. Then a glue was made by thoroughly boiling buffalo cow hoofs which was then plastered over the outside. Burned flint was pounded and pulverized and sprinkled over the sticky surface.

Pipes Stone pipes of every conceivable shape and variety were made by the Eastern Dakota who had an abundant supply of catlinite in their famous quarry at Pipestone, Minnesota.[114] In the earliest times, the pipes were roughly blocked into shape by means of stone tools and then bored out with a drill made of an arrow-head of stone fastened to the end of a long stick. It is rather significant that the Indians refer to the stone drill head as an arrow-point only and goes to prove the old theory that among the Indians as among the whites, one implement

112. Skinner in "A Sketch of Eastern Dakota Ethnology" (p. 165) stated that he obtained a specimen for the American Museum of Natural History.

113. Skinner in "A Sketch of Eastern Dakota Ethnology" (p. 165) stated that types of all these objects were collected for the American Museum of Natural History. Others he reported were in the Museum of the American Indian, Heye Foundation.

114. Skinner in "A Sketch of Eastern Dakota Ethnology" (p. 168) noted that the Eastern Dakota had controlled the catlinite quarries of Couteau des Prairies from time immemorial.

might serve a number of uses. At later times metal implements shaped like screw drivers were used for this purpose and then augers. I have, myself, assisted an old Sisseton named Tiyomanipi (walks in the middle of the tipi) in boring out a catlinite pipe bowl with an old screw driver. Inlaying in stone and in metal was practiced at quite an early date.

Woven Bags All the divisions of the Eastern Dakota used basswood fiber bags woven in the typical Central Algonkian style.[115]

Parfleches Among the Santee, small barrel-shaped parfleches were used to carry objects, especially on horseback. The Wahpeton and Sisseton used parfleches of the box and envelope type and probably also the flat type found on the prairie.[116]

Vegetal Food Indian turnip or tipsina, is sliced, dried, and preserved for future use, when it is boiled with dried meat. Squashes were cut and dried in strings. Corn was braided, dried and hung over horizontal bars outside the lodge to dry. It was then prepared in various ways being hulled with lye obtained from wood ashes or ground into flour in wooden mortars of the horizontal type. A specimen of this variety of mortar with its crude pestle, which like others seen among the Eastern Dakota, were not constricted in the middle for a grip, was obtained from a Wahpeton woman, but others were seen in Sisseton families.[117] Green corn was roasted or it was scraped from the cob and dried on mats or skins for future use.

Buffalo Hunting Buffalo were formerly abundant only periodically; when they were scarce, scouts were sent out to look for them on the prairie. When the scouts were sent out to look for the buffalo they might be gone a day or more, so the akicita went through the village and announced to the people to be very quiet so the buffalo could not hear or smell them. Boys and girls were not allowed to play or make any noise. No dancing was permitted. Even the dogs seemed to know enough to keep quiet. When the scouts were seen returning over the

115. Skinner in "A Sketch of Eastern Dakota Ethnology" (p. 166) went on to say that the square woven bags were formerly intended for all purposes but were most recently used to hold medicines. He also noted that woven tobacco pouches of the Menomini and Ojibwe style, square and worn around the neck, were used.

116. Skinner in "A Sketch of Eastern Dakota Ethnology"(p. 166) also stated that these parfleches were painted with angular figures.

117. Skinner in "A Sketch of Eastern Dakota Ethnology" (p. 166) found the mortar and pestles common to the Central Algonkian, not the vertical variety of the Southern Siouans.

hill they would raise their blankets as a sign of good news. If they had seen the buffalo then the people yelled and the dogs barked.

If the scouts were successful in locating the buffalo, they would return with the news, going to the council lodge or tiyotipi. There the councilors and leader came together with their akicita or officers who executed the orders. These akicita were called *waawanyaka* or overseers and were selected from the braves by the council. Their office only lasted during the buffalo hunt and had no reference to their position in any of the warrior societies. Sometimes the men might be chosen from half a dozen different societies. However, when one division of the Eastern Sioux, say the Wahpeton, was camped by itself, they might make use of an organization, the *tokana*, for instance, if they chose.

A herald was selected to tell the people that buffalo had been found, and after the announcement of the discovery of the buffalo by the scouts to the council, the herald would call through the village that the people must get their running horses ready, clean their guns, and prepare their arrows for the signal. These running horses were not hobbled or staked out on the prairie with the ordinary steeds but were kept close to the lodges where they were carefully watched and tended. After a while the herald would pass through camp again, announcing that everyone should start for the place where the buffalo had been seen. The cavalcade started slowly, the warriors leading their running horses to keep them fresh. The akicita led the expedition, and it was their duty to punish those who went ahead of the main body by killing the culprits' horses, whipping them with a club, whip, or gun, and breaking their weapons.

When the buffalo were sighted, the leader would prepare his gun and then yell "Hukahe" when all was ready. The hunters then mounted their running horses and charged the herd in a body, picking out and shooting the best buffalo. It was thought that orphan boys were the cleverest and best hunters and very wealthy men who owned two or three running horses would hire orphans to ride for them during the hunt.

After the buffalo had been killed, the men usually did the skinning unless the main body of the women had arrived there in time. They would work two and two and brought off all they could of the buffalo meat, hoofs, horns, tongue, head, and entrails. The latter were often eaten raw with the liver. The liver, sprinkled with gall, was prized as a dainty and devoured raw on the spot.

In packing the horse to bring back the meat to camp, the buffalo were quartered and tied with thongs on the ponies' backs.[118] Some of the horses were said to have been able to carry as many as two buffalo each. What they could not carry off they covered with grass and left until night or the next day. In order to keep the coyotes from stealing it, the Indians would take a bladder, blow it up, put shot inside, take gunpowder and blow it on the hide or meat and this would look like fire at night.

After a hunt, someone from Heyoka tipi would come to gather tongues and hearts. If a sun dance was to be held, someone was sent out to gather these articles for the host.[119] After a successful surround of buffalo, the people all gave the Medicine Feasts and Heyoka and Buffalo Dances were started at the same time.

Another method of hunting buffalo was to drive them out on the ice where they were awkward and could be easily shot.

Tanning—Preparing Buffalo Robes The buffalo hides were first stretched on the ground and pegged down with the hair side down. They were then scraped with a toothed bone, or later, metal scraper, to get off the meat and subcutaneous tissue. They were washed, dried, and smoked. For leather, after the tissue had been removed, the hide was reversed and the hair removed with a hoe-shaped scraper of elkhorn with a metal blade. Then a semilunar-shaped chopper was brought to bear on the hide and it was thoroughly scraped after which it was rubbed down with a buffalo hip bone. It was then made into a bag and smoked over a fire of rotten wood. The writer observed a scraper in the possession of a Sisseton woman upon which the number of hides tanned was marked on the elkhorn handle by a series of dots and the number of tipis made of their skins were also figured in crude drawings.[120]

Deer skin was prepared differently from buffalo hide. It was fleshed immediately after the deer was skinned by being stretched and worked in the same way as the buffalo skin. The hair was cut off with a knife and was thrown over the upper end of a log driven obliquely into the

118. Skinner in "A Sketch of Eastern Dakota Ethnology" (p. 166) stated that the pack straps were of the Ojibwe style, usually made of moosehide, with the center piece that passes over the forehead still retaining the hair.

119. See Skinner, "Sun Dance of the Sisseton Dakota," 383–85. Logically this information on the Sun Dance would be included with this ethnology in the material on ceremonies, according with Skinner's outline, page 199, above.

120. Skinner in "A Sketch of Eastern Dakota Ethnology" (p. 167) said the buffalo-tanning method was in the Plains style.

ground. It was then scraped with a semilunar metal scraper and then thoroughly rubbed and pounded with a stone implement, an example of which was obtained from a Wahpeton woman. It is identical with the pitted hammerstones found in the neighborhood of New York City on archaeological sites.[121] After this, a solution of deer brains was applied by washing. The skin was then stretched and pulled with the hands to render it pliable as it dried. It was also rubbed back and forth over a twisted rope and then made into a bag, suspended over a tripod which was set up over a hole in the ground where a smoky fire was made to cure it.[122]

Games

Sliding Game. Icasdohe This game was played on the ice. A trough or alley a few inches wide and about thirty feet long was made and at either end horizontal bars were set up upon which prizes are hung. Women divided in parties of two and chose either goal. Two sticks were set up at each end and the parties alternated in rolling a small round stone up each alley trying to knock over the sticks, which were about an inch high. Those who were successful in bowling over the most sticks get the prize.

Snow Snake or Psidohanpe This game was played by pushing a wooden shaft down a slide, made in the snow, similar to that used in the preceding game. The shafts were thrown or pushed for distance.

Ice Game or Hutanicutepi This was played with a stick made something like that used for the game of snow snake. A head was carved to resemble that of a pickerel and on its back a human face was made. The stick was slid over the ice, the player making his stick glide the farthest, won the game.

Bowl and Dice or Kansu This was a woman's game, and was played with a wooden bowl in which were shaken plum seeds blackened on one side and white on the other.[123] Some were carved to represent birds or animals. According to the way they fell the count was made.

121. Skinner in "A Sketch of Eastern Dakota Ethnology" (p. 166) stressed that these double-pitted hammerstones were found in ancient Indian village sites all over the East, together with a rubbing and sharpening stone.

122. Skinner in "A Sketch of Eastern Dakota Ethnology" (p. 167) stated that the method of dressing deer hides was like the Northern and Central Algonkian method.

123 Wallis ("Canadian Dakota," 37) called this "Plum Stones" played with eight stones.

Snow Arrow or Mantka The details were not learned.[124]

Lacrosse or Takapsica This game was played with little sticks made with a small net at one end in regular Central Algonkian style. It had but little ceremonial aspects of the Menomini game. The only ceremony. The goal posts were half a mile or a mile apart. The two contesting sides could put in any number so long as they were equal. They met in the center of the field, the ball was thrown in the air, then all scrambled for it, attempting to bring it down and throw it against the opponent's goal. No one was supposed to be angry if hurt, although this game was very rough. Usually the players tied eagle down on their hair. According to some of the old accounts (see Catlin[125]) the Santee played this game on the ice. Women sometimes played against other women but the sexes never mingled.

A *winkta* (or berdache) once took part in a woman's game. He borrowed paint from Jingling-cloud's grandmother, who was a relative of his, and colored his legs and arms gray. A winkta was supposed to be especially adept at all woman's games just as in woman's arts.

Moccasin Game[126] Four animal skins about five inches broad by ten inches long, usually dog, badger, or skunk, were laid on the ground and the players divided, four men on each side. The leader, who had to

124. Written on four-by-seven-inch lined notebook paper in Amos Oneroad's hand, found in the Skinner Collection, is the following: "*Mantka:-Snow arrow.* This was boys and men's game, played in winter on prairie or ice. the head is conical both ways the head side longer and rounded point, which is burnt & hardened the front side is about two and a half inches long to the longest part and then slants off about an inch where its cut off and in the center a hole is bored and the handle not longer than a lead pencil is put on, and it is very limber, the snow arrow is made chiefly from hard wood. One kind of snow arrow is made of one piece the head resembling the head of a pickerel which is played on the ice, the other is played on the prairie, holding the handle at the end and with a gull swing and bounce on the mound prepared for it if its icy so much the better, the one that is thrown and bounced the farthest is the winner, the only ceremony before the game is from a brave hero relating some deed of notable account, and that his favorite side will be able to accomplish it like wise and then he throws the ball."

125. George Catlin was an artist and author of *Letters and Notes on the Manners, Customs, and Conditions of the North American Indians* (Philadelphia, 1841; New York, Dover Publications, 1973). See Wallis ("Canadian Dakota," 38) on lacrosse.

126. Wallis ("Canadian Dakota," 37) called this "hunt the slipper" and said it could be played with from one to four moccasins or mittens. Howard (*Canadian Sioux*, 90–92) called this "ĥaŋpa ap'eda" or "to strike the moccasin" (eastern dialect) or "ĥaŋpa maĥeyuzapi" or "to mix up inside moccasins" (middle dialect) and said it was still customary to play in North Dakota and Canada in the month of January.

guess where the opposing side was going to hide the bead or bullet, had a long stick to strike the moccasin where he thought it had been placed. The leader of the other side then tried to hide a bead in one of the moccasins. A pile of sticks was heaped in the center between the parties and every time the guesser was right he received four of them. When he failed to guess correctly he gave back two to the other side, and lost his turn. The game was kept up until one side had only two sticks left. Then the winner returned all his pile but six and if the loser still failed to get the bead on the next trial, the game was over and the winner made the loser give presents for from one to ten sticks from his pile. Horses, clothes, horse equipment, etc., were given. One of the favorite songs was "When I see you, I laugh," lines supposed to be about a girl.

Kicking Game or Nakicitanpi This is a rough game played by the boys, who divide into equal sides and kick each other on the shins and thighs alternately. Those who are knocked over and are unable to rise are gently kicked by the winner who nicknames them. The side knocking over the most opponents wins. Sometimes the game is played more roughly. Those who are thrown down are attacked by their opponents who bump their knees into the faces of the prostrate players. If a man is approached by one of the other side and lies down without any resistance he is spared, unless it has been declared before staring that no quarter will be given. This game is said to usually wind up in a free-for-all fight.

Hoop and Javelin[127] or Tahuka canhdeska Several hoops laced with rawhide and graded in size, perhaps as many as eight in all being used, are thrown so as to run along the ground and are speared at by the players. Sides are chosen which line up abreast, standing opposite each other. The leader of one side goes between them and throws the hoops, beginning with the large one, while the players on the other side try to transfix them with their spears. The small hoop is thrown last, and the object is to drive the spear or javelin through the small circle left in the center of the web and called the eye. When the hoops are all pinned by one side the players on that side snatch them up and pursue those on the other, throwing the hoops at them and trying to hit the fleeing players. If a man on the losing side is hit by a hoop which afterwards

127. Howard (Canadian Sioux, 89) reported that the older games of lacrosse, shinny, and various archery games had not been played for years by the Canadian Sioux and were scarcely remembered. However, Sam Buffalo and George Bear remembered hoop and pole being played at Round Plain, Sask., and Birdtail, Man.

rolls away he tries to spear it, and if successful he throws it back. The winning side then rests while the others throw the hoops again. This is considered a "brave" game and not beneath the notice of warriors.

Shinny[128] or Takapopa This was played by women as well as men. It was similar to the proverbial double ball game of the Central Algonkian.

Cat's Cradle Cat's cradle was a common game and many different forms of twisting the string were known.

Basdohampi A shaft of weed or ash was thrown over the ground by taking it by one end and shooting it across the instep or the foot might be raised from the ground and held in various awkward positions.

Tops Whipping tops of horn or wood were beaten on the ice or on the ground.[129]

Darts Throwing darts, feathered on one end, were hurled at a mark.

War Games In playing this game, grass spikes or burrs were pulled off their parent weeds in bunches. The grass spikes were wet and twisted together and the children used them to throw at each other. They would stick to the clothing or to the flesh like little arrows. The game had no formal rules.

Coasting For coasting, a flat piece of wood like a barrel stave was taken and a rawhide thong tied to one end. The children would stand on the other end while they held the thong tight and slid down hill. They guided the sled with a stick.

Bow and Arrow Game Miniature bow and arrows were made of dry stalks of grass. They were used to war and also to see who could shoot the farthest.

Races Sticks were set up for goals sometimes as far as one or two miles apart and horsemen watched at the start and finished while the contestants raced from one post to the other. Prizes for the first four places usually consisted of guns, quivers, arrows, bows, spears, etc.

Test of Bravery This was a game which was played by boys. Pith was dampened and placed on the skin of the bare arms and hands and set

128. Wallis ("Canadian Dakota," 37) quoted Neill ("Dakota Land and Dakota Life," 280–81) saying it was played on a smooth place. Each player had a stick three or four feet long and crooked at the lower end, with deer strings tied across forming a pocket. The ball was made of a rounded knot of wood or clay covered with hide. Stakes were set at a distance of a quarter- or half-mile as bounds.

129. Sam Buffalo, in Howard (*Canadian Sioux*, 89), called tops "ćaŋka waćipi," "wood they cause to dance." They were made from bison horn tips with a plum in the hollow upper end for balance and lashed with a rawhide whip to make them spin.

on fire. Those who could let it burn down to the skin until it went out were considered the bravest. Jingling-cloud has scars on his arms and hands from playing this game.

Hand Stick Game This is known perhaps to the Sisseton and to a few Wahpeton, but is more common among the Teton. Jingling-cloud has seen it played at Rosebud, where an Indian named Short-bull got into the center between the two contestants, counted his coups and announced that he hoped his side would win. Two play at once. In this particular game they had thirty-two cartridge shells. They shook their hands and waved them back and forth with many tricks of legerdemain while the opponent tried to guess in which hand the bullet is held.[130]

--

130. Howard (*Canadian Sioux*, 92–93) gave a description provided by John Goodwill for the Canadian Dakota. Wallis ("Canadian Dakota," 37–38) also mentioned the foot race and pony fight in addition to the games included here.

*Sisseton and Wahpeton
Tales and Folklore*

Introduction

The following stories were obtained in part from Mr. Amos Oneroad, a full blooded Wahpeton Dakota, whose native name is Maȟpiyasna or Jingling Cloud, who comes from a long line of distinguished Eastern Dakota, numbering among his ancestors Standing Buffalo, Blue Medicine [Spirit] and Jingling Cloud. They were recorded in English during the summer of 1922 while Mr. Oneroad was acting as the writer's assistant in the Department of Anthropology of the Public Museum of the City of Milwaukee.

Mr. Oneroad has been an intimate friend of the writer's since 1913. In 1914 he acted as the writer's guide and interpreter among the remnant of the various groups of Eastern Dakota residing near Sisseton, S.D., on behalf of the American Museum of Natural History of New York. A small collection of Wahpeton myths and tales was gathered by the writer at that time, and, with the permission of the American Museum of Natural History those stories which do not duplicate Mr. Oneroad's contributions have been added to the manuscript.

Mr. Oneroad had access to the writer's collection of Ioway myths and tales, and has endeavored to give the Wahpeton versions of all of these with which he was acquainted, so that the document is valuable for comparison with the Ioway manuscript. The entire series has been edited by the writer.

The Wahpeton are one of the seven primary divisions of the Sioux or Dakota nation, and are closely related to the Wahpekute group, who took part in the famous Inkpaduta troubles in northern Iowa.

Wahpeton customs concerning the narration of these tales are mostly obsolete.[1] However it is known that in former times the usual

---

1. See George Lankford, "The Unfulfilled Promise of North American Indian Folklore," in *Handbook of American Folklore*, Richard M. Dorson, ed. (Bloomington: Indiana University Press, 1983), 18–24. Wilson D. Wallis, "Beliefs and Tales of the Canadian Dakota," *Journal of American Folklore* 36 (1924): 56–57, also mentioned this local rule for not telling tales in the summer. He reported it was limited to stories "which are recognized as not true but valued for the pleasure of the tale." He reported his informant did so in deference and slept out in a tent to show the belief had no foundation, only to awaken to a snake crawling toward him.

tabu against telling the stories in warm weather was in force, the Indians fearing that those who violated the rule would have snakes or toads creep into bed with them. The convention[al] ending of each story is said to have been: "This is the end of the tail of the elk."

Alanson Skinner
Curator of Anthropology
Public Museum of the City of Milwaukee
May 10, 1924

THE ADVENTURES OF IKTOMI

1. Iktomi and His Member

In the remote long ago, so the old Dakota people narrate, Iktomi was even more mischievous than later on in his history.[2] On this account he carried his member, which was of abnormal size, wrapped up in a blanket made of raccoon skin.[3]

2. Iktomi and the Bathing Girls

Once as Iktomi was strolling along he saw two girls in swimming on the opposite side of a lake. He immediately uncoiled his member, and submerging it beneath the water thrust it into the body of one of the girls whom he held a prisoner while the other fled screaming up the bank. Attracted by the commotion the grandmother of the girls came down and waded out to the captive. She felt all over her body until she discovered what it was that held her fast. The old woman pulled it free, exclaiming as she did so: "It is only Iktomi." Some versions say that the sisters were twin fresh water clams.

3. Iktomi and the Mysterious Raccoon

After his adventure with the girls Iktomi proceeded on his journey. When night fell he camped on his trail, covering himself with his raccoon skin robe. He slept soundly after the days [sic] adventures, and thought of what might happen the following day. When he awoke the sun had risen diagonally in the heavens, and as he looked into the clear sky he saw something fluttering, very different from his feathered friends when they make ready to pounce on their prey. Iktomi watched it for some time, and could not make out what it was, so he rubbed his eyes, arose, and went on his way. As he ascended a knoll he saw, in the distance ahead of him, a raccoon walking slowly along.

2. "In the remote long ago, so the old Dakota people narrate," Black Elk told Neihardt this beginning signals "Ehani Woyakapi" or legend, but since the old people are mentioned it may signal "Ohunkakapi" or fiction made up by old people. Perhaps it signals both. This is not a hard and fast rule but a general introduction as is "once upon a time." See also Raymond J. De Mallie, ed., *The Sixth Grandfather: Black Elk's Teachings Given to John G. Neihardt* (Lincoln: University of Nebraska Press, 1984), 376.

3. In Iktomi tales, "member" is a euphemism for penis.

Iktomi ran after the animal, but the raccoon ran on also, keeping an equal distance ahead of him. He reduced his pace, puffing to get his breath, and so did the raccoon. He descended the other side of the knoll, but the raccoon was at the foot before him. Now it dawned on Iktomi that he missed something, and on examining himself he found that during the night the recollection of his exploit the day before had caused his member to enlarge, and that his raccoon skin blanket had been caught on the tip of it like a war standard. When he discovered what was the matter Iktomi coiled up his member, and wrapping it in his raccoon skin blanket, went on his way again.[4]

4. Iktomi and the Gopher
As Iktomi journeyed a gopher peeped at him from its burrow, and was amused at his ridiculous appearance. The gopher began to laugh and sing:
> "Look! Iktomi is packing his member!"
> "Look! Iktomi is packing his member!"
This made Iktomi so angry that he said: "Keep quiet, or I'll poke you with it."
Nevertheless, the gopher kept on singing:
> "Look! Iktomi is packing his member!"
Iktomi at first paid no attention, but Gopher was so persistent with his singing that Iktomi from being annoyed became very angry.
"I'll punch you to death!" he cried in his rage, and uncoiled his member and thrust it after the gopher into his burrow. The passage was long and had had many turns, but he pushed his member down its entire length. Meantime Gopher had run up a little side passage, and he began to gnaw at Iktomi's member, until he bit it off close to his body. Iktomi did not care much about his loss, as it made him feel considerably lighter.[5]

5. Iktomi Is Caught in a Skull
Iktomi travelled on across the prairie until he heard a sound of people singing, and dancing. He stopped and went back a little ways. Then he

4. Deloria (*Dakota Texts*, 36-43) also presented a tale where Iktomi wraps up in a raccoon skin, but the story has variations and is more elaborate. Also see a variant in Barbara Babcock, "A Tolerated Margin of Mess: The Trickster and His Tales Reconsidered," in *Critical Essays on Native American Literature*, ed. Andrew Wiget (Boston: G. K. Hall & Co., 1975), 169, episode 7.
5. Babcock, "Tolerated Margin of Mess," 170, includes a variant in episode 15.

thought it sounded to his right, then all around. At last, as he listened and looked, he found that the sounds came from the buffalo skull that lay on the prairie. His little brothers the mice were having a frolic and every one was happy. Iktomi lay down and peeped in and said, "Brothers, I would like to join you in your good time." The spokesman of the mice replied: "Oh, Iktomi, you might spoil our fun."

But Iktomi said again, "Brothers, I would like to join you in your good time."

"Oh no, Iktomi," said the leader of the mice, "You might spoil our fun."

However, Iktomi persisted until they said that he might come in, so he forced his head into the opening for the spinal cord at the base of the skull.[6] The singing and dancing ceased, and though Iktomi looked, he could see no one, for the mice thought it was time to make their exit when he entered.

Poor Iktomi now found that his head was imprisoned in the skull, and he had to feel his way like a blind man. He would feel of each tree that he bumped against and ask it to direct him on his way. Certain trees grew on the high bank and broke his prisoning cap. Then Iktomi pretended to be angry and scolded the steep bank for crushing his buffalo skull. "Why, I had no headaches when I wore that on my head he said."[7]

6. Iktomi and the Elk

Iktomi once spied a herd of elk taking a noonday siesta, so he said to himself, "Now I shall have some elk meat."

With his bow and his quiver full of arrows he cat pawed his way slowly and softly toward them. Some of the animals were sleeping, and others were chewing their cud. Iktomi took an arrow between his thumb and forefinger, set it in its place and aimed at the nearest elk and shot it. Just then a breeze puffed it over the heads of the herd. The

6. Stith Thompson, *Tales of the North American Indians* (Bloomington: Indiana University Press, 1966) made a list of motifs he found. He noted repetitious motifs within Skinner's tales. Hereafter Thompson's motifs are noted by his designated number, description, and note number, e.g., Thompson: J2152 Trickster puts on buffalo skull 86.

7. Deloria (*Dakota Texts*, 43–46) gave a version of this episode. She commented that she heard various endings and could not tell which was "the correct version." Alternate endings included shattering the skull, soaking the skull so it would stretch, drowning, building a fire to burn it off, and burning himself.

elk at once knew who it was, and one called, "Iktomi, you almost shot me in the eye."

"Brothers," cried Iktomi, "that was some hunter passing by. He almost shot me first." Of course, it was a poor excuse, but Iktomi had to say something. "Oh brothers, make me one of you," he begged.

"Oh no, Iktomi, you'll get us into trouble."

But Iktomi begged and insisted until they agreed. The elk brought up a model, a buck of the younger type, but after Iktomi had examined it he felt that it was too good for him, and he made his own selection, a poor, lean old buck with very large antlers. Before he had been transformed the elk told him a certain sign that all the elk know, and when it is given they are all accustomed to rise up and follow the leader and do as he does. After the instruction was given, Iktomi was made to lie down with the herd. In a little while the old buck who was leader gave a short snappy grunt and they sprang up with speed. Iktomi sprang up with the rest, and to his astonishment he was transformed into an old buck, according to his wishes. They fed for sometime and then they came to a grove of shady oaks. It was in the fall and nature had clothed herself in brilliant and beautiful colors. The leaves shook in the gentle breeze, a leaf fluttered here and there through the air, and a number of acorns fell, only to be promptly munched by the herd. Iktomi was the one who slept while the others ate.

Another breeze came up and more acorns fell to be quickly gulped down by the hungry ones. The wind grew stronger and stronger and at length the leader gave a sharp whistle of distress. Iktomi heard and sprang up with the rest of the herd. The elk stampeded to a knoll snorting as they ran. Iktomi was at the tail end of the herd. As he came up he cried: "Someone shot me with a bullet, but I shook it off." The elk all knew that it was only an acorn that fell on him.

They all fed by a river and at intervals walked over to the tall grass to rest again, but as they were dozing, the same signal of danger was given by Iktomi and they raced off for life. When the herd assembled again Iktomi was the last one to join them. They asked him what it was that had frightened him.

"My brothers," said Iktomi, "I was the farthest away from the herd, and I saw a man with a shield on his back and a spear in his hand crawling up on us."

But one of the elk had seen it too, and he spoke up and said that it was only Turtle out foraging.

The herd followed the leader towards the woods, and Iktomi, as usual, walked by himself. Some hunters had been watching the herd for some time, and not knowing their hiding place the elk passed near them. They shot at the herd but the elk made their escape. Iktomi was the last one, and the men gave chase, shooting as they ran. Iktomi's antlers were so large that now and then they were caught between trees, or in the branches, so that the hunters caught up to him and shot an arrow into him, which knocked him down. When he came to himself he was Iktomi again. He looked at the hunters gathered around, and said, "Brothers, what has happened to you?"[8]

7. Iktomi and the Nighthawk

Iktomi stood and watched the nighthawk as it soared up into the sky. Every now and then it fluttered and uttered its harsh cry, then, all of a sudden it would swoop down and spread its wings out, producing a booming sound.[9]

Iktomi was pleased and thought that he would like to be a bird, so as the nighthawk came down and lit on a rock that stood near, he walked over and begged it to turn him into a night hawk too. At first the bird didn't want to do it, but Iktomi begged and coaxed and finally persuaded the nighthawk, who said: "Watch me and do as I do," and from the rock the nighthawk rose with its horse cry of "Pish," and flew away. Iktomi did the same, and found that he could fly with perfect ease, following his feathered friend into the air, swooping, booming, and rising again. The nighthawk flew off in one direction and Iktomi took another. He thought that he would like to boom again, so he did, and then again. Then he thought he ought to go higher than ever before and swooped and boomed so loud that it reverberated over the hills and vales, so that Iktomi was very proud. Then he rose to go still higher than ever before. He soared like a small speck, and then he swooped down, intending to boom when he was only a few feet above the ground. When the proper time came he tried to spread his wings, but his power was gone, and he fell to the earth so hard that it knocked him senseless, and when he came to himself he was Iktomi again.

8. See Wallis, "Beliefs and Tales," 97–98: "Spider is Outwitted by the Elk." In this tale and the next, Iktomi receives permission to transform into one of "them" (the elk and the nighthawk).

9. A nighthawk, generally just before a thunderstorm, sweeps down and then makes a sudden turn upward with a curious explosive sound. See Deloria, *Dakota Texts*, 76.

8. *Iktomi and the Turkey Buzzard*

Iktomi's last misfortune had not been over more than a few days when he saw Turkey Buzzard sailing above the treetops looking for food. Iktomi cried out to him, "He! Brother! Let me ride on your back."

So the bird said that he would let Iktomi ride for a little while until his wings grew tired. When Iktomi was once on his back he urged the Turkey Buzzard to go higher and higher, so the buzzard soared upward in great spirals, and would then turn and glide downward, as it was getting tired of carrying Iktomi's weight on his flight. Still Iktomi urged the buzzard to fly, until finally the bird grew angry, and as he flew over the tree tops he saw a large stub broken off some distance from the ground, so he dumped Iktomi into it.[10]

Iktomi was imprisoned in the hollow stub for a long time, how long he did not know. After a while he heard voices, not far away, and he knew them to be the voices of women who had come for firewood. Iktomi then remembered his raccoon skin robe, he wrapped it tightly around himself, and began to sing:

"I am a large fat raccoon! I am a large fat raccoon!"

He kept this up until he was heard by one of the women. "Ah, I hear a voice," said she, "It seems to say, 'I am a large fat raccoon.'"

They all stopped their work and listened, and they could hear it clearly, "I am a large fat raccoon."

"Where did it come from?" asked one of the women, and they began to search until they found and chopped the dead tree. They took turns, and by and by they could see the fur of the raccoon, and hear from within the voice of Iktomi, crying: "I am a fat raccoon! Cut the hole larger. I am a large fat raccoon!"

Now the women could see the raccoon skin moving inside the hollow, for Iktomi was preparing to spring out. They backed [*sic*] the hole larger, and all at once Iktomi leaped forth with the exclamation, "Look out! You are killing yourselves!" The women were sorry that they had worked so laboriously for nothing, but Iktomi walked away grinning tauntingly.[11]

---

10. Thompson: K1041 Trickster carried by birds and dropped (borrowed feathers) 80. Babcock, "Tolerated Margin of Mess," 169, includes a variant in episode 8.

11. Deloria (*Dakota Texts*, 43–46) includes a similar tale that varied the story line a little—the bird was a hawk. Wallis, "Beliefs and Tales,"73–75: "Spider and Hedja [Buzzard]" is similar but incorporates Skinner's spider and raccoon tale.

9. Iktomi Has Revenge upon the Buzzard

Iktomi thought over the trick that the Buzzard had played upon him, and came to the conclusion that he must punish the bird severely. He decided to turn himself into the carcass of an elk, so, finding a place suitable for his snare, Iktomi lay down and turned himself into a dead bull elk. The wolves and coyotes came and ate from the carcass, as did all the lesser carnivorous animals. Even the feathered ones came.

The Buzzard was suspicious, however, and he soared in great circles until he was satisfied, then he sailed down and began to eat the meat bit by bit, biting the buttocks of the elk. Finally he ate a large cavity and on stretching his neck inside to get another bite, Iktomi caused the hole to snap together, and caught the buzzard by the neck.

Iktomi now sprang up in his own human form, and began to dance with the Buzzard hanging from his back.

"I have a real live feather

[Page 9, the end of "Iktomi Has Revenge upon the Buzzard" and beginning of "Iktomi and the Ducks," is missing from the original manuscript.]

"You dance with shut eyes
Whoever shall look
Hence forth will be red eyed,
Hence forth will be red eyed."

Iktomi took his position at the door, and all the birds began to dance with their eyes firmly closed. When the dance was at its height Iktomi added the words, "I too, join myself," so that all the birds would think that he was also dancing. As a matter of fact, however, he was standing there and grabbing the largest birds as they passed by and wringing their necks. One big swan was too tough to kill at once, and he screamed and honked, so that the woodduck became alarmed and peeped and cried out, "Open your eyes! Iktomi is wringing your necks!"

All the birds fled flapping and screeching for the door, and Iktomi tried to head them off, but they knocked him down and trampled over him to freedom. But the woodduck, who did not obey Iktomi's instructions, has had red eyes ever since.[12]

12. T. T. Waterman, "The Explanatory Element in the Folk-Tales of the North-American Indians," *Journal of American Folklore* 27 (1914): 44, compared explanations for the "dancing bird" motif and found the Dakota attribute an origin explanation to the woodduck's red eyes. See also Peter Hunter, *Word Carrier*, June 1889, for a comparable tale.

Iktomi was well satisfied with his kill that day, and he selected a spot under some trees for his meal. There he built a fire and began to cook the fattest ones of the birds. Some he put in his kettle, some he stuck on a spit near the fire, while others he buried in the coals. As the fowls cooked Iktomi squatted by the fire, and skimmed and tasted the grease with a feather. As he was doing this he heard two limbs overhead rubbing and squeaking and it annoyed him very much. He looked up and said: "If you don't stop that I will come up there and take you apart." The noise kept on, and Iktomi climbed up, but as he took hold of the limbs his hand slipped in between them and he was caught. He pulled and pulled, but he was held fast. He looked down and saw that his meal was now nearly cooked, and just then some wolves passed that way. Iktomi called to them: "My younger brothers! I have some waterfowls here that are almost cooked. Don't take and eat them."

"Ah," said the wolves to each other. "Iktomi says that he has something for us to eat over there."

They came over and ate all the birds in the kettle, leaving only the bones. They ate those that were on the spits also, and smacked their lips and made ready to go. Just then Iktomi called, "My brothers, don't eat those that are in the ashes."

"Ah," said the wolves, "Iktomi says he has some hidden for us in the ashes," so they ate there also leaving only the bones.

Just then the wind blew and the limbs moved again, releasing Iktomi, who came down to find nothing but the bones, which he gnawed hungrily. He was no better off than before, indeed, he was hungrier.[13]

11. Iktomi and the Artichoke

Iktomi felt hungry, and naturally turned his footsteps towards the woodland. At the edge of the woods near a slough he discovered an artichoke, where these plants grew in abundance.

"Artichoke, what is your name?" asked Iktomi.

---

13. Deloria (*Dakota Texts*, 19–25) had this tale involving pheasants rather than ducks. Frank B. Linderman, *Indian Why Stories: Sparks from War Eagle's Lodge-Fire* (New York: Charles Scribner's Sons, 1915), 17–23, has a version called "How the Ducks Got Their Fine Feathers," which has similar motifs. Riggs (*Dakota Grammar, Texts, and Ethnography*, 110–14) collected a version of this from David Grey Cloud called "Bad Song" that he said corresponded with Omaha and Ponca tales. See Babcock, "Tolerated Margin of Mess,"169, version in episode 6. Wallis, "Beliefs and Tales," 93: "Spider, the Ducks, the Child, and the Mink" contains this motif.

"You have said it," answered the plant. "Artichoke is my name."

"People usually have more than one name," replied Iktomi, and he seized on and thrust it in his mouth, and began to munch it.

"I am also called the 'Defecator,'" cried the plant.

"Pshaw," answered Iktomi with a sneer, "A thing like you couldn't be a defecator!" And he ate his fill and went away.

Presently the artichoke began to work upon him and he began to be loose in the bowels. "Why, I begin to believe that little root was right," said Iktomi to himself. He began to break wind. "Yes, I am beginning to be convinced. No[w] the concussions of his flatulency jarred him, "Yes, in a way I believe it," he said. Then the concussions grew faster and harder, and Iktomi began to be blown off the ground at every discharge. He grabbed hold of a sapling, but still his legs were both lifted up into the air. He then saw that it was a mistake to have ridiculed the artichoke. His breech-clout was split by the discharge, and the tree that he held was torn out by the roots. Still he clung fast. "Yes, I kind of believe it," he said. Then there was a great explosion that rolled him over and shattered the tree trunk to pieces. When Iktomi, who was knocked unconscious, came to, he sat up and scratched his bushy head. Half of his breech-clout was gone and the tree was a pile of fragments. "Well," said he thoughtfully, "I kind of believe that Artichoke's name is in harmony with what it can do."[14]

12. Iktomi and the Roseberries

Iktomi was still hungry, and the roseberries were ripe. He picked a handful and asked them: "Roseberries, what is your name?" They replied, "You have said it. Roseberries is our name."[15]

"Well," said Iktomi, "It is customary for people to have more than one name."

"We are also called buttocks-itchers, oh Iktomi."

"What, a thing like you make my buttocks itch?" asked Iktomi with a scornful look, and he ate to repletion, swallowing seeds and all. Then he went on into the woods. Presently his buttocks began to itch. "Why," said he, "I kind of believe that what those Roseberries told me was true." He began to scratch himself, and the more he scratched the

14. Thompson: J2153 Trickster eats medicines that physic him 109h; Babcock, "Tolerated Margin of Mess," 169, variant in episode 11.

15. Roseberries were the humblest of foods, common and disdained, except during famine. See Deloria, *Dakota Texts*, 198.

more it itched.[16] Finally, he could stand it no longer, so he backed up against a tree and rubbed and scratched until the skin came off. Then he thought of another plan. "I'll build a fire and stand over it." This he did, and presently he began to feel better, he piled on more wood, and the itching was much relieved. He went on through the woods, wandering here and there. As he went he presently came across a trail of drops of fresh blood, and thought that it must be a deer that someone had wounded. He followed it until he discovered entrails strung along the ground, and he picked up one end of these and began to eat them. As he was very hungry, he ate a lot but just about the time that he was filled up he came back to the fireplace that he had built, and discovered that he had been eating his own intestines. The fire had burned him until his bowels fell out and this had relieved his itching. He stood there spitting in disgust for a moment and then exclaimed: "Why, I kind of believe that the Roseberries were right."

13. Iktomi and the Two Girls

Iktomi had not met any human beings since the women had chopped down the hollow tree into which he had fallen and so released him. He went on until he came to a lake on the opposite side of which he saw two girls in swimming. He watched them for a moment, and then said to himself, "I've got something for those girls." Then he plunged in and swam under the water until he came close to where the maidens were, then he popped out his head and said: "I am a mysterious being and anyone who licks my buttocks will have a long life."

He submerged himself again, and then rose again saying: "I am a mysterious being, and anyone who licks my buttocks will have a long life."

The girls heard him and one said to the other, "Cousin, I will be the first one, so they both obeyed the order of the mysterious being, who vanished and again stuck out his head at a distance. Then the girls saw that it was Iktomi who had duped them and they threatened and scolded him but he only laughed and swam back to where he had come from.

14. Iktomi and the Raccoon Family

Once, when Iktomi was travelling along a trail he came to a lodge whence smoke issued from the top. He stopped and listened, and he

16. Thompson: J2154 Trickster eats scratch-berries 109k. Waterman ("Folk-Tales of the North-American Indians," 47) compared the explanations of this motif.

could hear two women (raccoons) talking within. Then he took one of his testicles and tossed it through the smoke hole, and listened again. One of the women said, "Cousin, I am going to eat that plum" and she took it up and bit it in two and swallowed it.

Then Iktomi took the other and threw it in, and the other woman caught it up and swallowed it. Then he lifted the flap and went in and sat at the place reserved for visitors. He sat there perspiring and fanning himself with a wing, and the two asked him, "Where did you get those juicy plums that you gave us, brother?"

Iktomi looked wise and nodded his head towards the western horizon: "You see that brilliant red colored cloud yonder? Well, right beneath it in a ravine are plum trees loaded down with this fruit and it is their reflection that you see in the sky."

The women took their bags and went out to gather the plums, but finally returned without the fruit, for Iktomi had directed them astray. However, he pointed out the place where he said the ravine was, and they started out again. Peeping through the door. Iktomi finally saw them disappear from sight. "Now I am going to have some food," said he. So he started up the fire, filled the kettle with water and taking his knife he cut off the heads of the baby raccoons, singed their bodies, cut them up and dropped them in the kettle. After a while he went out and began digging in the hillside until he had made a tunnel right through the hill. Then he came back to the tipi and ate heartily of the flesh of the baby raccoons. When he was satisfied, he took some of the grease and smeared it over the mouths of the heads that he had cut off and stuck them back in the cradleboards and waited the return of the mother raccoons.[17]

He was almost asleep when he heard them coming, talking and laughing, and bringing their bags full of plums. When they entered, Iktomi said: "My sisters, while you were gone a badger came this way with her young ones, and I killed them and cooked them. I ate some and some I left for you to eat. Don't take up your babies. I fed them and put them to sleep. Eat first and then you can nurse your babies.

The two raccoon women were hungry after their long walk, so they started to eat, while Iktomi crouched, ready to leap for the door. At last one of the women finished, and took up her cradleboard. When she did so her baby's head fell off and rolled away. Iktomi began to laugh, "I'll tell you what has happened. You have eaten your own ba-

17. Thompson: G400-G599 The child and the cannibal 268; Babcock, "Tolerated Margin of Mess," 170, variant in episode 12. Wallis, "Beliefs and Tales," 67–68: "Spider and Raccoon" is a contest tale where again the Spider triumphs.

bies!" Then he fled for his life out of the door. Both women screamed in sorrow and rage and shouted, "Wicked scoundrel, Iktomi, you have killed our children!"[18]

One of the women snatched up a knife and the other a pole which happened to lie there, a short pole or a digging stick used in gathering prairie turnips. They chased Iktomi but he outran them and crawled into the tunnel that he had dug through the hill. He came out of the opposite end and then blocked it up and going to the water he washed himself. He gathered wild sage and made himself a headdress and arm bands, belt and garters and returning approached the women from another direction. "My younger sisters, what are you trying to do? And what are you crying about?" he asked.

The raccoon women told him what Iktomi had done to them and how they had driven him into this hole for refuge. "My younger sisters, do you but wait out here, and I will go in and kill Iktomi, then you can go in and drag him out."

Iktomi removed his sagebrush regalia and crawled in. Then with shouts and yells he made believe that he was fighting a desperate battle. He scratched his cheeks until the blood ran, then, covered with dirt and sweat, he crawled out again.

"My younger sisters, that was a terrible battle! But at last I prevailed because I am handsomer and stronger than Iktomi. I have indeed killed him and his body lies in there. My younger sisters, now that he is dead, go in both of you and do what you please with his body."

The two raccoon women then crawled into the tunnel and as soon as they were out of sight Iktomi stuffed the mouth of the hole with dry grass. Then he took his flint and struck off a spark on a piece of punk. From within came a voice: "Brother, are you striking a flint?"

"No, my younger sisters, that is only a woodpecker rattling on a tree."

As the fire started to catch, Iktomi began to blow on it and a voice from within called out as before: "Brother are you blowing a fire?"

"No, my younger sisters, that is only the wind in the tree-tops."

The fire caught well, so he piled on more grass, until a great smoke began to rise, and Iktomi had to fan it very fast to keep the smoke in. There were screams from within, but finally these died away and he knew that the raccoons were smothered. Then Iktomi crawled in himself and pulled them out, already singed. He tied them on a branch and

18. Thompson: G61 Relative's flesh unwittingly eaten 98, 226.

then went down by the mouth of a river that emptied into a large round lake, searching for a good spot to cook his dinner. As he turned a bend of the river he heard a voice crying: "I'll wear a coat! I'll wear a coat! From the flexible pickerel skin! I'll wear a coat! I'll wear a coat! Head him off there, Iktomi! I'll wear a coat! I'll wear a coat from the flexible pickerel skin!"

It was none other than Mink who was out fishing.

"Oh brother Mink," cried Iktomi, "I have something here good to eat. Raccoons two I have killed on the way, and if you will go and bring your very best cooking pot, we'll have a feast here."

So Mink went off at once, and brought his elder brother Iktomi what he thought was the very best cooking pot, but the sight of it only made Iktomi angry. "Go again! Take this back and fetch me the very best one that you can see!" he ordered. So Mink scurried away and brought him his next best kettle. Iktomi shook his head: "Do you call that the best?" Mink was abashed and surprised but at Iktomi's order he hurried back with a still poorer one. This one Iktomi again refused saying: "You watch here and I'll go myself and get what I call the very best cooking pot." Soon he was back, bearing the pot of his choice, but it leaked through a number of holes. So Iktomi made plaster with his spittle and clay and stopped them up with that.

When the meal was almost cooked, Iktomi looked foolishly at Mink. "Brother," said he, "let us have a race around this lake. Whoever wins shall get all the meat and the looser shall have the bones and the soup. Mink was very hungry and did not like the idea of a competition but as Iktomi kept on urging him, he hesitated. "Brother," said Iktomi, "I will tie some stones to my ankle, and then I can't run so fast." So at last, Mink agreed and they set out to run around the lake. When they were half way round, Iktomi could see the steam rising from the pot and as Mink was then away in the lead, he cut loose the stones and began to gain. Mink, however, repeated some magic words, and ice formed so that he was able to run across the lake.[19]

"Brother Mink! What did you say? Wait for me, and we will feast together," cried Iktomi in alarm.

"I said, 'Open ice and close again,'" cried Mink and the ice let Iktomi through and then closed over his head. Iktomi sank to the bottom and wandered all over the lower world. It looked very different there. After a while he met pickerel and said, "Brother, tell me, where is the

19. Thompson: K115 Trickster's race 90.

shore?" The Pickerel answered him saying: "When I was young with my brethren, we used to play close to the shore but when we grew up we left it, and I no longer know where it is."

Iktomi wandered on until he met Sucker and he asked him where the shore was and Sucker made him the same reply that Pickerel did. So Iktomi wandered on until he met Perch and he made the same inquiry of him and again received the same reply. At length he came across a little pinhead minnow and asked him. The Pinhead made reply: "When I was young I used to play near the shore but when I grew up I left it and now I no longer know where the shore is." With his answer Pinhead swam away and disappeared. Iktomi turned to walk away and as he turned, BANG! he struck his head, and when he came to, he was lying on his back looking up. Pinhead had deceived him, for they were at the shore itself, and Iktomi had banged his head against the rocks. "Now I know where I am," he said.

Iktomi looked up again and there he saw Mink sitting in the fork of a tree, eating the last of his meal with a pleased expression on his face.

"Oh pray, brother," cried Iktomi, "give me a bite?"

The Mink took a sharp bone and skewering a piece of meat replied, "Now close your eyes, Iktomi, and I will drop this into your mouth." Iktomi, was delighted for he was very hungry so he shut his eyes and opened his mouth. Mink threw down the meat on the sharp bone with such force that it knocked Iktomi unconscious. When he came to he saw that Mink had finished and gone off. It was some time before Iktomi was able to drag himself about. When he had recovered, he discovered that Mink had eaten the soup as well as the meat and had left only bones for Iktomi. This is the end of the Elk's tail.[20]

15. *Iktomi and the Fox*
One time Iktomi met his friend Fox.[21] He already had a scheme nicely planned out, and was only too glad to share it with his friend. The idea

20. "This is the end of the tail of the elk," Skinner says is the conventional ending of each story.

21. Oneroad to Skinner, March 20, 1924: "A parable. It had to do with a Red Fox. The story is similar to Uŋktomi getting his power from the skunk as you will recall that Iktomi practiced to be a good shot and use up the shots before he knew it, there were only five shots in this case it we match [*sic*] that Redfox bought of a Paleface, because he wanted power and honor among his people. he was foxy and paid a large sum for the matches. but Paleface he too" [the note is unfinished].

was this: Iktomi had a large family and among his children was a girl just about entering womanhood.

Iktomi said to his wife: "When I am dead and gone, dress me up in my best clothes, wrap me in buffalo rawhide, and hang me on a limb of a tree in the woods. Afterwards two young men will come to court you and your eldest daughter. He will wear a buckskin suit, a bow, a quiver full of arrows, and wear feathers in his hair. The other will wear a deerskin suit likewise, but he will have two feathers in his hair and bear a lance in his hand. Do you take him for your husband and give your daughter to the other one." So Iktomi proposed to his friend the Fox that the latter should dress according to his prophecy and carry a lance, while Iktomi should pretend to sicken and die, but should escape to join Fox disguised as the other young man with the bow, and that they should approach Iktomi's widow when Fox should marry her, and Iktomi his own daughter.[22]

"I shall be very sick soon," said Iktomi to Fox, "And I shall die." So it came about that Iktomi feigned illness and seemed to pass away. Everything was carried out as Iktomi had instructed his wife except that the buffalo hide was not long enough.

"Mother, what shall we do?" asked Iktomi's daughter, "Father is tall, and our rawhide is not long enough. Shall we chop off his legs? We can't bend them."

When Iktomi heard these words he was alarmed and cried out: "Bend them!" This they succeeded in doing. Then they carried him to the tree that had been selected and hung him up and they mourned greatly according to custom.

A few days after the funeral, one of the boy's [boys] came home and said to his mother: "I was over at the tree where my father is buried and under the place where we hung him there were already bleached bones lying white on the ground."

"Ah," said the old woman, "Those are the bones of your father!" So she went over to the tree and saw for herself that what the boy had reported was true.

The following day two young men appeared at their camp according to Iktomi's prediction and the widow obeyed the sacred words of her dead husband. To the young man with the deerskin suit, the bow, and the quiver full of arrows, with one feather on his head, she gave

22. Thompson: T411.1 Lecherous father 109p.

her daughter to wife, and she took the other, who wore two feathers in his hair and bore a spear, in his hand to be her own husband.

The daughter and her husband moved into a new lodge that was prepared for them. It was soon noticed that her husband was not so young as they had at first supposed, but rather elderly, whereas the widow's man was rather young, and very swift of foot. They hunted every day and the younger man was very successful and brought in more game by far than his 'son-in-law.'

One evening one of the boys came to his mother and said: "I just popped into sister's lodge and saw sister and her husband lying there, and brother-in-law has a scar on his thigh exactly like the one father used to have on his."

The woman grew suspicious at once, for she had suspected something was wrong from the very start, so she took her turnip digging-stick and looked in for herself, and lo! it was Iktomi! The old woman struck him a heavy blow on the back, "Hau! That is right, old woman, just help me to have coition with your daughter," cried Iktomi.[23]

16. Iktomi and the Hare

Iktomi met his brother, the Hare, and they travelled together until the sun set, when they came to a place to camp for the night.[24] As they were ready to go to bed Iktomi said to the Hare: "Brother, I would like to lie with you and when I am through, you can then lie with me."

"No," answered Hare, "Let me lie with you first, then you can lie with me."

"Oh no, my younger brother, I will be first and then you may follow."

"No, Iktomi, I want to be first and you can come afterwards."

"Oh no, younger brother! Consider, I spoke first so I am to be first, and when I am through I will let you have your turn."

The Hare still objected and after Iktomi had thought it over for a while he agreed and so they lay down and covered themselves with Iktomi's raccoon skin robe. But when Hare had finished and Iktomi demanded his turn, Hare hopped off a little ways and laughed at him.

---

23. Deloria (*Dakota Texts,* 11–19) called this tale "Iktomi Marries his Daughter." Wallis, "Beliefs and Tales," 92: "Spider Pretends to Die" is this same motif, and the "Spider and Fox" (p. 68) is a contest tale whereby the Spider triumphs again.

24. The Hare is perhaps the same Maśtiŋa character of the tales following the Iktomi tales.

Iktomi coaxed and coaxed him, but he would not return. Finally, he ran over the knoll and vanished in the darkness.

The next day Iktomi got up and went his way, but soon his stomach began to feel strange, so he bent over and a young rabbit sprang from his body and dashed off into the bushes.

"Come here, my child!" called Iktomi, but the hare fled into the undergrowth and Iktomi went on his way. Presently he was again taken with strange pains and again gave birth to a little rabbit. This happened a third time, but the fourth time Iktomi was ready and he took off his raccoon skin robe, cut holes all round the border and laced it up to make a bag, then he sat down over it holding the string in his hand and when he felt something leave his body he pulled the string tight and snatching up a stick he began to beat it exclaiming, "You with the split lip, large brown eyes, and long ears!" as he did so.

Presently he was through with his rage and he opened the bag to let the little rabbit out but to his astonishment he found that he had only dunged into his robe and beaten it in. Chagrined, Iktomi went on and soon came to a large boulder standing on the prairie. He spoke to it: "Oh my Grandfather, you who have stood here from time immemorial with nothing to shelter you from the heat and the cold, I give you my raccoon skin blanket!" And with these words he threw the robe over the rock and went on his way.

It is said that many things happened and that Iktomi went here and there and did this and that but that he finally came back to the rock one day and found that the rains had washed his raccoon robe clean again. For a while Iktomi stood silently regarding it, then he exclaimed: "My grandfather, you have had my raccoon skin for some time, and now I need it again!" With these words he took the raccoon skin off the rock, his grandfather.[25]

17. *Iktomi Visits the Squirrel*

Iktomi went to visit his little brother, the squirrel. As he drew near the lodge, the baby squirrel peeped out through a hole and told their father: "Iktomi is coming! Iktomi is coming!" Just then he opened the door flap, walked in, and sat down.

Squirrel promptly told his wife to prepare something to eat for his

25. "Tuŋkaŋ" in Dakota is the word for "grandfather" and in sacred language is the word for "a stone" regarded as sacred. This outrageous behavior or breaking of convention signals humor through licensed sacrilege. Wallis, "Beliefs and Tales," 96: "Spider and Rabbit" is comparable.

elder brother Iktomi. She fussed around, although Squirrel knew that they had no food in their home. Presently Squirrel called to her, "Bring me an awl and you stand here and hold the big wooden bowl." With the awl in his hand, Squirrel climbed to the top of their lodge and then stabbed himself in one of his testicles, whereupon wild beans gushed forth and filled up the bowl. With magic words he closed the wound, and stabbed the other testicle, upon which wild rice flowed forth. Then he likewise healed the new wound, while Iktomi stood bewildered.

"Here, my elder brother, you had better have something to eat before you go," said Squirrel. It was a good meal and as Iktomi left he said: "My younger brother, you must visit me in my home sometime."

The next day Iktomi's family saw Squirrel approaching the lodge, so they swept the guest place for him, and when he entered, they showed him to his seat with due ceremony. "Alas," said Iktomi's wife, "we have nothing to offer our younger brother to eat."

"I will look after that," answered Iktomi, "Give me the awl and you come here and hold that wooden bowl." The woman obeyed and with the awl in hand he climbed up one of the lodge poles, in imitation of what the Squirrel had done.[26] He told his wife to hold the bowl ready and with the awl he stabbed one of his testicles. But instead of wild beans, blood squirted out and Iktomi howled in pain.

"Alas, my elder brother," said Squirrel, "You attempted to follow my example and now see the trouble that you are in." He went to the aid of Iktomi, healed the wound and by his accustomed magic, brought beans and rice from his own testicles. Iktomi, as usual, had an excuse ready: "My younger brother, this would not have happened except that my wife is undergoing her courses, and therefore my medicine has gone back on me."[27]

18. Iktomi and the Beaver

Iktomi went to visit his younger brother the Beaver. Beaver was very cordial and presently he said to his wife: "What shall we give our elder brother to eat?" He looked all around as though he were searching for something as he spoke. Finally he called up his children and taking the youngest one, he said to his wife: "You comb her hair, paint her face,

26. Waterman ("Folk-Tales of the North-American Indians," 45) compares explanations for the "imitating host" motif. Wallis, "Beliefs and Tales," 88–89: "Spider and Squirrel" lengthens this same motif; it is one of his few tales where the Spider is foolish and not the victor over another being.

27. It is suggested that the menstrual cycle interferes with "medicine."

put on her buckskin dress and her porcupine quilled moccasins, and then bring her to me."

The wife obeyed. She took the child, combed her hair, painted her face, put on her buckskin dress and her porcupine quilled moccasins and brought her back to her father. Then the old Beaver said: "Make ready your fire and the cooking pot."

All this time Iktomi sat and looked on wondering what was going to happen next. He saw the Beaver kill and dress his child and cook it. It was served to them and just before they began to eat Beaver said to Iktomi, "Iktomi, when you eat, don't break any of the bones."

"I wonder what he means by that?" thought Iktomi and just to see what would happen he secretly broke or took part of the ankle bones. When the meal was finished, Beaver collected all the bones, took them down to the water and threw them in. Then he walked back, came in, and sat down. Just then something was heard and Iktomi looked over towards the water and saw the baby Beaver coming towards them crying and limping, saying, "Father, Iktomi has disjointed my ankle." Beaver was annoyed and looking over at Iktomi he said: "Elder Brother, I told you to be careful and not disjoint any bones."

"Alas, my younger brother," responded Iktomi, "I didn't mean to do it, it was only a slip of the jaw."[28]

After a while Iktomi rose to go: "You had better come over to my lodge soon," he said to Beaver.

Sometime later Beaver paid a return visit to Iktomi and Iktomi imitated what Beaver had done as nearly as was possible. He had his youngest child prepared and killed to make a meal for his guest, but he did not have Beaver's power and the child did not revive and had it not been for Beaver who restored her to life when Iktomi failed, he would never have brought her back.[29]

19. Iktomi and the Buffalo

Iktomi had been out hunting every day but it seemed as if the game had all disappeared. He was unable to find any tracks and he finally became so tired that he climbed up on a high bluff where he could overlook the region round about and sat there watching. It went up in the air, straight, like smoke, so he shaded his eyes and looked again. It

28. Thompson: E32 Resuscitated eaten animal 1 1 4a.

29. Wallis, "Beliefs and Tales," 62: "Spider and Beaver" is an outwitting motif whereby the spider triumphs.

seemed as if the dust cloud was moving like a whirlwind, but it was not. Finally, as it moved on across the prairie, Iktomi saw that it was a herd of buffalo. Iktomi was delighted, and he took out his ce and said: "Mi-ce, do you see that herd of buffalo out on the plain?"[30] He shook it and repeated, "Mi-ce, do you see that herd of buffalo? Do you see that herd of buffalo?"

All at once his ce answered: "I see, I see, I see, I see," Iktomi was amused that it answered him, but it continued to repeat, "I see, I see, I see, I see," until he began to feel uneasy.[31]

"Mi-ce, you have seen enough, stop now!" He ordered but it was no use, it kept right on repeating: "I see, I see, I see, I see." Iktomi wondered how he could silence it. He took it in his hand and squeezed it and it would stop for the time being, but as soon as he relaxed his grip it would cry out: "I see, I see, I see, I see!" He tried burying it in the earth of a mole hill but it puffed off the loose earth. He tried wading waist deep into the water, but that failed to stop it for the water bubbled up "I see, I see, I see, I see!"

"What in the world can I do to stop you?" asked Iktomi, at last.

"Take me to our mother-in-law and let her hold me in her hand and I will stop," said the ce.

Iktomi knew that it would be a great disgrace among his people to do this, but there seemed to be no other way to stop it, so he went to his mother-in-law and covering his face with his raccoon skin robe he told her what he wanted. She at once complied with his request and from that time on his ce stopped saying, "I see, I see, I see, I see."[32]

30. "Će" is Dakota for "penis" and "mi" is Dakota for "my" or "mine."

31. Thompson: D998, D161 03, H451 Talking privates 83a, 83b.

32. Skinner's version seems to play on the sounds of "miće" and "I see." Deloria (*Dakota Texts*, 8–11) has a tale of Iktomi violating the convention of mother-in-law avoidance when he takes her on the warpath and returns years later with a host of children. See Thompson: T41 7 Lecherous son-in-law 109s. Wallis, "Beliefs and Tales," 62–63: "Buffalo and Spider" uses the triumph of the small over the large motif.

THE ADVENTURES OF MASTINA, THE HARE

1. Hare and His Grandmother

The Hare and his grandmother lived alone in a little hut. One day he said, "Grandmother, I am going out hunting," and taking his bag he went over to the dancing ground of the prairie chickens. The birds saw him from a distance and cried out, "Oh here comes Mastina. Wonder what he has in that bag?"[33]

However, Hare used his utmost skill and cunning and finally lured them all into his bag. Then hurriedly tying it up, he carried it back to his grandmother's lodge. He was very hungry, so he told his grandmother to watch the bag while he went to gather some firewood, at a little distance from the hut.

While he was gone, Uncina, the grandmother, became curious to know what kind of game her grandson had brought in. She opened the bag a little and the prairie chickens began to talk to her.

"Oh grandmother! We were having a good time on the brow of the hill when Mastina joined us and lured us into his bag," they said, and they begged and coaxed her to open it a little wider. The old lady did this, and they burst forth and each tried to be first to escape by flying through the smoke hole. In the confusion they knocked each other down with their wings, and grandmother was bowled over also, but she managed to get up and yelling to Mastina she seized hold of two legs, crying, "Hurry up, grandson, I have caught two!"

Hare came running back but when he got there he saw that she had only succeeded in catching one lean bird by both legs! He killed it and began to pluck it, raging at his grandmother who sat on the opposite side of the lodge. When he started to draw the bird he took out the entrails and threw them across the lodge into his grandmother's lap: "Uncina," he cried, "You have become catamenial! The medicine bags

33. "Maśtiŋća" is Dakota for rabbit; "maśtina" is Oneroad's word for the hare. Skinner's note, inserted at this point, stated that grandmother was {Called Kunsi, Kunsitku, or Unci} in Dakota. The suffix "-na" is a diminutive. Skinner also noted: {Siyo, a prairie chicken, siyo-owaci [is literally] Prairie Chicken Dance-ground [in Dakota]} [Skinner's notes].

are inside and you must observe the custom of our people. Be gone and stay away until you are through with your purification."[34]

When the fire and the water were ready and the bird was boiling, Mastina told his grandmother that he wanted to invite his friends to partake of the feast, so he went out and began to call them in, the animal people, addressing each by name. Then he went back in the lodge and began to move the door flap, making noises as though persons were arriving, and he was showing them their respective places: "You sit over there, and you over here" he would cry, talking and answering himself with the voices of different people. The old grandmother thought that Mastina must have a great many guests to eat of one little prairie chicken.

Then the visitors appeared to leave, one by one, as they came, each one telling Mastina that the feast was very good. When they had all gone, Hare called to his grandmother saying: "Uncina, come in now and partake of my feast," meaning only his leavings.

2. Hare and the Bear Hunt

The Hare went out hunting with his grandmother. It was winter and he carried his sleigh with him. After a while he killed a large bear and cut it up into quarters and smaller pieces, not too heavy to be carried by one person. He said then to his grandmother: "What will you carry, Uncina?"

"Oh I am subject to the headache and if I carry the head I may have it again, so I don't want to carry the head."

"Then carry one of the forelegs."

"Oh grandson, I have had sore arms and if I carry a foreleg, I may have sore arms again."

"Uncina, carry the ribs."

"No, grandson. I have had a sore side and if I carry the ribs I may have a sore side again."

"Well then, carry the hindquarters."

"All right, grandson, I will carry the hindquarters."

Mastina bundled up the meat into two or three loads, and took the first one and hurried home. Then he went back for another load and

34. {While a woman is catamenial all the medicine bags and war charms and sacred ceremonial clothing are taken from the lodge and hung on poles at some distance away, or on trees. After her period, the Dakota woman must go to some remote pond or river and there plunge in and cleanse herself. Even in winter she must cut a hole in the ice and bathe} [Skinner's note].

brought that to the lodge. In the meantime he had forgotten all about his grandmother, but now he remembered and wondered where she could be, for she had long since started home by another path with her load. Mastina searched and finally from the other side of a hill he heard sounds like his grandmother's laughter. He was surprised, for this was something unusual. He trailed her to the spot and saw his grandmother coasting down hill on the hindquarters of the bear, and having connections with them at the same time, and this was what was causing her laughter.

3. Hare and the Early Riser

The Hare rose in the morning as usual and looked over his line of traps, only to find that someone had been there before him, but he could not tell from the footprints whom it might be. On his return he told his grandmother all about the hunter who got up earlier than he did. She only told him to rise earlier.

Next morning Hare did arise earlier, but as on the day before he found his rival's footprints, showing that he had been there before him. He reported to his grandmother, who only said: "Mastina, go still earlier." The next morning Mastina set a snare in the trail of the hunter who had preceded him and on the fourth morning he rose earlier than ever before to go the rounds of his traps. As he approached his snare he heard strange sounds and saw flashes of light streaking across the horizon, through the branches and leaves of the trees. Mastina was amazed at this unwanted sight and as he came nearer a flash struck him and scorched his body so that he had to go and stand behind a tree.

From where he was hidden he could see the early riser shake his yellow locks and saw them flash again. The atmosphere was very hot and sultry.

"Ha," thought Hare, "This must be somebody who has power!"

Just then the Early Riser caught sight of Mastina and said in a gruff tone, "Let me loose, you are holding back the day."

However, Mastina ran home to tell his grandmother all that had happened. Grandmother was greatly excited and said: "Make haste and turn him lose, that is the sun."

Mastina ran to obey, but in loosing the Early Riser his beautiful fur was burnt brown as a punishment and so it has remained until this day.

OTHER STORIES

1. The Child of Love

There was once a camp in which lived a young man who was known as "The Child of Love."[35] His father was a noted leader, and the young man had many brothers and sisters. It was a camp where everybody was happy and there were dances every night, but everyone noticed that this young man was not happy at all. He was never seen at any of the merrymakings. It was suspected that there was something wrong with him, but no one, not even his intimate friends, knew what it was for the young man kept all his troubles to himself.

This young man had the best buckskin leggings and shirt. He was handsome and his companions were proud of him, yet he was very sad, especially in the evenings, when he would not even tell his parents why it was but one night he spoke to his grandmother: "My Grandmother," he said, "my heart is heavy. Every night when I am just falling asleep, and sometimes just after I have dozed off, someone comes and stands over me and micturates on me. It is a young woman."

"Aha," said his grandmother, "Now I see why my grandson has been sad these many days. Tonight when you go to your bed, have some red paint ready in a bowl and when she comes throw it on her body and her face."

The Child of Love did as he was told. Just as he was about to fall asleep, someone entered softly and stood over the young man, and he

35. Ruth Landes, *The Mystic Lake Sioux* (Madison: University of Wisconsin Press, 1968), 136, said a "beloved-child" was a child "born after parents' travail of some sort and consequently honored in public ceremonies and consecrated to ethical ideals." Walker (*Lakota Belief,* 300) said they were ones who had been honored by the "Hunka" ceremony. Deloria (*Dakota Texts,* 110, 175) said a boy-beloved was a great honor and carried heavy obligation. Parents who wished to declare their child beloved must first give away many presents in the child's name. Then they must always be the foremost in doing kind deeds to the poor and needy in the child's honor. In return, the entire tribe set great store by the child. It ensured him the deference and recognition of the people and affection as one on whose account many had benefited. He was often raised in a separate decorated tipi where the poor always found welcome and food. This Skinner tale incorporates another told to Riggs (*Dakota Grammar, Texts, and Ethnography,* 130–43) by Michael Renville called "The Younger Brother" or "The Unvisited Island."

roused himself up and threw the paint all over her legs, body, and face. The girl, frightened, whirled around and fled in the darkness. That night the young man slept well and when he rose in the morning he looked handsomer than ever. He told his grandmother what had happened and she said: "My grandson, you tell your father and mother to prepare a feast and a dance. Watch the women who come closely, and you will be able to identify the girl who has done this deed of shame to you, by the paint that clings to her."

His parents were quite willing to give a feast and a dance in the young man's honor, and when everything was ready they sent an old man as a herald to invite the people to attend the dance given for The Child of Love. No one was to stay home, old and young alike were requested to come. The dancing place was selected, and the people came singly and in crowds, in their best costumes and with painted faces. The dancing began and the young man went over to watch. He stood in the crowd with some of his companions talking and looking on. Presently, during the dance he spied a girl who was smeared with red paint and it was one of his own sisters. The young man was greatly astonished.[36]

He went home and sat a while in silence and presently he heard footsteps of some one coming softly but he did not look up to see who it was until he heard a voice saying, "My younger brother, I have come from another village and I hear that your people are having a good time. What makes you so sad, my younger brother? Especially when all your people are rejoicing."

The young man looked up and saw that it was Iktomi who was speaking: "Iktomi, I have something for you to do and it must be done right away." With these words he took his bow and his quiver full of arrows and handed them to the newcomer. "Do as I tell you. Take these weapons and go over to yonder dance. Watch for a girl who has a very peculiar smear of scarlet paint on her face and who dances differently from all the rest; take one of the arrows and with a careful aim shoot her through the heart then run back here as quickly as you can and your life will be spared."

At first Iktomi did not want to do what the young man ordered, but when the Child of Love insisted and told him who he was and why, he took the bow and arrows and walked over among the crowd. The people saw him and cried: "Here comes Iktomi. Wonder what he has in

36. Thompson: T41 5 Brother and sister incest 8.

mind now? Why is he carrying that bow and arrows?" Just then the singers beat on their drum, and the dance began again. Iktomi saw a girl with a peculiar smear of scarlet paint dancing differently from the rest, so with speed he sent his arrow to her heart.

There was great confusion and the bystanders yelled: "It is Iktomi! Iktomi did it!" And there was great tumult, the crowd swayed to and fro, and the women wept over the girl. The men gave chase to Iktomi who ran half way back to the lodge of the Child of Love who had promised him protection, and the young man came out of his lodge and stood with his hand stretched forth. The crowd came to a stand still and the young man said: "I am the cause of this tragedy and no one shall dare to harm Iktomi; he shall have his freedom in peace."

The crowd dispersed, the young man turned back to his lodge and Iktomi went on his way. The camp soon learned the cause of the murder, and they buried the young woman on the outskirts of the settlement, and covered her grave with sod. Then they went about their daily duties and forgot about the unfortunate happening.

In the meantime the grave of the girl opened and more sods had to be cast on. Yet again, in a few days it opened again and the body was pushed up so that it had to be covered again until it looked like a sod mound from a distance in clear view of the camp. Still the body was thrust up until it became too high for the people to put more sod on it so they built up a scaffold and then they discovered that a hawthorn tree had grown up from below through the channel left where the arrow had pierced her heart and had raised her body up in full view. It seemed to the people that this was a punishment meted out to the girl as a warning to those who lead immoral lives. Since that time a hawthorn tree has always been used to point out as a warning to naughty children. This particular hawthorn tree grew high and the girl on her scaffold was held aloft as a warning in full sight of the camp.

One day the young man said to his parents that he must go on a long journey and would not return for sometime. His mother made moccasins for him and when everything was ready he gathered up his pets. These were four in number, two birds and two mammals, a burrowing owl and a kite, an otter and a fisher. The latter was his most intimate companion, and it was carried in a pocket that he had made on his breast for safety. The young man left the tribe and went off for a long ways without seeing anyone. As he journeyed along with his pets they came to the foot of a large hill and the owl said to him, "Father, I would like to live here." So the young man agreed and they left the owl there and went on.

After a time they came to a large lake and on one side of it there was a high bluff with many springs gushing from it to run down to the lake. "Father," said the otter, "I want to stay here." The young man answered, "yes, you can stay and make your home here."

They continued on their way along the lake shore until they came to groves of pine and cedar growing on high rocks where the land looked rough and rugged. Here the Kite thought it was a suitable abode for him and permission was granted him to dwell there by the young man.

The young man and the fisher continued their travels along the sandy shore that fringed the rough country, until they heard in the distance ahead of them the voice of a woman calling and saw a wooded point jutting out into the lake. As he came closer he saw that the point was really an island, and he could hear the woman still calling, just out of sight ahead of them. When he came nearer he could see a canoe, partly grounded on the shore, and an old woman standing there, leaning on a cane and gazing out towards the island. At her feet was a pack about the length of a man wrapped in the fresh inner bark of basswood and fresh leaves. To the young man it seemed very suspicious.

As he approached the old woman said to the young man: "My grandchild, I have waited long for someone to take me over to yonder island, and now you are come to paddle me over there."

The youth hesitated a moment, and then agreed. The old woman had some bundles, some of which lay on the beach and some were already in the canoe. She said to him: "Put the big pack in first." It was very heavy, but the youth managed to put it in. He was still filled with wonder at its size, weight, and shape, and did not know what to make of it. The old woman herself put her little bundles into the craft. Then the youth said, "Wait a moment, until I shift your big pack to a better place." He took up the suspicious pack as though he were going to put it in the other end of the canoe, but as he was about to lay it down again, he dropped it in the deep water, and springing into the canoe, shoved it out on the lake, looking back he saw the old woman glaring at him with piercing eyes, saying: "You save your life by your wits!"

It seems that the old woman was a witch, and the bundles were her evil medicines. In the large pack was concealed a man with a short handled lance with which he stabbed the youths whom the old woman inveigled into coming to her assistance. She lived on the bodies of those whom she was able to murder.[37]

The young man paddled out towards the island, which seemed quite large. He wondered if the old woman was really calling to someone there. When he reached the shore he pulled up his canoe and scouted around on the beach. He saw human tracks, deer tracks, and those of smaller animals. Then he came to a path that led through the woods, and so, as he naturally wanted to know where it led to, he followed it. After a while he came to a clearing, in which he saw a large lodge, and not far away was a smaller hut. On closer inspection this hut brought forth a new surprise. It was made of human skins! Just then the youth saw the door flap moved, and a gray haired woman peered out under her shading palm. "Who is here? Who has come to visit my daughters?" she exclaimed. With these words she looked towards the woods and yelled: "Come home! Your man is here now! Come home, your man is here now!"

The youth observed that the old woman's attire consisted of an old tattered deerskin dress. Her hood was of human skin taken from the front of a man. For earrings she wore a testicle and a mentula.[38] The young man realized that he was in great danger, and the fisher in his bosom began to snarl, "Father! Here is danger!"

In answer to the old hag's summons two young women now appeared at the edge of the opening. The old woman began to mumble and scold the girls: "Why didn't you come at once when I called you? Your man is here and he is very hungry. Give him something to eat at once." With these words she hobbled back into her hut.

The girls signed to the young man to enter the large lodge, and this he did, going directly to the guest place, in the rear, opposite the doorway, while the girls took their stations on opposite sides of the lodge, making it apparent to the youth that each owned half of the building. Inside the wigwam was decorated with beautiful colors. On one half the lodge were drawn pictures of human beings, on the other pictures of animals.

The young woman on whose side were the human drawings sud-

37. Waterman ("Folk-Tales of the North-American Indians," 43) compared the explanation of this motif between differing tribes. He said the Dakota explanation for the "fiendish woman" was that women cannot kill people by magic. Wallis ("Beliefs and Tales," 80–81) includes this motif in the Iktomi tale, "Spider and Young Man."

38. Mentula is another term for penis.

denly said: "Sister, I will serve the man with my food first." Whereupon
the other sang under her breath:

> *"Ecin   chan   ni   waste   ke   nakaes eo"*[39]
> To think   the acts   thy   good   art   indeed
> That is: "Indeed I think thy acts art good."

The youth watched every move that his hostess made and presently
she brought him a wooden bowl filled with sliced human flesh, which
she had boiled and offered him with broth. She placed a big wooden la-
dle in it and passed it to her guest.

The youth took up the spoon and stirred the broth until it cooled
and bending his head, he watched the woman, while he fed the soup a
spoonful at a time to the fisher in his breast. When it was all gone he
pushed the empty bowl back to the woman, who thought that he had
eaten it himself. The other woman on whose side of the lodge the animal drawings were, sang again, saying:

> *"Wica kin, miye woyute ica   waku kte."*
> Man   the   I   food   real   serve shall [40]
> That is: "I shall serve the man real food."

With these words she whispered to the youth: "I am all right, don't
be afraid of me," and he saw her prepare real venison with her own
cooking utensils. This time he took the bowl and spoon and ate the
meal.[41]

Now the woods became dark and the youth knew that the sun had
gone down. He began to get drowsy and sleepy after his days of tramp-
ing. The women began to prepare their beds and the one who had first
fed him said: "Sister, I will sleep with the man first." And he heard her
song in reply:

> *Ecin   chan niwasteka nakaes."*
> To think   acts   thy good   indeed
> That is: "Indeed, to think thy acts art good."

When her bed was ready, the girl motioned to the youth to join her.
She had a blanket which she called Maȟpiya-sina, or Cloud Blanket
and she called to her sister to cover them up. The Cloud Blanket was
very light at first, but as the youth lay there, he was nearly smothered.

---

39. The Dakota word for "the act" is "śkaŋ" or "haŋ." It is unclear why "chan,"
which means "tree; woods; day or night; or when," is used. Also "ke" generally signi-
fies the future tense of the first person. Later the adjective "niwaśteka" or "your good"
is used and should be used here instead of "ni waśte ke."

40. The Dakota word for "real" is "ȟca" or "hecaȟca" not "ica."

41. Thompson: G532 Help from ogre's child 171.

Then he heard the chattering of teeth. He happened to remember that he had in his medicine pouch a gland of musk from a badger's ear, wrapped up in buckskin. He felt for and opened it and when the foul odor of the musk arose, the woman called, "Sister, open the blanket, this man has broken wind." Thus he got a good breath of fresh air. Meantime he heard the gritting of teeth once more, and he decided that it came from his companion's vagina.[42] So he found a deerbone in his pouch, and thrust it in. The hard bone broke the teeth and the woman screamed saying, "Sister! This man has killed me!" Meanwhile he heard the old woman grumbling outside, saying, "I thought you had finished the man by this time." This was one way in which they killed youths who came to visit them.

The girl threw off the Cloud Blanket and ran out of the lodge, whereupon the youth went over and got into bed with her sister, who said that she was a normal woman.

Now the girl from whom he had broken the teeth did not die, so the youth dwelt with them both, and each had a child. He continued to live with them until his two sons were able to walk and wander out in the woods alone. Then the youth began to think of his parents and he told his wives that he thought they would go and visit the people. They made ready for the home journey and they went over to the mainland in the canoe and thence started out on foot. When they came to the rocky country, the youth found the kite, who had discovered a mate and had raised a family. He was satisfied, so the youth told him to remain where he was.

When they came to the springy bluff, they found the otter living in luxury. He presented the travelers with fresh and dried fish, and, as he preferred to remain there, they left him and went on.

When they came to the land at the foot of the great hill, there they met the owl and his family living happily. He chose to remain there, and today, on your rambles over the prairie, you may see him, in the land of his choice.

The homeward journey was slow, because of the children, but finally, the young man said to his family: "We are not far from the camp of my people," and he selected a permanent camping ground, pitched his tent, and told his wives that if the evening was quiet they ought to be able to hear the noise of the home camp. However, although the

42. Thompson: F547.1 Vagina dentata 115. Waterman ("Folk-Tales of the North-American Indians," 49–50) compares the "toothed vagina" motif explanations.

evening was quiet, no sound was heard, so early the next morning the youth set out alone to visit his people.

When he drew near to the camp he wondered if it had been moved but, when he came up on a hill overlooking the site, he saw at a glance that they must have had an epidemic or a panic, for the tents were still standing in part. Others were scattered on the ground, while household goods were blown and tossed everywhere. Where his father's dwelling had been he saw two small brown tents, and from one there rose a curl of smoke.[43]

The youth walked slowly towards the tents, with a heavy heart. As he came close, his mother met him, crying, and he noticed that she was covered with sores, as though she had been burnt all over. When the other members of the family appeared, he noticed that they were in the same condition, and this is what they told him: "Soon after you had gone your sister whom Iktomi killed and who was later placed aloft on the scaffold returned as a ghost every evening. She would approach the people and ask, 'Has my elder brother returned?' and when we answered 'No,' she snatches up a firebrand and burns one or two people until they die, and we are the only ones who are left."

The youth then said to them: "Tonight I shall change myself into an old stump, and when my sister comes to ask you about me, answer her as usual, that I have not yet returned. Then she will notice the old stump, and say: 'Why this stump was never here before!' Then mother, you reply, 'Yes, that has stood here always.' Then walk over to it and say, 'Don't you remember how I used to take bark and burn it?' Then take a bit of bark and strip it off and she will say: 'Why won't he come now?' Then she will grab a firebrand to burn you as before."

The old people understood what their son meant to do, and as he said he would do, he transformed himself into an old stump, and just before twilight the scaffold where the dead girl lay shook slightly, and the girl's ghost descended and came over to her father's tent and said: "Has my elder brother returned yet?" Her mother answered, "No." Then she looked around and saw the stump and said again: "Why, that stump never stood here before." But her mother returned, "Yes, it has been there all the time. Don't you remember how I used to burn the bark?" And she walked over and peeled some as though she were going to use it. Whereupon the girl cried: "Is my elder brother ever going

43 A skin tipi in long use or that is old becomes smoke tanned and was usually discarded or reused by the poor.

to return here?" and snatched up a firebrand, when the stump rose up as her brother ready to defend his people, with a bow and arrow of magic power.[44]

The ghost screamed and fled towards the scaffold whence she had come, but the magic arrow passed through her swiftly and she vanished at its foot.

Then the Child of Love said: "Don't worry about her coming again," and he told his family that he would now return to his camp and in a few days he would bring back his wives and family and some food. When he got to the place where his wives were they noticed that he had changed, and seemed sad once more. He did not tell them what he had found, but the next day he went back to his parents with a load of tipsinna, deer meat, and healing herbs.[45] He found them already improved in their condition and left them, promising to return again.

That night the women in the Child of Love's camp said: "Someone is coming!" The stranger drew nearer and nearer, and the women did not know him. He entered the camp and said: "My younger brother! Is it well with thee? You have been gone a long time, and I have been looking for you in every camp."

It was Iktomi, and he played with the little boys and then the women started to joke with him, as their brother-in-law. They pinched him and he would laugh, and exclaim, "My younger brother, my sisters-in-law are getting reckless!" The young man said nothing and finally the two wives seized Iktomi by the legs and arms and stretched him over the fire. Iktomi laughed at first, but his laugh soon changed to pitiful cries, and these died away. When he was dead they took out his heart and laid it to one side, while they burned his body to ashes. Then they took his heart and sliced and dried it in the sun. When it was cured, they made it into pemmican.[46]

All this time the heart of the youth was filled with wonder and suspicion. He thought of his encounter with the witch who ate people and his first meeting with the girls, and he wondered if their appetite for human flesh had reawakened. But he could not fathom their hearts nor their thoughts.

After a while the two women set off over the hills without a word. The young man was left sadder and more puzzled than ever. Day after

44. Thompson: D1 841.3 Burning magically evaded 1 2 0.

45. Tipsiŋna is a prairie turnip, a bulbous root eaten in the beginning of the summer.

46. Thompson: D251 Trickster becomes a dish 1 00.

day he sat there, thinking over the past. Finally, however, the women returned loaded with tipsinna, which they prepared by peeling back the
skin and braiding it to dry. Others they sliced and dried for winter use.

After a few days the women visited the camp of their husband's people. They took with them the dried heart of Iktomi, and at each thresh-
old they dropped a few particles of it, and a few more at the scaffold.
The next day they went there again, and they saw that maggots were
swarming wherever the pemmican had been spread.

"Ah, sister," said the elder girl, "Our prediction is coming to pass."

Next day they returned with more tipsinna, prepared and ready to
store away, and this time they saw tiny persons where the maggots had
been. Men and women, they were trying to stand, but flopped over and
over. They went home very happy that night, and in a few days they
heard noises at the old camp as though it were peopled again, and they
could hear dogs barking. They also heard the clear voice of a herald
announcing something, and the sound of singing and the beating of a
drum.

"Sister," said the elder wife, "our words have come true." They told
the youth that his people had all been restored, and early the next
morning he went over and found that his people really were alive
again. Then he saw and understood why his wives had burnt Iktomi
alive and made pemmican of his heart. The young man and his family then joined the camp, and lived among his people once more.[47]

2. The Mouse and the Buffalo

A mouse met a buffalo out on the prairie, and challenged him, saying:

"*Tatanka ci huhu.*"

"Buffalo-bull, I will cohabit with you."[48]

This angered the bison, who bellowed in reply: "Keep quiet, or I will
crush you with my hoofs!"

But the mouse sang as before, and the bison answered: "Keep quiet,
or I will crush you under my heels."

For the third time the mouse sang his insulting song, and the bison
was beginning to get very angry, pawing the dirt until the dust rose

47. Deloria (*Dakota Texts*, 175–81) said "Incest" also was about a boy who was
tempted by his own sister, who was punished, but he became the tree.

48. The noun "hu" means bones (particularly of the legs). Riggs says the verb "hu"
means to have intercourse with a female. "Huhu" denotes repetitive action. Therefore, the statement to the bull carries a double insult with either possible translation.

like smoke, and shaking his head, while he advanced towards the mouse. "I told you to keep quiet, or I will crush you under my heel!"

Ever alert, the mouse sang his song for the fourth time, and the buffalo charged on him, but the mouse escaped by leaping through the split hoof of the huge bull, climbed up his tail, and ran through his buttocks into his body, where it gnawed the buffalo's heart until it fell over dead.[49] Then the mouse came out and sat on the carcass and sang:

"*Isan au, wasanka bawakse kte!*"

Knife bring, arrows not dried I cut shall.[50]

That is, "Bring a knife! I shall cut arrow shafts!" This song he kept repeating, each time a little louder than before.

It happened that a fox was passing on the other side of the hill and he heard the call, and pricked up his ears in surprise, saying: "What is that? Listen! Ah, he says 'Isan au, wasanka bawakse kte!' That is, 'Bring a knife, I shall butcher beef.'" Again the mouse sang, "Bring a knife, I shall cut arrow sticks!"

"Yes," cried the Fox, "Now I hear! He said: 'Bring a knife, I shall butcher beef'"[51] and he ran over the hill and found his friend Mouse sitting on the dead buffalo. Mouse was glad to see Fox, and they cut up the game. Mouse said: "Let us build a straw hut. You get the poles and I will gather the straw."

So they worked hard, and soon built a lodge, and there they lived happily, eating and sleeping, until they had devoured the buffalo.

3. The Legend of Hoop Ravine

The Indians had gone into winter quarters at the foot of Hoop Ravine.[52] It was a severe winter, and the struggle to keep alive was desperate, and the famine was great. In the early spring that followed two young men who were friends strolled out towards Thunder Claw

49. Thompson: K952 Monster killed from within 159; Q478 Eaten Heart 241.

50. There is not a negative indicator in the Dakota sentence.

51. {There seems to be a play on words here. Probably a pun on "wasaŋka," which is made to appear to mean arrowshafts and beef. "Tado" is the usual word for the latter, however} [Skinner's note]. It is also likely a word play on "wasaŋka" and "tataŋka." "Wasaŋka" means arrows and "tataŋka" means male buffalo.

52. Garcia to Anderson, February 22, 1994. Garcia found that Hoop Ravine or Hoop Hollow or as it is called in the Sisseton Claims, Circular Ravine, is located seven miles west of Peever, S.Dak. The Dakota name for it is supposedly "Kaksiza Canhdeska." It is located north of Big Coolie where two different streams circle about, each forming about a half of the circle.

Print Lake.[53] They wandered around on the east side, eating roseberries, and filling their hunting bags until they were ready to come
home. Just then there appeared buffalo coming over the ridge to the
south straight towards them. "Friend," cried one, "the buffalo are coming right this way."

They watched until they were quite sure that there was no mistake,
then one said to the other, "Friend, we must in some way waylay them.
Remember, we are in the midst of famine." They hid themselves in the
tall grass. One youth had a bow and a quiver full of arrows, while the
other, having only a few arrows, naturally depended on the first to do
the killing. They lay flat on their bellies, never taking their eyes off the
approaching animals. Presently the buffalo came close enough for the
youths to see that they were two young buffalo cows.

The first youth straightened his arrow and took careful aim. He let
fly his arrow, and one of the cows bawled and fell over dead. The other
ran on a few paces and then turned back as though to take a last look
at her companion, then wheeled, and ran off, dodging the hunters, and
finally escaped over a distant knoll.

It was getting along towards evening, and the youths wanted to get
back home before sunset. They worked fast to skin and quarter the animal. The less fortunate hunter said, "Friend, I would like to take the
tongue." The other answered, "No, my friend, that is my packstring
knot." Later the unfortunate youth said: "Friend, I should like to take
the heart," but again, he was answered, "No, my friend, that is my packstring knot." They continued the butchering, and at length the unfortunate youth said, "Friend, I should like to take the liver." But the reply
was as before, "No, my friend, that is my packstring knot."[54]

53. Thunder Claw Print Lake could be Wakinyan Oye in Dakota. Joseph N. Nicol-
let translated it as "Lighting's Track" and referred to three small lakes near Big Stone
Lake; see Nicollet, *Hydrographical Basin of the Upper Mississippi River, 1843* (St. Paul:
Minnesota Historical Society, 1976). A Thunder Bird Rock is eight miles northwest of
Browns Valley and is reported as having the imprint of ancient bird claws or of a
"Thunder Bird"; see *Brown's Valley: 125 Years, 1866–1991* (Browns Valley, Minn.:
Browns Valley Town and Country Club History Committee, 1991), 56. Morris called it
"Big Slough"; high upon the ridge on its eastern bank is the ridge that separates it
from the southern branch of the Minnesota River—there is a granite rock on whose
face is what appears to be the print of a great bird; see Morris, *Historical Stories*, 27.

54. The tongues, the portions on one side of the ribs, and the tenderloins of all
buffalo were taken by the akicita to the tiyotipi, cooked by four poor men, and fed to
everyone. The tongue and the heart were cooked in special feasts and given to the
poor. The liver was given as an honor to someone to eat. See Lowie, "Dance Associations," 135, and Wallis, "Canadian Dakota."

Whether the second youth was joking or not, his companion took his replies seriously, and stopped and wiped his knife on the grass and put it back in his case. Then he said: "Friend, this is a time of famine. All of us alike are suffering from [lack of] food. When you return home bear the news well. I care not what becomes of me, I am going to trail that other buffalo to the end."

The other youth was surprised at this, and cried; "No, my friend, do not go. Take the tongue and whatever you will."

"No," said the unfortunate youth, "that is your packstring knot. The meat is all yours. What I have said is well." With these words he walked off, although his comrade coaxed and begged him to stay.

The prairie was wet from melted snow, and the hoof prints of the buffalo cow could be seen clearly. In some places her feet had sunk deep and the tracks were filled with water. The sun had sunk, but the hunter did not slacken his strides. The trail led on parallel with the Coteau des prairies, the great ridge that runs across the Dakotas. Although it was dusk he could still see the tracks, and he thought that maybe the cow would stop somewhere to feed and there would be a chance of overtaking it.

It was now getting dark, yet the Coteau was still visible along the horizon. He knew that he could go no further, so he determined to camp for the night and go on in the morning. Just as he had decided to do this he saw a tent ahead of him, with sparks flying out of the smoke hole. He thought: "It is good. Someone is camping here, and I can rest for the night."

He hesitated outside a moment, then, without a word he raised the door flap and went in and sat down. There was a woman there sitting on one side, combing her hair, and he waited some time until she had finished her toilet. Then she spoke: "Well, I will give you some food, but I don't know whether you will eat it or not." Saying this, she handed him a bowl full of mashed wild cherries mixed with a little meat and tallow.[55] The youth thought: "This little bowl full is nothing." But he began to eat, and soon found that he was unable to eat it all. There was always enough there.[56] When he could eat no more he handed the

55. The right side of the tipi looking in is the family side. Relatives and guests sit on the left side. The space immediately to the left of the doorway was where the elderly and those coming to "seek house" with the purpose of getting something to eat sat. Pemmican was the choice food, considered the mark of honor for the donor or recipient. See Deloria, *Dakota Texts,* 112, 96.

56. Thompson: D1 032 Inexhaustible food-supply 210.

bowl back to the woman, who seemed surprised, and remarked: "A little bowl full, and you couldn't eat it up!" With these words she dumped the contents into her hand and devoured it.

The woman continued to sit opposite the man, and neither spoke a word. Every now and then she would poke up the fire and make it burn brighter. The young man, tired by his exertions, soon fell asleep. When he awoke he found himself alone, sleeping on the prairie. There was no sign of a tent there. He thought that he must have been dreaming and rubbed his eyes. There were the hoof prints looking as fresh as if they had been made that very morning. He followed them, and they lead northwest along the edge of the Coteau des prairies. All day he saw no one, nor any animals.

At night he followed the tracks over a ridge, and as he descended the other side to a broad prairie, it became dark, and just as he felt that he couldn't go any further he saw a tent ahead of him. "Someone must have been hunting out here," he thought, "I'll stop here for the night," and he walked in. There was the same woman sitting combing her hair.

"I am going to give you something to eat," she said, as before. "But whether you will eat it or not, I cannot tell." With these words she handed him bowl full of turnips. He was hungry, and tried to eat it up, but he could not finish it. So he handed back the bowl with just as much in it as there was before. The girl took the bowl with a surprised look, and said: "A little bowl full, and you gave it up!" She tipped it over in her palm and put the remainder in her mouth.

They remained sitting opposite each other as before, and neither spoke, although every now and then the woman would poke the fire to make it burn brighter. The young man, being tired, fell asleep, and did not awaken until the next morning, when he found himself alone, as before. He was ready to go, however, for he expected to overtake the buffalo some time during the day, for the hoof prints were fresh.

Refreshed with food and a nights [sic] rest he hurried on over the rolling country, and at night fall he stood on a high elevation and gazed over the surrounding country, then he hastened down the slope. It was dark when he got to the bottom, and he began to look for a suitable place to sleep, when he saw a tipi in the distance with sparks flying up through the smoke hole, so he decided to go there and spend the night. He approached the tent as before, and entering sat down as usual in the guest place. The same woman was there, combing her hair. When she was through she said: "I am going to give you some food. Maybe you will eat it, and maybe not." So saying she handed him a little bowl full of raspberries, and although he was very hungry, he was unable to finish it all, and when he handed it back it looked as though it wasn't touched. The woman took the bowl, exclaiming, "Such a little bowl full, and you gave it up!" Whereupon she dumped its contents into the palm of her hand, and disposed of it all in a single bite.

Again they sat silent opposite each other, with the woman once in a while poking up the fire to make it lighter. The youth soon dropped off to sleep, and when he awoke in the morning he was alone. Again he travelled all day, and found the tipi at night. This time the woman fed a bowl full of wild potatoes that magically stayed replenished, and with her customary remark finished them herself.

This time the youth was not very tired, and he sat there watching the woman by the firelight, while she sewed upon a pair of moccasins. Suddenly she looked up and spoke to him: "Young man, whence came ye? Where are you going, and why do you follow the hoof prints of the buffalo cow?"

The young man answered her, saying: "Our people are in the midst of a great famine this winter at their winter encampment at Hoop Ravine. My friend and I went over to Thunder-claws Print Lake to gather roseberries, and along towards evening we saw two buffalo cows. My friend shot one, the one on the left. The other cow ran on, but returned to her companion and then ran away, circling till she was out of reach of shot. Then she fled north along the base of the Coteau des prairies. We butchered the cow he killed, and I asked my friend to give me the tongue, but he replied: 'No, my friend, that is my pack thong knot.' Then I begged for the heart and he answered: 'No, my friend, that is my pack thong knot.' Then I requested him to give me the liver, and he said: 'No, my friend, that is my pack thong knot.' Then I made my last plea for the kidneys, and had the same answer, 'No, my friend, that is my pack thong knot.'"

"So I stopped right there and said: "Friend, this is a time of famine when all alike are suffering for want of food. When you return home, bear the news well. I care not what becomes of me, I am going to trail the other buffalo cow to the end."

"When he head heard my speech he coaxed me to take the tongue or whatever I wanted, but I answered, 'No, my friend, that is your pack thong knot. It is well, what I have said,' so I came on, and followed the trail all these days until now I am here."

The woman nodded and made reply: "Hau, young man, you have

spoken the truth. I am the buffalo cow you are trailing, and we are near to the end of our journey. Listen, and you will hear the voices of my people, who are patiently waiting for my return."[57]

The youth bent low and listened, and he could hear the distant rumbling as of thunder, and he knew that it was but a day's journey to the main herd of buffalo.

Then the young woman spoke again: "This is my story. My friend and I were sent on a dangerous expedition to Makato-oze (Mankato, Minn.) and on our return trip she was shot by your friend. Our object was to get the blue earth paint that is found in that locality, and she had it in her mouth when she fell, so I ran back and took it. Tomorrow, before the sun is at its zenith you shall see my people, and, if you will do what I tell you, both you and your people shall be made happy. We shall go, and when we have arrived at the last ridge you must remain and wait until the chief sends his messenger for you. Then you shall tell them all the tale of your adventures. The famine, your friend, and your trailing of the buffalo cow to the end. The Chief will surely answer you favorably, and, if he will permit me to do so, I shall go home with you as your companion." Then the buffalo woman looked out of the tipi and said, "See, Wica-akiyuhapi (Urea [Ursa] Major) is overhead. Now it is time to be going."

They saw the approach of dawn and the coming of the morning star. "Follow me," said the buffalo woman, and they set out and he noticed that they ran magically, seeming to glide over the tops of the grasses. The journey seemed much easier, the sun rose more glorious in the land of the buffalo than it does at Hoop Ravine, in the land of the Indian people. "I must be near the end of my trail," thought the youth.[58]

The sun rose still higher and higher, and the ridge which the buffalo woman had mentioned was in sight. In a few moments they were standing on the promontory of the ridge, and looking ahead as far as the eye could see the earth was a dark with bison as though a prairie fire had swept through that section of land.

"Now wait for me [and] the messenger here," said the buffalo woman, and she became a buffalo again and descended the slope. She ran over the prairie towards the herd and disappeared among them, and he could hear the bawling of the animals like the pealing of

57. Thompson: D651 Transformation to escape death 117b.
58. Thompson: F0 Journeys to other worlds 192.

distant thunder. He knew instinctively that the buffalo were cheering and applauding their heroine.

Now all was silent. "She must be speaking at their council, telling about her adventures and the loss of her companion. What will they say about that?" thought the youth, and he began to tremble lest her plea for him and his people should be rejected. At that very moment there came the thunderous bellowing of the bison to his ears. This time it was not rejoicing, but distress that he detected in its sound. He could see great clouds of dust rise, and the herd seemed to waver. Then it was quiet again. Suddenly, the solid herd opened, and out shot a black object with the speed of an arrow. It came straight towards him, and as he saw it approach it resolved itself into the messenger: "Hau," said the buffalo, coming up to him, "You are wanted to appear before our great chief. He is waiting."

Accompanied by the buffalo the youth walked down and crossed the prairie, while the eyes of all the buffalo were upon them. The great herd seemed to give way as they approached, and it opened and closed in again behind them. On every side they were surrounded by the buffalo. Smooth horns, bent horns, and even little spring calves wrinkled their black noses at them, for it is a saying of the buffalo people that "It is better to smell than to see."

At last they came to the midst of a large circle that was carefully guarded by akicita (Soldiers or Braves), and in the center of the circle was a lone lodge. The Messenger led the way to it, followed by the youth, and they entered the tipi. Just opposite the door sat the chief, and, from his immense size the youth knew at once that he must be the ruler of the plains. Servants brought him something to eat, and he was given a pipe to smoke, and he looked around and saw that the leaders of the Buffalo Nation were all assembled.[59] The youth discovered that he had been seated next to his friend the Buffalo woman, and that the father and mother of the cow whom his friend had shot were there, in mourning, with their faces blackened with charcoal.

In that great assembly were mostly old bulls, though close behind them were the smooth horns, who were being trained by their elders. He saw also the sacred pipe, freshly painted with the blue earth that the Buffalo cow woman had brought with her from Mankato. It was

59. This echoes of the "mythical Tataŋka (buffalo) Republic," which became the nickname of Fort Sisseton (Wadsworth) and was where a herd of 3,000 buffalo were discovered in 1865. This is the Buffalo Woman motif. See Blackthunder, *Ehanna Woyakapi,* 49.

leaning from a crotched stick in the center of the lodge. Finally the old chief addressed him, saying: "Stranger, speak. Tell us what is in your heart, and what has brought you to our country. We desire to listen to the message that you bring from your people."

"Hau, oh chief!" answered the youth. "Our people are in the midst of a great famine at their winter encampment at Hoop Ravine. My friend and I went over eastward to Thunder Claw's Print Lake to pick roseberries and towards evening we saw two buffalo cows coming. My friend shot one."

Here the old chief grunted, and the councilors bellowed until their mournful cries shook the earth.

"The other cow ran back to her companion and circled around within arrow range."

At this point the buffalo bellowed again in tones of thunder, cheering the courage of the cow.

"Then she fled north along the foot of the Coteau des prairies, and we butchered the cow." The young man then went on to tell how he had asked his partner for a share of the meat and how he had been refused, and how he had then pursued the escaped cow and his adventures until he came to this very spot.

"Stranger," said the chief, when he had finished, "You have spoken well. You have told the truth. What is your wish? Tell us, that it may be granted to you."

The Buffalo woman leaned forward and whispered something in his ear, and he replied: "I want my people to make the chase four times."

The Chief nodded and said: "Where and how do you wish your people to make the chase?"

Again the Buffalo woman prompted him, and he said: "I wish that four successive herds should follow the west bottoms of the Coteau des prairies, crossing over at Turkey Buzzard Knoll and descending south of Big Coulee straight to Otter Tail Lake (Lake Traverse). Then north, following the east base of the Coteau."

"Hau," said the Chief. "As for you, your reward shall be to take our heroine with you as your wife. We lack two very precious ornaments to decorate our pipe. We desire an eagle feather and a strip of red broadcloth. These we desire you to furnish."[60]

60. Oneroad and Skinner describe this token as "war honors awarded horses." Thompson: B600 Animal marriages 3.

At this moment the chief was interrupted by the appearance of the messenger accompanied by a young bull of the smooth horn class. Two other young smooth horns began to pull off his beautiful hair, and when they were through he was a singed scabby bull.[61] Two netted gaming hoops he carried, concealed on either flank.

"Now," said the old chief: "This is the singed bull who is to avenge the death of our heroine. When he arrives at your village, be ready with the eagle plume and the red broadcloth. The bull's life will be spared in spite of many shots, until he has accomplished his mission. As soon as he receives the fatal wound, run to him, wrap up his head in the broadcloth and attach the plume to it. What I have spoken shall be true. Go now to your home, and take our heroine with you."

The youth and the Buffalo woman went slowly away, and all eyes were upon them. The herd divided and they passed through, and it closed again behind them as they went out onto the broad prairie. The woman took the two magic netted gaming hoops and rolled them ahead of them and they went on at great speed, passing the singed bull as they ran. "That is my cousin," said the Buffalo woman, "and he is on his way."

They passed on, and before sunset they had arrived at the north end of the Coteau. They seemed to glide over it, and as the sun sank they were already at a hill west of and overlooking Hoop Ravine. They saw that when they arrived at the creek bank the youth said to the woman: "Wait here until I send some one." Then he took the path and followed it until he came to the camp circle. Finally he found his father's house and entered, saying: "Father, it is I who have returned."

His family had all mourned him as dead, and his father answered, "You boys all say this, but it is not so." Then some one poked up the fire and then indeed they saw that it was their son who had gone off on the trail of the buffalo cow.

"My sister," said the young man, "Your sister-in-law is waiting down at the water." At once the girls ran down to meet her, and in the meantime his father and mother who had mourned his death began to rejoice aloud, and the people came running to their lodge to see what was the matter.

When the young man had told his story the people were very

---

61. {A note by Mr. Oneroad says that a buffalo bull, whether young or old, that had been singed in a prairie fire was always very vicious, and was exceedingly dreaded by the Indians} [Skinner's note].

happy, especially when he showed his wife, and predicted the coming of four great herds of buffalo.

Only a few days later, at dawn, the Buffalo woman said to her husband: "Go up on the hill. My cousin is coming." So the young man put on his moccasins and ran up on the hill. Near the north end of Drywood Lake and on the east side stands a hill that looms above the rest. The youth ran and stood there, and he saw the singed bull, surrounded by a pack of wolves making a running fight. He ran back and aroused the camp. All the men went out to meet the bull. The youth took his roll of red broadcloth and wrapped it up with his eagle feather. He took his wife with him, and other women joined the party, but they went slower than the warriors. When they arrived at the knoll the sun was quite high, and the men, who had outdistanced them were at the other end of the lake shooting at the bull, who was holding his own. No matter how well the men aimed their arrows they did not seem to be able to hit their target, and each time they shot the bull charged ferociously.

Presently the youth's friend, who had slain the cow and refused him a share, arrived, and announced his name aloud that all might hear and know. "I am the one who is to slay this buffalo" he proclaimed, and, while all eyes were upon him, he took his arrow and placed it against his bowstring, aimed, and shot. At that moment the bull charged, and struck the young man and split him in two. Thus the cow was avenged, and the bull fell dying. The youth ran up with his cloth and feather and laid them on the head of the bull, while he and his wife stood guard over them.

Now the hungry Indians cut the meat in small bits and distributed it. As they carried it off over the hill and the young couple were left alone they heard the angry challenging bellow of a bull, and behold the buffalo was restored to life once more! It stood there, pawing and tearing the turf and throwing the sods over its back. It ran its smooth horns into the black soil, and the dust eddied up around it. Then it turned and swiftly ran away around the lake. Then the young couple went back to wait the coming of the herd.

During the following summer the words of the Buffalo chief were amply fulfilled. The buffalo came to the people four times, so that they could make the chase, and all had supplies of meat to last until the spring.

A few years after this the Buffalo woman said to her husband: "I must soon leave you and your people." Soon the time came, and they walked together to the knoll at Drywood Lake, and as they stood there she said: "Next summer about this time we shall meet here for the last time. Then I shall return to my people and you to yours. I shall bear posterity among my people and you among yours." So saying they parted, and she became a buffalo cow as she walked away.

Next summer Hoop Ravine camp moved to Otter Tail Lake. The young man was watching a game of Hoop and Javelin when suddenly he remembered something. He ran to his tipi and dressed in his best, and ascended the Coteau to its summit. As he arrived there he met his Buffalo wife, and they stood there talking for sometime, then separated and went their ways. What they said, no one knows, but this is the legend of Hoop Ravine as it was given to me.[62]

4. *Raccoon and the Crawfish*

The Raccoon (Wica-ite-hdega) awoke from his slumber. He shook his fur and stretched himself. He was hungry, so he began to sing a song dedicated to himself, as he considered his face, his paws, his back, and his tail.

> *Sisi   ma-stosto,   Sisi   ma-stosto*
> Paw   my smooth,   paw   my smooth,   (bis)
> *Wica   ite   ma   hdehdega*
> Raccoon   face   my   spotted
> *Uta   kin   iwa   hpaye*
> Acorn   carrying   in consequence of   I fell
>   [the]   [iwahpaya = I fell down]
> *Manica   - pamdu   sinte   awa   hdu   sdohan*
> Pocket-gopher   hills   tail   upon   mine   drag along
> [to snow upon]

Literally:

> My smooth paw, my smooth paw.
> My smooth paw, my smooth paw.
> My spotted raccoon face.
> My spotted raccoon face.
> I fell in consequence of carrying the acorn
> I fell in consequence of carrying the acorn

62. Another version called "Wohpe and the Gift of the Pipe" was collected by James R. Walker in 1914; Walker, *Lakota Belief and Ritual*, 109–12, 148–50. See also De Mallie, ed., *Sixth Grandfather*, 283–85, and Powers, *Oglala Religion*, 81–83. See Waterman, "Folk-Tales of the North-American Indians," 42, for a comparison of the explanations in other tribes' tales using the motif of the Buffalo wife.

My tail drags along on the pocket-gopher hill
My tail drags along on the pocket-gopher hill.

He stretched again, yawned, sniffed, and saw a beautiful lake ahead of him. Softly he trod his way until he stood over on the high bank of the lake, and he thought over where the most likely places were to find cranberries, artichokes, and the black-haw berries that made him sick when he climbed for them. He looked at the lake shore below him, and then he thought of fresh crawfishes, and his mouth watered, so he sang again.

> *Wapapake,   wapapake*
> I shall bark, I shall bark
> *potpanke   yud [yuta]   unyanpi   kte*
> Cranberries   eat   we go   shall
> *Heca   wata   eca   cuwi   omaokuye*
> Suchlike to eat truly   internal   mine sweeten
>   [side]   [with help or sick]
> *Pangi   yud   unyanpi   kte*
> Artichoke eat   we go   shall
> *Heca   wata   eca   cuwi   omatage*
> Suchlike to eat   truly   internal   mine bitter
> *Mna   yud   unyanpi   kte*
> Blackhaws eat   we go   shall
> *Heca   wata   eca   cuwi   omasde*
> Suchlike to eat   truly   internal   mine fuse [grease]
> *Matuska yud   unyanpi   kte*
> Crawfish   to eat we go   shall
> *Heca   wata   eca   cuwi   omawaste.*
> Suchlike to eat   truly   internal   my good.

Literally:
"I shall bark, I shall bark!
We shall go to eat cranberries.
Truly, to eat suchlike sweetens my insides.
We shall go to eat artichokes,
Truly, to eat suchlike makes my insides bitter.
We shall go to eat blackhaws,
Truly, to eat suchlike fuses my insides.
We shall go to eat crawfishes,
Truly, to eat suchlike refreshes my insides!"

He thought of this and that as he came down to the shore, his old hunting ground. "I know what I will do," he said to himself, "I will lie down on the sand and pretend that I am dead."

So the raccoon lay down as though he were dead. Presently the crawfishes began to appear on the scene. They began to examine raccoon's carcass, for at first they did not know what it was. They felt it, smelled it, and pinched it, and finally one, who seemed to be wiser than the rest, remarked: "People, this is Raccoon, our enemy, who used to crush and chew us up. He is dead." And they re-examined the carcass. "Sure enough," they agreed, "He is dead. Let us dance around his body, now that we have no enemy to fear."

By this time every crawfish, old or young, had heard the news, and came to see the excitement. They began to beat the drum, and to dance to the song that the drummers sang.

> *Wica   unya   huhugapi   ece*
> Raccoon you   crushed us   always
> *Wanji   den   ta   wanke*
> One   here   dead lies
> *Wohiya   wohiya*
> Conquered, conquered
> *Ha   hin   mina   kokiju*
> Skin   hair   with   cover   united
>   [knife or my-you—to come together]

Literally:

> "You Raccoon that always crushed us
> One (of your people) lies here dead.
> Conquered! Conquered!
> Unite to cover ourselves with fur,
> Unite to cover ourselves with fur

Just when the festivities were at their height Raccoon jumped up and began to crunch and gulp down the crawfishes. He swallowed old and young until none were left to tell the tale of that eventful day. Raccoon looked around to see if any had been overlooked, but there was no sign of anything along the shore. He felt very well satisfied with his bountiful meal.

Just then his stomach began to feel uneasy, and suddenly he heard a muffled voice, crying. It seemed to be that of a crawfish. He could see no one. The voice continued, saying: "Wica, cesdi!" (Raccoon, evacuate!)

"Oh," said Raccoon, "That must be one of them in my stomach. One that I failed to crush!"

Again the voice cried pitifully: "Wica, cesdi!"

"No," replied Raccoon, "Not until I have digested your pinchers!"

However, the crawfish began to twist, and turn, and crawl, and pinch until he began to afflict Raccoon with internal pains. At last Raccoon was obliged to evacuate him, and there must have been more than one crawfish left alive in his stomach, for from these who escaped the crawfish people again replenished the earth with their kind.[63]

5. Turtle and his Warparty

It was announced that Turtle and his warriors were going on the warpath to make war on the enemy. There were Bladder, Dragon-fly, Fire-brand, Grasshopper, Dung, Squirrel, and Turtle himself. The party left early in the spring as soon as warm weather set in. Dung was the first victim. He could not stand the warmth, and crumbled in the rays of the sun. So one of the party ceased to follow the footsteps of their leader.[64]

The remaining six travelled on until they came to a patch of woodland, when Bladder was pricked by a thorn and burst. Thus another warrior laid down his life.[65]

The five survivors proceeded full of vigor. They came to a river, and all crossed it successfully save Firebrand. He was extinguished with smoke and hissing. He disappeared in the current and sank to the bottom.

Turtle encouraged his warriors, telling them to fear nothing, four even four could accomplish something. The path lay through a bog, however, and Grasshopper's legs were caught in the mire and pulled off, so he too was left behind, never to see the enemy's country, nor to share in bringing home war trophies to his people.

Now there were only three warriors left to travel on. Dragonfly, bereaved by the loss of his near relative, Grasshopper, wept. He tried to wipe his nose, but in attempting to do so he pulled off his own head.

Squirrel and Turtle kept bravely on alone. They were now in the outskirts of the enemy's country, so they proceeded cautiously, watching and examining every object which appeared the least suspicious. Finally, when they heard voices, they halted, and Turtle gave Squirrel his plans and issued his orders and instructions.

63. {Menomini, Potawatomi, Fox, Ojibway, Ioway, Omaha} [Skinner's note].

64. Thompson: F1027 Turtle's war party 108.

65. Bladders were blown up and allowed to dry and, among other things, used like oiled paper to carry greasy food or as children's balloons. See Deloria, *Dakota Texts,* 79.

"I will enter the camp and make myself known," said Turtle, "If anything happens, you keep on watch from the tree tops and come to me."

With these words they parted, the Turtle [Squirrel] taking his station in the tree top, while Turtle strolled into the camp all alone. Almost at once he was captured by some boys, who carried him into the village to show him to the people. Turtle stood calmly while the crowd surrounded him, some laughing, some gesticulating to one another. Turtle couldn't stand to be jeered at, so he boldly announced: "I have come to make war!"

The people understood him, and the old men councilled that since he had announced himself to be an enemy he should be treated as such. It was decided that he must die, and he was to be thrown into a kettle of hot water.

"But," said someone, "Perhaps we had better not do that, for if we cast him in he will kick and upset the pot, and someone may be scalded. That will not be good."

So the elders councilled again. This time they agreed to chop his head off, thinking that that would be the easiest way to get rid of him. They got an axe, and one man pulled out his head and neck while another raised the axe to take his life. Just as he swung his weapon, Turtle pulled his head in, and the man who was holding it had one of his fingers cut off. Thus Turtle counted a coup.

"Throw him in the air, and the fall will surely kill him," shouted someone in the crowd. This sounded good, so they selected a strong man who tossed him high in the air, like a lacrosse ball. But Turtle fell down on a lodge and broke through the roof and fell on a sleeping child and killed it. Thus he counted a second coup.

By this time the crowd was getting restless and the women were wailing, and the elders didn't know what to do. "Let us drown him," suggested someone. When he heard these words Turtle began to exhibit signs of fear. He thrust out his head and cried: "I am afraid of water!"

"Listen," said every one, "He says that he is afraid of water. Now we will get rid of him, this Turtle who comes to make war."[66]

They took him to the water and threw him in. Turtle scrambled for the shore, "Inh! Inh!" Surely it appeared that he was afraid of water, for he swam back every time that they threw him in. "Let us cast him in the deep water," said someone, so they threw him as far as they could, and he sank out of sight. "Ah, surely he will be drowned this time," said

66. Thompson: ĸ581 Drowning punishment for turtle 108.

all the people, and they thronged the shore to watch. Just then Turtle stuck out his head in the middle of the lake, and raising his arm as far as he could, he showed two fingers to let the people know that he had counted two coups, and he called to the crowd: "This is where I came from." Then he dove again, and presently came up once more to show his two fingers and taunt them with: "This is where I came from."

He kept this up until the crowd was angry and fell into a great commotion. They called upon two pelicans to come and drink the lake dry. The pelicans drank until they had drained the lake, all but a little pool in the center, and Turtle began to get excited. He kept diving and coming up again. The people began to shout and cheer, but just then, before anyone noticed what was happening, Squirrel rushed up and shot both of the pelicans, and the water all ran back into the lake again. This saved Turtle, and Squirrel retreated again to his tree top.

Such is the tale of Turtle and his war party.[67]

6. The Woodpecker and the Crane

The woodpecker was in his winter quarters, a large hollow tree, when, late in the autumn a visitor came to talk with him about staying there for the winter. The woodpecker, being a non-migratory bird, knew by experience what northern winters are, and, like a good, wise, elder brother he said: "You had better fly south where it is warm. The winters here are cold, and I have not enough food laid by for both of us."[68]

The visitor, who was Crane, answered: "Yes, brother, but I want to stay up here for the winter. I have enough food stored up for the cold weather."

The woodpecker again spoke, saying: "My younger brother, hear me, and listen well to what I say. We have hard winters, and your legs are too long. You will freeze."

But the crane answered: "Brother, I am going to stay up here and live with you in this hollow tree for the winter. I have enough food to last till spring."

The woodpecker saw that it was no use to argue with Crane, so he said: "All right, then. You may stay with me for the winter. Bring your supplies up here."

67. {Menomini, Ojibway, Potawatomi, Ioway} [Skinner's note]. Deloria (*Dakota Texts*, 77–80) also has a variant of this tale. The ending of the tale exclaims whence came the saying "Like a turtle about to be thrown into water" whenever someone pretends to hold back from the very thing he wants.

68. This echoes the grasshopper-and-the-ant motif.

So the crane was happy to think that he was to stay north for once. He went home and brought back his supplies. Most of it was psincinca or "young wild rice," an esculent bulb or root which grows along the rivers and lakes. He piled it up in a corner of Woodpecker's abode, and then he went back and brought some more.

Soon after this the cold weather came, and snow began to fall. That day the Woodpecker and the Crane stayed inside, and they built a fire. The crane did not seem to mind his first cold day. The next day was fine and the crane went outside and made tracks in the snow. He thought that the woodpecker must have been telling him something that wasn't so. Day after day he would go out and walk on the snow bank, and, although every now and then there came a storm, he thought that it was an easy winter. It did not seem so cold as he expected.

The two birds were very happy, and along towards midwinter the days were warm and the snow began to melt, and the crane waded in the pools of water that formed here and there. He thought surely spring had come, so he ran into the house and told his brother that spring had come and he had even waded in the water. He took out his winter supplies and dumped them in a pile.

"Brother, what are you doing?" asked woodpecker.

"Why, spring is here now, you know. I have been down to the lake and waded in the water."

"No, my younger brother! This is not spring. Don't throw away your food, bring it in again. We will have more winter yet, with lots of storms."

But the crane knew too much about the weather, so the woodpecker said again: "Brother, when we have some more wintry days you will wish that you hadn't stayed up here. You will long for your psincinca."

But the crane only laughed and went out to wade in the water until he came in for the night, to sleep and dream of the fine weather that was coming in the morning. But next day he awoke to find that a storm had come during the night, and woodpecker had been up for some time and had a fire blazing. The crane looked out and he couldn't see anything. The storm kept up all day, and the crane had nothing to eat. The next morning the wind was still blowing, and Crane was very hungry. He ran out to where he had thrown his roots, and he was able, by aid of his long slender bill to dig them out, one by one. But they were now frozen as hard as pebbles. Then his legs began to get numb, and he had a hard time to get back. He found the woodpecker sitting by the fire, cracking a nut.

"I told you what was coming," said the latter, "But you didn't believe me. Better stay inside, we will still have more stormy days before winter is gone."

Crane made no reply. He sat before the fire, thinking of the warm south where his relatives must have been for some time, and he hung his head. Day after day he sat there, poking the fire with his long bill, until the fire turned his bill black, and burnt the top of his head red. He used his wing to brush up the ashes, and the sparks burnt the feathers black, and his beautiful white plumage was smoked to a dull gray color. All these changes came to him as a punishment for staying behind his people when they went south. And today, if you chance to see a sandhill crane, you will notice the black bill, red top, and dull gray color of the bird, with the wing feathers tipped with black. This is the history of his change, for once he had beautiful plumage, like his elder brother the Whooping crane.

All this time the woodpecker had not been idle, and as he rattled and cracked his nuts he thought of his younger brother the crane. "I'll invite my friend to come here for the purpose of asking those who are adventurous to go after the spring," he thought.

That night the guests came in, one by one, until woodpecker's lodge was crowded. Came the bear, panther, lynx, fisher, otter, mink, weasel, timber wolf, prairie wolf, coyote, fox, porcupine, raccoon, squirrel, golden eagle, kite, and, last of all, the tadpole. It was indeed a great gathering, and the result of the council which they held was that the tadpole, fox, otter, and kite were selected to go after the spring weather.

When the day set arrived the brave men set forth on their dangerous quest. It took many days before they arrived at the home of spring weather, which was inside a great enclosure. The door keepers were two mountain lions (panthers or pumas), and so the warriors paused and talked over who was to first attempt to go in. The lot fell upon Tadpole, who was instructed to try to slip through the door unnoticed. He was then to go to the chief, who was called the "Keeper of the Sun-flower," and make himself known. The kite and the otter were to wait outside, and, while the tadpole excited commotion, Fox was to sneak in also.

Kite and Otter recognized some of their summer friends inside, but the door-keepers were not pleased at all. Otter presently began to feel very uncomfortable in his warm winter fur, but Kite did not seem to mind. Meanwhile, Tadpole passed in and being so small that no one noticed him, he made his way straight to the Keeper of the Sun-flower.

When Tadpole got to the Keeper of the Sun-flower he began to mumble something, but as he had no mouth he could not be understood, so a great crowd of excited spectators gathered around, and soon his deformity was noticed, and all began to exclaim, "He has no mouth!" and that drew still more people to the place. Even the door keepers became curious and left their posts, and this gave Fox his chance to slip in.

Tadpole kept on mumbling away, until someone cried, "Let us cut a mouth for him. He has some news that he is anxious to tell us!" So they cut a mouth for him, but, before he could speak, someone cried: "Fox has stolen the Sun-flower!" And everybody rushed to the scene. Sure enough, the Sun-flower was gone, and all who were good runners began to make chase. Fox tied the Sun-flower to the end of his tail and ran slowly to deceive his pursuers. He was in the lead, and the crowd was headed by the two panther door keepers. Fox played all the tricks he was capable of, and caused great excitement because of his narrow escapes. As the spring travelled wherever the Sun-flower was taken, the birds were free to go, and they went as they pleased, in flocks or in pairs.

For two days Fox ran on, carrying the Sun-flower at his tail's tip. The Indians say that he still carries the scent of sun-flowers at the tip of his tail. Finally he grew tired, and otter took the flower, and ran over the frozen lakes and along water courses, dodging his pursuers. The ice behind him melted, and torrential floods followed, yet the best runners among the enemy, headed still by the mountain lions, were close behind. Now the kite swooped down and picked up the flower, and, with a speed surpassing all animals and most birds he disappeared from their sight. The last stretch was finished, and the kite brought the sun-flower to the hollow tree abode of the woodpecker and the sandhill crane. He was received with great joy.[69]

The next day the crane left the hollow tree and walked down to the lake shore in search of food. There he stood, watching the coming of his feathered friends, the water birds. He found that he was unable to fly, because his wing feathers were so badly burnt, so he ran up and down the lake shore, happy to think that spring had come again at last. Such is the tale of the sandhill crane who wintered in the north land with his elder brother the woodpecker.

69. Thompson: A1151 Theft of the seasons 60a.

7. The Mysterious Man

The events told in this story occurred near Big Coulee on the old Sisseton Agency in South Dakota. This strange man is said to have had physical endurance beyond comparison with any other man. He had the power to reincarnate himself. He was desperate when attacked, but quiet when unmolested.

This man had the reputation of taking women and girls of marriageable age and fleeing with them to remote places for many months or sometimes years before he would revisit his people. He was very much feared on account of this habit, and his name was dreaded throughout the various Dakota camps.

Men in defending their women had shot their arrows into his body with no effect whatever. They had stabbed him with their knives, and clubbed him and left him for dead. They would move and hide their camps for safety, but there was no eluding him when the passion to steal a woman came upon him.

A certain woman whose two daughters were married to a warrior were encamped on what is now the James River. She had heard that her children were not treated right by their husband, so she started to go to them from her camp at Mde-ipaksan (Bent Lake, the middle stretch of Big Stone Lake, now known as Hartford Beach). She arrived at her son-in-law's and was directed to his lodge by the other villagers. She met her daughters, and remained with them for sometime. Meantime she told them secretly why she had come so far, and that she was ready to take them home. She had them make new moccasins, repair old ones, and pack up a supply of buffalo pemmican. The men were always away hunting, so this went unnoticed. When she was ready, one day the herald announced that the men were to go on a hunting expedition for two or three days, and were to take sufficient provisions for that time. That very night the three women made their departure, travelling all night until daybreak, when they came to a ravine at the foot of the Coteau des prairies, where they hid. At night they travelled on over the rolling ridge, and at dawn they rested for a short time and then moved on.

The older woman knew the way and thought that they were now safe, but, when they were a little ways west of the Big Coulee, they came on the Mysterious Man quite unexpectedly. He gave them no opportunity to speak, but said: "There is my camp yonder, and I am well supplied with buffalo meat," and he led them to his tipi for the night.

At night, however, the three women escaped again, but the next day they were overtaken and headed off by the man, who seized one and cried: "This is the one I will keep as my wife!" The girl screamed, and all three of the women attacked the man. The old woman was brave and steady. She grappled with the man and tried desperately to throw him down, and held her own for some time, when she signalled her daughters that she was weakening. Then the girls pounced upon him, thrusting and slashing his back until the blood gushed forth. The man turned to them with a surprised look, exclaiming: "Wan! De camape ye!" (Look! She stabbed me!) He grew weak from loss of blood, and they fell on him and cut off his head.

The mother told her daughters to run on towards the Big Coulee, which was not far off, and she followed, carrying the head of the man, as a trophy. As they entered the coulee the old woman threw the head down and it rolled to the bottom. They looked back and saw their headless enemy running around as though looking for something, and the old woman cries: "He is trying to find his head!"

They fled down the sloping side of the Big Coulee, and headed for Bent Lake. Nothing was ever again heard of the Mysterious Man after this encounter, which ended his career.

8. *The Man Who Was Changed into a Pickerel*[70]

Two young men, friends, who were travelling on the warpath alone together, arrived at the shore of a lake now said to be at Stillwater, Minnesota. Tired and hungry they stopped for a short rest, and, when one of them went to get water he found a dead pickerel washed up on the shore. He examined it, and, as it looked fresh, he called to his companion: "Friend, here is a pickerel that has just dies [died]. We will cook it."

"You had better not do that," replied the other, but the youth who had found the fish said that he was hungry, and so he made a fire and boiled the fish, that they might have soup. When he had finished, he tasted it, and said that it was good, but the other insisted: "I cannot partake of that fish."

The first young man urged and coaxed his partner, who finally said "I will have to eat it, if you won't give up." The first youth was somewhat confused, and repeated: "This soup is good, and you ought to have some." Again said the other, "I will eat it, if you don't give up."

70. The second rule of the ten rules of life reminds one that water is sacred and, therefore, requires a red-feather sacrifice before dipping it up for the medicine feast. If this ceremony is omitted, it is cautioned that a pickerel will swallow the offender or drag him into the water. See Skinner's 1920 article on the Medicine Dance.

"No," replied the first, "I won't give up!" So between them they ate the fish and drank the broth. A little while after it was finished the young man who had demurred said to the other: "My friend, will you bring me a drink of water?"

The friend brought him the water, but, in a little while, he said again: "My friend, will you bring me a drink of water?" And again his friend went after some for him.

The second youth kept up his requests for water so long that the other finally said: "My friend, I am getting tired of hauling water. I will take you down to the water, and you can drink all you want."

"Yes," said the other, "My friend, I knew that you were going to get tired and give up."

So the thirsty youth was carried down to the lake's edge to drink all he wanted. The sun was setting, and the other man prepared for the night by carrying in firewood. He sat by the fire alone for a long time, and then, as darkness gathered he went down to see how his companion was making out. He found the other youth still lying there drinking, and, as he stared at him he discovered that his chum's ankles had been changed into pickerel's fins![71]

Speechless with amazement he returned to his campfire. The next morning he was awakened by his companion's voice calling, "Friend, come down now and look at me." He went down and what he saw made him weep. During the night his friend had been transformed into a pickerel, all but his head!

"Go back to our people," said the fishman, "and tell them about this strange thing which has taken place. Next summer at this season bring them here to make sacrificial gifts, and pay homage, and I will lie across the lake."

With these words his head became that of a pickerel also, and slowly and gracefully the giant fish moved his fins and glided off into the water. The water ripples, and the waves dashed against the shores.

The young man stood at the water's edge weeping for a time, and then returned to his people. The next summer, as they had been instructed, the people came to the spot. They saw the fireplace, and in the middle of the lake the waves rose and parted at the exact spot where the great fish lay.[72] The people sacrificed by throwing into the lake beautiful robes, deerskin shirts, moccasins, or anything that they had which was rare and valuable. Each year they visited the spot, and some

71. Thompson: D550 Transformation by eating or drinking 132a.
72. Thompson: D1551 Magic parting of waters 15b.

go even yet, as they can still see the resting place of the pickerel where the waves part in the center of the lake, down to this very day.

9. *The Mysterious Turtle*

Some hunters were out after game and found a very large turtle on the prairie. They jokingly said to one another: "Let us get on its back and see if it can carry us," so they all jumped on its back, and it started to walk off with them. The hunters thought that it was great fun to ride on the back of such an enormous turtle, but it was no fun when they found that they were stuck there and could not get off.

The turtle walked right straight to a lake, and walked on under water, and finally came up on the opposite shore alone. The hunters were all drowned.

10. *The Toad Who Stole a Boy*

In a village there lived a woman who had twins. One was a boy and the other was a black dog. It happened that once, when she went visiting her friends, she left the baby boy in charge of the black dog at home. She made a long visit, saying that the babe was fast asleep. Just then she heard the dog give a sharp yelp, and jumping up she ran back. But it was too late, when she got to her lodge she found it empty, but there was a piece of flesh scorching in the fire.

The whole camp searched, but they found no trace of either boy or dog. The woman mourned day after day, and the days turned into months and years, and still the woman could be heard wailing as she rambled in the woods. The people at length became accustomed to hearing her, and no longer paid her any attention. There was, however, a young man, who lived away from all others, who followed a different mode of life, and who had never seen a human being. He heard her each day, and it touched him deeply.

This young man had grown up amidst the forest, and he was as timid as a fawn. Yet, down in his human heart there was a yearning for the love of a human mother. He was kept in the family of an old Toad Woman, and when he came home and told her about his feelings, she said: "That is only an old drudge (wiwatoksu) who you hear. You must not pay any attention to her."

The next day he went out in the woods again, having as his only companion a black dog. He heard the wailing again, and slowly made his way towards it, keeping out of sight as he did so. As they approached his dog began to bristle and snarl, and ran towards the scene.

The youth followed, and when he got there he found a woman in a low tree, where she had climbed out of reach of the dog. He spoke to her.

"Why is it that you wail so sorrowfully? I have heard you weeping many a day."

"Many years ago," answered the woman, "I was happy. I had a baby boy and a black dog. While I was gone visiting the Toad Woman came and stole both of them, but before she got away the dog bit a piece out of her thigh and left it burning in the fire. I have been weeping for them ever since but I believe that you are the pair for whom I have been mourning."

The young man stood there listening to her, while the dog was on its hind legs, with its paws on the trunk of the tree, barking. The woman spoke again: "It shall be proved that you are the stolen pair," and so saying she squeezed her breast and the milk ran down on the trunk of the tree. Whereupon the dog smelled it, and eagerly licked it up. Then it began to whine and wag its tail. "You are my two children lost long ago," said the woman. And she came down from the tree. "There is one more proof that I need. If this woman whom you claim as your mother has a scar on her right thigh, then she is surely the Toad Woman who stole you both."

The young man well understood what was said and she spoke again: "When you go back home pretend that you are ill, and get the Toad Woman to dance and expose her thighs. Then you will see if she has that scar as I suspect." Then they parted, being sure that their separation had come to an end.

The young man went home and pretended to be very sick. He did all sorts of queer things, and wanted everything. "Mother," said he to the old Toad Woman, "dance for me." The old woman complied.

"Show me your thighs," he begged.

"Yes," said the Toad Woman, "When he is sick he wants everything done his way."

The youth saw that she had a scar on her right thigh, and he said: "Mother, why is it that my brothers and sisters are so different from me?" and she answered him: "Why, they are only a mixture of various species of frog progeny."

But now the youth had seen and understood all that had happened. He left the old Toad Woman and was reunited with his real mother.[73]

73. Cornelius Matthews, *The Enchanted Moccasin and Other Legends of the American Indians* (New York: G. P. Putnam's Sons, 1877), 90–97, contains a version of "The Toad Woman."

11. *The Flying Man*

In a certain village lived a man who had four sons, all of whom had grown to young manhood. The father was very proud of his boys, as they were all handsome and manly. It so happened that one night, after they had all gone to bed, a great horned owl lit on the ridge pole and hooted, and then flew away in the darkness. The next morning the eldest boy complained of a headache. At first no one thought it was serious, but it developed until they were unable to help him, and, after lingering delirious for a time, the young man died. He was buried under the earth, and his father mourned according to the custom of his people cutting his hair below the ears, blackening his face, and going barefoot. Each morning he would sing the death song, and wail until the woodlands reverberated.

Not long after the death of the eldest youth the great horned owl again came and hooted from the ridge pole. This time the next to eldest boy took sick and died, and was buried beside his brother. At dawn each day the father wailed beside the two graves.

A few days later the great horned owl came again as before, hooted from the ridge pole and flew off in the darkness. The sign was now known to the family to mean death, and soon the third of the brothers followed the other two to the grave and the spirit world beyond. He too was buried with the others. As the father wailed over the graves in the morning he noticed a small hole bored in the earth at the head of each grave.

[It was] Not long after the third death that the owls [sic] call was heard again. The father noticed, as he had before that just before it was given he could hear the cries of different birds of prey and of carnivorous animals. Like the rest, the youngest boy died, and the father had his body laid in the branches of a tree, not far from the graves of the others. He went there in the evening and took his position concealed, with his gun loaded with shot.

It was not long before the man heard the growling of a wildcat, drawing nearer and nearer. Then followed the long drawn howl of a timber wolf, and the shrill cry of a hawk, as it flew half way between the tree tops and disappeared. Then came the chattering of the bill of a great horned owl as it swooped from the darkness right to the head of the corpse, where it lit, turning its head from side to side and peering towards the ground.

The man watched every move of the bird, and, as he looked, all of a sudden the owl changed into a man and began to unwrap the covering of the corpse. He aimed carefully, fired, and his enemy toppled off its perch and fell to the ground, fatally wounded, and exclaiming: "Oh, you have brought ill fate and misery upon me!"

The man was clothed as a witch. He was naked, but on each ankle were tied tiny globular buckskin packets of herbs and roots. The same things were on his wrists, and to his elbows, wrists, and ankles, were attached the skins of animals and birds. He also wore a charm necklace and belt. As the man who shot him came up, he cried: "I am near the end, but before I go I'll inform you as to the use of these medicines."[74]

He explained each bundle carefully, telling its use, and its remedy, and how to turn oneself into the various animals and birds. When he had finished he lapsed into silence forever. The man who shot him understood it all now. The holes in the graves in the earth had been made by the witch who had changed himself into a snake and had taken the tongues of his victims as charms. After sitting there waiting until it grew very dark, the bereaved father cut off the witches arms and legs and buried them. Then he carried home some of the flesh and cooked it, telling everyone that it was from a bear that he had shot for a medicine feast. Then he sent invitations to the most dreaded shamans in the camp, including the father of the witch whom he had killed.

One by one the shamans came, each bringing his wooden bowl, and the father seated them in the customary circle, according to their rank. The host then addressed them, telling them that the feast he was giving was in honor of his dead, and that, while he was unable to feast them sumptuously he was able to offer them the flesh of a four footed mammal (a ceremonial circumlocution for the bear), for the occasion. Then acting as waiter himself, he began to serve them soup and meat in their wooden feasting bowls. As he did so, each called him by the usual courteous term of ceremonial address on such occasions, "my grandson," or, "my nephew." Then they began eating, immediately imitating the animals which were their dream guardians as they did so, growling and smacking their lips. However, the most notorious of all the wicked shamans took only one or two bites and then hung his head and refused to eat any more. He was the father of the witch who was killed, and was very suspicious, suspecting the whole thing.[75]

74. Thompson: D651 Transformation to kill enemies 26 and B500 Magic power from animal 146b.

75. Thompson: G61 Relative's flesh unwittingly eaten 98, 226.

When they were half through their host, to their surprise, turned on them in rage and defiance saying: "You witches claim to be terrible and you certainly are." With these words he brought forth the bundle containing the head of the owl man whom he had shot, and unwrapped it before them. They gave one look, and with the medicine cry, "E-ho-ho-ho-ho!" they vanished into the darkness.

12. Star Born

Two young women were lying on their backs on the prairie one evening, gazing into the sky, and one of them said: "I wish that that bright star would be my husband." Said the other: "I wish that star yonder, which is less bright, would be mine."[76] No sooner had they spoken these words when they were bodily taken up into the sky, fulfilling all their longings.[77]

The first speaker married the bright star of her choice, who was an old man. The other married the dimmer star, who turned out to be a young man. In that land there were many tipsina (prairie turnips) and the girl who married the elder man wanted to dig them, but her husband forbad her to do so, saying that the people of that country never used them.[78]

One day, while building her tipi, she found that she had set up her tent over a large turnip. She was curious about it, so she took her knife and just as she pulled it up by the stalk, she fell through the hole it left, down to the earth, and her body burst open.[79] An old man was passing by, and he saw her lying there, and her child was still alive and kicking. He felt very sad at the sight, and picked up the baby and put it under

76. Thompson: c15 Wish for star husband realized 193. For the version collected from Michael Renville called "Star Falls," see Riggs, *Dakota Grammar, Texts, and Ethnography,* 83–94. Wallis ("Beliefs and Tales," 85–88) found this motif incorporated into the Canadian Dakota "Trickster Cycle" in "Spider and Thunder Boy." For the Neihardt version, "Falling Star," see De Mallie, ed., *Sixth Grandfather,* 395–409. De Mallie says Beckwith identified a variant; see Martha Warren Beckwith, "Mythology of the Oglala Dakota," *Journal of American Folklore* 43 (Oct.–Dec. 1930): 377–98. George Bird Grinnell, "Falling Star," *Journal of American Folklore* 34 (1921): 308–15, has a variant. This tale has many different heroes. See Gladys A. Reichard, "Literary Types and Dissemination of Myths," *Journal of American Folklore* 34 (1921): 269–307, for a study of this tale in several tribes. Waterman ("Folk-Tales of the North-American Indians," 49) tabulated various explanations of this tale.

77. Thompson: F15 Visit to land of stars 118c.

78. Thompson: c211 Taboo: eating in other world 217c.

79. Thompson: A211 Woman who fell from the sky 27.

his robe and took it home.[80] When he got to his lodge he said to his wife: "I saw something today which made my heart ache."

"What was it?" queried the old woman.

"As I was walking over the prairie I saw a young woman lying dead with her body burst open, and a baby boy lying there, crying and kicking."

"Old man," said his wife, "Why didn't you bring him home?"

"Here he is," said the old man, and he took the tiny babe from under his blanket and gave it to her.

"Old man, we will raise this child," she cried.

"Very well, old woman, we will roll him over the top of our house," he answered, and he threw the baby up through the smoke hole and it rolled down the roof. Presently a child crawled in. The old man seized it and threw it through the smoke hole again and it rolled to the ground. Then a little boy walked in. The old man threw him through the smoke hole and a youth walked in bearing a handful of fresh cut shoots. "Father," he said, "Make me some arrows." The old man, however, threw him through the smoke hole once more, and a young man entered with fresh saplings, saying: "Father, make me some arrows."[81]

The old man was now satisfied, so he made a bow and some arrows for the young man. The youth became a great hunter, and in a little while he was able to supply them with all the provisions that they needed.

Then the old man said to his wife: "Old woman, I am going to make an announcement, because my heart is filled with gladness." So he went up on top of the ridge pole and proclaimed to the people: "I have enough provisions; I even chew the fat of kidneys."[82]

It is said that this old man was the meadow lark. The yellow on his breast represents the breaking dawn, and the black half moon shape spot there represents the smooth horned buffalo.

Soon after this Star Born, the young man said to his grandfather: "I am going on a visit to other villages." To this his grandfather replied: "When one is young, that is the time to travel." So Star Born went away to visit a neighboring village.

80. Thompson: T581 Child removed from dead mother 152, 166i.

81. Thompson: D1890 Magic aging 50b.

82. To be able to chew the fat of the kidneys denoted a fresh kill whereby a certain fat near the sternum was eaten in honor. See the Legend of Hoop Ravine and Deloria, *Dakota Texts*, 236.

As he approached he saw that the men were enjoying a game of hoop and javelin, so he stood there watching. Finally he met a young man about his own age, who said to him, "Kicuna (friend[83]) let us go to my home." The two went home together, and when they entered the lodge the host, who had been raised by his grandmother, said to her: "Grandmother! I have brought my friend. Give him something to eat."

"What shall I do, my grandson?"

"What is the matter?" asked the youth, and the grandmother replied: "When anyone from this village goes after water they never return."

"My friend," said Star Born, "get the water pots and we will fetch some."

On hearing these words the old woman was very sad, and in pitiful tones she said: "My grand child, you whom I have raised in spite of great obstacles!"

"Grandmother," answered Star Born, "You worry yourself over trifles."

The two young men carried their pots to the water and stood there after filling them, and as they looked around they could see many other brimming water pots deserted on the water's edge. Star Born raised his voice in challenge: "Where is the one who destroys those who come after water? Where are you? I am here to get water."

All of a sudden they were engulfed. And when they came to they were in a large, long room where there were many young men and women. Some were already dead, and others were in the agony of dissolution. "What are you all doing here?" asked Star Born, and they answered, "You have heard of those who went after water and never returned? We are the ones."

There was something hanging overhead, swinging to and fro. They were told to look out, for this was the heart of the monster fish that had swallowed them. Star Born took out his knife and began to cut into it, bit by bit. Suddenly, with a tremendous shock the giant pickerel leaped and fell dead upon the shore. Star Born cut a hole in its side and let out all the young people who were imprisoned there.[84] The people were made happy over the return of those who they had lost, and they offered Star Born the choice of two beautiful young girls as wives, but he

83. The Riggs dictionary lists a "kicuwa" as meaning friend, but "kicuna" is not entered.

84. Thompson:F913 Victims rescued when swallower is killed 159a.

declined to accept, and bestowed them on his friend, saying: "I must travel," and he left the camp.

Star Born soon arrived at another village, where he stood, watching the youths and men indulging in the hoop and javelin game. A young man came up and spoke to him and watched with him, until the other said to Star Born: "My friend, I will take you home." So they went to the former's lodge, where he dwelt with his grandmother who had raised him.

"Grandmother," said the youth, "I have invited a friend of mine to our lodge. Do give him something to eat."

"What can I do, grandson? We people here barely manage to exist. When anyone goes after wood he never returns, and for that reason we dread to haul wood."

"My friend," said Star Born, "Get the thongs and we will gather wood."

The old grandmother began to sob, saying: "My grandson! You whom I have raised with hardship, toil and difficulty."

"Grandmother," retorted Star Born, "You do worry about little things."

They took the packstraps and went out to the forest where they gathered wood and strolled about. Finally, Star Born cried aloud: "Who are you who is so powerful and destroys all the youths who come after wood?"

All at once they were engulfed, and when they came to they found themselves in a long house full of men and women. "What are you doing here?" they asked. And the reply was: "We came after wood, and something brought us here." Star Born asked them "What was it?" and they replied: "This is the thing," and pointed to a small dark hole.

Star Born took his bow and arrows and shot bolt after bolt into the dark cavern, and then a door seemed to open, and they all walked out. It was the owl's ear in which they were kept.

The people were made happy by the restoration of their young people, and, to show their gratitude, they brought out two of their prettiest girls and offered them to Star Born as wives, but he declined to accept the offer, and presented them to his friend, saying: "I want to travel, and must now be going." So off he went to the next settlement.

Star Born soon arrived at the next village, and stood on the outskirts watching the men and boys playing hoop and javelin. As he was looking on a young man came up to him, and said: "My friend, shall we watch this game together?" They watched the game until they were tired, when the young stranger said: "My friend, we will go to my home."

The strange youth had been raised by his grandmother, and when they got to his lodge he said: "Grandmother, I have brought a friend home with me. Do give him something to eat."

"Alas, grandson," replied the old woman, "Where can I get the food that you speak of?"

"Why do you speak thus?" asked Star Born.

"Why," said the old woman, "The people here are very successful in their buffalo hunts, but lately Waziya (The God of the North) comes along and takes the meat for himself by force. Therefore the people are half starved."

"Grandmother," said Star Born, "You go over to Waziya's lodge and say: 'My grandson who has travelled from afar has come to visit me, but I have no food to set before him.'"

The old woman went over to Waziya's lodge as she had been bidden, and stood at a distance and called: "My grandson who has travelled from afar has come to visit me, but I have no food to set before him."

But Waziya, in a gruff, unmerciful voice growled back: "You are a bad malevolent old woman. Get out! What do you mean by disturbing me?"

The old grandmother came home crying, and Star Born said, "Grandma, what did Waziya say to you?"

"Oh grandson, he almost killed me!"

"My friend," said Star Born to the other youth, "Get the pack straps."

The poor old woman dreaded to see them go, but Star Born said: "My grandmother, you worry about little things."

They walked right over to Waziya's lodge, where the meat was hung outside to dry. They took enough to make a load, and the youth brought it home, while Star Born went over to Waziya's house and entered, thus saying to the North God: "Waziya, what do you mean by talking so rudely when I sent my grandmother over here?"

Waziya made no reply, but glared furiously at Star Born. Behind him his terrible Ice Bow was hanging peacefully. Star Born looked at it. "Waziya, what is that bow for?" he asked.

"Don't touch it," replied Waziya. "Whoever touches it breaks his arm."

"All right," replied Star Born, "I will see if it breaks my arm." And he took down the Ice Bow and pulled the string back so far that it snapped and broke. Star Born left Waziya in consternation and went back.

In the morning the people made another great chase of the buffalo and slaughtered many that day. But, while they were butchering, Waziya appeared, taking away their meat, and packing it in his blanket above his belt. When he came to where Star Born was at work, he paused, and asked: "Who is butchering here?" Star Born replied boldly, "I am."

"Who bore ye that you boast of yourself?" asked Waziya.

"Rather, who bore ye to boast of yourself," replied Star Born.

Waziya, to show his power, retorted: "Whoever points his finger at me shall die."[85]

Mockingly answered Star Born: "I shall point my finger to see if I die," and he did point at Waziya, but nothing happened to him. "Now," said Star Born, "Whoever points his finger at me, the flesh of his hand to his elbow will rot."

"Ho," said Waziya, "I will point my finger to see if my forearm decays."

And Waziya stretched out his hand and it was decayed. Then he stretched out the other and that one was rotted also.

Then Star Born sliced Waziya's blanket with his knife, and the buffalo meat all fell out. He told the people to gather up their own and take it home.

Next morning a herald announced that Waziya's wife had mended his blanket, and that he was about to shake it. Waziya stood facing the north, shaking it. The north wind brought snowflakes as large as a tent, and it continued to snow until the village was out of sight. Then the people began to murmur against Star Born, saying: "We were at least accustomed to live and exist until this young man came and caused us to perish."

Star Born said to his grandmother, "Announce that I want a fan." She made tunnels to the other lodges and bore the message. "What is this for?" grumbled the people. But they sent him a fan. Then Star Born dug his way to the roof, and facing the south, he began fanning himself, and the warm south wind sprang up and melted the snow to water. Waziya and his family were all smothered to death, except the youngest who hid in the frosted tent pole and so escaped. That is why we have the cold god still existing today.[86]

85. Thompson: D2062 Death by pointing 242a and D1701.1 Contest in magic 182.
86. Thompson: A1150 Determination of the seasons 60.

13. The Origin of the Medicine Dance

The Great Mysterious One (Wakan Tanka) descended from above in a rainbow upon the deep sea. "I will make two Powers to be leaders of the Medicine Dance and preserve it for mankind," he said.

He took his right lower rib and sunk it in the water, and in a moment there rose a male Unktehi[87] (Underworld Panther). He took his left lower rib and sunk that, and there rose a female Unktehi. Then the Great Mystery said: "You twain shall be leaders in the grand Medicine Dances and all the rituals and ceremonies pertaining to them, which must be preserved and followed by the Indians." After saying these words the Great Mystery ascended in the rainbow again, and went back into the heavens.

The two monsters floated on the mighty sea. The female monster spoke first. She seemed to be more intelligent than the other: "There is no earth, but we shall cause it to appear." Through their magic they caused several animals to appear. These were the otter and the muskrat, the loon and the grebe. The loon was first commanded to dive in search of black soil. He obeyed, and was submerged for a long time. When he came up he floated breast up, and his life was gone. The two monsters gave the medicine cry: "E-ho-ho-ho-ho!" Blew their sacred roots on the on the loon, and laid it to one side.

The otter was ordered to dive next, and he stayed under the water even longer than the loon had done, but the otter likewise appeared on the surface dead. As before the monsters gave the medicine cry, and, after blowing their sacred roots upon it, laid it to one side.

Now the grebe dived. The bubbles and ripples died away, and he stayed down longer than the other two had done, but he too came up breast first. Again the monsters gave their medicine cry, blew their roots upon him, and laid him to one side.

Last of all was that small animal the muskrat, who also went in search of black mud.[88] It stayed down a very long time, and the female monster said to her mate: "This time our prediction will be verified." Just then up popped the muskrat, floating with its back up, showing

87. Oneroad specified that this was a four-footed, long-tailed monster with shiny horns, somewhat resembling a buffalo, but their heads were white like snow.

88. See Alan Dundes, "Structural Typology in North American Indian Folktales," in *The Study of Folklore*, Alan Dundes, ed. (Englewood Cliffs, N.J.: Prentice-Hall, 1965), for an analysis of tale variants; he found "four" to be a stable and significant number. Here the fourth animal was successful on the fourth dive and later four times a year made a sacrifice to Unktehi.

that it was still alive. They picked it up with the medicine cry, and between its paws, in the hollow, they found black earth, and they blew their sacred roots upon the muskrat, and laid him with the rest.

Then said the female monster: "Henceforth, this shall be west." And, as she was wiser than the male, she took the black earth and threw it towards the west, and they moved off in that direction.[89] The animals were sent ahead to scout and carry back the news when they came in sight of land. As the monsters swam the noise of their going was like the swift rushing rapids of a river. It was the muskrat again who first sighted the land and brought the news. "It is true, what we have said," cried the monsters, and they landed in a large round bay that resembled a lodge in shape.[90]

The male and female Unktehi took their positions at the west shore of this bay, facing the east, and called upon the animals and birds to participate in the first Medicine Dance. The two powerful monsters sang different songs, and the animals and birds, changing into human form, began to dance. The first missiles that they used to shoot their magic into each other were the claws of eagles and other birds, and of panthers, but, as these often actually killed their victims, they changed them into the carved shell missiles used today.

The Unktehi monsters showed the dancers how to restore those who had been shot, and bring them back to life again, and instructed them in the lore of the roots, the inner bark of trees, the plants, and seeds.[91] The animals were furthermore instructed how to appear to the Indians seeking guardians in dreams, and how to answer their prayers for help. The two Unktehi then said: "We leaders will lie beneath the ground with our ears spread out wide to hear the prayers and listen to the songs of the ceremonies. From our backs will grow the roots and herbs to heal the wounds and cure the sick." Then the two monsters sank under the soil and the birds and animals carried their secrets to the Indians, and instructed them in their dreams.

Thus it has come about that everything is wakan (mysterious or powerful) to the Indian that he does not understand. He sings certain songs for the different species of plants and herbs, approaching them

89. Thompson: A541 Divinity's departure for west 11.

90. See Reichard, "Literary Types," for a study of a tale that resembles the Earth-Diver tale, incorporating an origin explanation.

91. Thompson: A810 Primeval water 29; A540 Divinity teaches arts and crafts 12; D1880 Rejuvenation 50.

and covering them with white and red bird's down before he takes up the plant or herb that he wants to use for any given purpose.

The grasses and herbs appear like human beings to the Indian, and four times a year, a dog, covered with white and red down is thrown into the lake (or some other body of water) as a sacrifice to the Unktehi, who are ever listening to the songs and prayers of the Indians.[92]

92. See "Puberty, Fasting, and Dreaming," page 90, above, and tale following for comparative information on this ceremony. For this myth and the Medicine Dance ceremony, see Skinner, "Medicine Ceremony of the . . . Wahpeton Dakota."

TALES

The following tales are part of a series that were obtained from Mahpiyasna (Jingling-Cloud) and his brother Matomaza (Iron-Bear) during
the summer of 1914, mostly near the Sisseton Agency at Sisseton, South
Dakota. They present only a very few of the numerous tales known to
the Wahpeton Dakota. A number of stories duplicating those given in
the first part of this paper [Iktomi and Mastina tales] were also collected, but are omitted, as Mr. Oneroad's versions are always fuller.

14. A Migration Tale

The Eastern Dakota claim that the Sioux originated in the north, and
came south, until, somewhere to the southeast of their starting-point,
they were stopped by the ocean, where they scattered and went in different directions. They fought many tribes, and finally grew stronger,
and then traveled northwestward towards the prairie. When they
reached Minnesota and eastern South Dakota, they came upon the
Cheyenne, whom they drove out onto the prairies. The Cheyenne still
remember this, according to the Dakota, and declare that their ancestors lived at Enemy Swim Lake, South Dakota. The name of the lake
was derived from an incident that occurred in early times, when the
Cheyenne were attacked by some enemy from the north. There are
Eastern Dakota now living, who claim descent from the Cheyenne
who dwelt about Enemy Swim Lake, which is in northeastern South
Dakota, not far from Sisseton.

15. How a Heyoka Got His Medicine[93]

Once a Heyoka found the gas-inflated carcass of a buffalo, commonly
called a "whistle" by the Indians. Not far away he saw someone standing on a hill. He told him to go on and take the buffalo, adding, "I did
not shoot it." This one was a real Heyoka; and of course he was talking
backwards, and meant to tell the man that he had shot the buffalo, and

---

93 {The Heyoka are persons who, because of a vision of thunder, act always in an
anti-natural manner. When cold, they appear to be warm, and vice versa. They also
use "inverted speech" saying the opposite of what they mean, and acting accordingly.}
[Skinner's note].

therefore the Indian was not to take it. But the man failed to understand. He skinned the animal, and took its heart.[94]

That night his head ached, and his nose bled, his face turned black, and he went crazy. His companions desired [deserted?] him, for, learning what the trouble was, they were afraid. Lightning came, thunder roared, and passed over. The man sang all night; and the next morning, when the people looked at him, they saw that he was covered all over with black spiders, and that he was laughing, and crying, "He, he he! Get him, hit him, there he goes!" At sunrise he came out, took a tent-pin and rolled down one eye lid wither. Then he took another tent-pin for a flute, and began to act like one crazy. Later, when he had recovered, he told the people that the real Heyokas had come to him that night, and wanted to kill him, but one white Heyoka, who had a whistle, defended him.

Later he went to war, and, by order of the Heyoka, took with him a bow and arrows made from a great hickory tree, large enough to cover a man's body. He held the bow in front of him, and he was defended as though by a great tree. When the others shouted to him to step back, he went ahead. Once an arrow struck him between the fingers and went into his bow, but he was uninjured.

16. A Boy Joker

Some Oglala went to war.[95] In the party there were four middle-aged men and a boy about sixteen years old. The three men were brothers, and the boy was their cousin. He carried the moccasins and other baggage of the party, and it was the first time he went on the war path. The expedition was headed against the Crow. When they had gone part of their journey, they were out of tobacco; and a little distance away on the bank of a river, was a tipi in which a relative had died.[96] The tipi still stood by the river-bank, with the corpse and all its belongings in it. The

94. Wallis ("Canadian Dakota," 111–223) recorded several anecdotes on many clowns or Heyoka from his 1914 field work.

95. {Many stories are told of the Oglala and other Prairie Sioux merely in jest.} [Skinner's note].

96. Sometimes a lodge was erected around the burial place of a distinguished warrior and a rack set up with his clothing to view. See Hassrick, The Sioux, 333. Neihardt has a version called "Young Man Pretended to be a Ghost"; see De Mallie, ed., Sixth Grandfather, 346–47. Deloria (Dakota Texts, 227) reported that a burial scaffold with a tipi over it was for "only very specially favored people" and was usually avoided as an abode of a ghost.

warriors knew that there was tobacco in the dead man's pouch. They decided to get some at noon the next day.

That morning the boy told his brothers to carry the moccasins, while he went off to shoot a deer and have it ready. He succeeded in killing a buck, and carried it to the place opposite the tipi of the dead man, for he wished to take a swim there. He made a fire, put his meat on spits to roast, and stripped off for his plunge. When he came out of the water, he saw that the crayfishes had thrown out white clay in their mining operations, so he rubbed some on his hands and daubed it all over his body.

He observed that he looked like a ghost. So he crawled to the top of a hill, and went behind the tipi and entered. The corpse lay there all dried up and the tobacco hung on the center pole of the lodge. There the boy stood until his four relatives came up, wiped the perspiration from their faces, and said, "Eh! here lies our cousin. He was a powerful person; but here he lies, with no one to feed him or give him a smoke." The oldest had a little tobacco, which was just enough for a pipeful, so he offered it to the six directions and spoke to the spirit of the dead man. "Spirit, partake of this! When we get into the enemy's country, help up to take a running horse and two others, and help me to count at least the second coup!" Just then the hidden boy grunted. "Let this be a fine day!" continued the speaker; but the other three saw and were frightened, so they rushed from the lodge and the boy jumped out. The speaker dropped his pipe and fled, while the boy chased him. He overtook one of the brothers who fell over in terror. Then the boy hid in the brush, but another one looked up and saw him, and fell down. This happened several times, then the young fellow sneaked home, washed, and went back to the fire to eat. When the others recovered, they went back again, and once more smoked to the corpse of their cousin.

They saw the boy's footprint in the ashes, and the place where he had cut the tent in order to get in, so they returned to their camp, and said nothing about it. The boy asked them why they had been gone so long, and they said they had seen a bad sign and turned back. The boy was amused at this, and told of it long afterwards, when he was older.

17. Contest between Thunder-bird and Monster

A thunder-bird once pounced upon a bear that dwelt beneath the water, but was unable to carry it off or to let it go. An Indian, happening to pass that way was besought by each for aid. The thunderer promised the man seven wounds and success in battle; the bear, seven enemies' scalps. The man finally let the thunderer loose without injuring either and received both rewards.

18. A Witch Story

A man and his family, which contained six young men and boys, were startled at night by the cries of animals and birds. Finally they heard an owl fly against the tent poles. The morning after this had happened, the oldest son died, and the father buried him in the ground. He dressed in mourning and moved his tipi away from the camp-circle, blackened his face, and put mud on his head. A few nights later the same thing happened and the next son died. Then he knew that the owl was a witch.

Finally there was no one left but the youngest son, and the same manifestation came again. So the man loaded his gun and sat in the dark and he saw a horned owl come.[97] He fired at it, and when it fell, it turned into a man. He was not quite dead. "Well," said the wounded witch, "You are pretty smart to get me before I die. I will teach you my medicines." It seems that the witch had little packets tied around his wrist, his elbows, and over his shoulder.[98] With each packet went the skin of a certain bird or mammal. He told his captor how to use these, how to dress, and how to turn into an animal and go to another part of the country. When he had finished instructing the man, he died. His slayer knew who the witch was and thought he was a member of the Medicine Dance. He took all the evil medicines and wrapped them up in a bag, intending to slay the old man's sons. He butchered the witch, wrapped up the body in leaves as though it were a bear, and told his wife that he would bury his victim. A little later he brought home the supposed bear. Then he invited all the medicine men to a bear feast. His wife cooked the meat in a big kettle until the grease boiled over into the fire. That night the medicine men all came in response to the tobacco which had been sent them. They brought their medicines in their wooden bowls, sang their bear songs, and started to eat. The witch's son was there; and he held his head down, for he suspected something and feasted and drank very little. When they were through, the man lectured them severely, and said, "You do kill your own rela-

97. The owl is associated with transformation. Also see Wallis "Canadian Dakota," 98.

98. {This is the typical Central Algonkian witch-outfit.} [Skinner's note]. Thompson: B500 Magic power from animals 146c; D651 Transformation to kill enemies 26; D876 Magic provider destroyed 1 09z.

tives and eat human flesh, just as has always been said." In conclusion he brought out the head of the old witch, and told them what they had eaten. All the guests hung their heads and cried "E ho ho."[99]

[Note:] In a variant of this story, it is said that the children are not buried, although some narrators say that they were buried and the witch dug a hole by the head of each grave into which he went in the form of a snake and stole the lungs from the corpse. This version, however, has the bodies wrapped in buffalo hide and hung on a platform. The father sat near the scaffold with bow and arrow. He heard a distant noise like the cry of a kite, then of an eagle, then of a sparrow-hawk. Then he saw a bird flying like a speck. Presently there was the growling of a bear, then of a panther, then of a wildcat. Finally a horned owl rose from the ground, rolled its eyes. On looking closely, he saw that the owl had a man's hands and that it started to untie the thongs. So he shot the owl. The rest of the story is the same.

The coyote, bear, and other fast-walking animals were used as witch medicines. They could go to other tribes in two days, when it took ordinary people five days to travel there. Therefore they were used as scouts.

19. A Berdache Story

A boy was once very sick, and a winkta (berdache) learned of it and said he could cure him.[100] The boy objected violently to having anything to do with the berdache. He was overruled by his parents and did indeed get well. He was then obliged to marry the berdache as a reward. The berdache, whom he had married, was given new clothes by the boy's parents, and then went off to collect gifts for them. While he was gone, the boy died; and the berdache hearing of it, cut his hair, and returned in mourning with horses for the parents. They gave him gifts to end the mourning, and accepted his presents.

If they had had another son, then they would have been obliged to give him to him. If a berdache nicknames any person, then that person must use this name or he will become very ill. Mr. Oneroad's father, the late Peter Oneroad, was once nicknamed by a berdache, who called

99. Thompson: G61 Relative's flesh unwittingly eaten 98, 226.
100. The Riggs dictionary definition of "wiŋkta" is a hermaphrodite, a male or a female with traits of both sexes. This is a more flexible term indicating either a feminine male or a masculine female, whereas the term berdache is limited to a male. The term berdache is appropriate to the tale as it does seem to refer to a male. See page 88, above, for another version of this story.

him "Sack-of-flour" because he used some of his supplies as a pillow. This name clung to him for many years.

The story is told of some girls who teased a berdache, and were accordingly nicknamed by him. One of the women never mentioned the name until she was sick years afterwards, when it occurred to her to confess it, and she became well.

20. A War Story

The Eastern Dakota always spared prisoners who were brought inside of the camp-circle. Once an Ojibwa was brought in, and a young man of the Sisseton camp wanted to kill him. Mahpiyasna, the elder volunteered, if the council so decreed, to shoot the Sisseton rather than have this custom violated. The council decided upon his death, and Mahpiyasna shot him, although he had no grudge against the warrior. Afterwards Jingling-Cloud, the elder, supplied the family of this man with food, when he returned from his hunt, in order to show his good will. The Ojibwa was later taken a day and a half journey into the woods towards his own country, and released.

The following spring a letter, written on birch bark, was found near the Sioux camp. On the bark was scratched the figure of a man taking long steps, with foot prints that showed he was running. This referred to Iyangmani (Running-Walker) the Wahpeton chief. The other side showed a man with clouds over his head, and crooked lines running from them. This referred to Jingling-Cloud, and the whole meant that the Ojibway were coming to make peace with the Dakota through these two warriors. The Dakota prepared to receive them; and in a few days Ojibway scouts came in with their candipaḣta (tobacco-bundle), composed of little bags of tobacco, and the Dakota sent some back by them. Then the Ojibway approached, and peace was made.

When they drew near, those of the Wahpeton who had horses circled back and forth between their own people and Ojibway and both sides sang. The Sioux dedicated their songs to Running-Walker and Jingling-Cloud. When the two lines were near, they stopped facing each other, and the head chief on each side approached with tobacco; and the hunka-song [ancestor song], dedicated to the four winds, was sung, concluding with the words, "Long live Iyangmani and Mahpiyasna! As long as you two warriors live, no one will dare to run over us."

Meanwhile the chief brought out a pipe, which he offered wakan tanka and the four directions. When he had done this, he gave it to the opposing chief, and all the Ojibway took a whiff. Then the Ojibway prepared their pipe in their own way. After this everybody approached and shook hands. The Ojibway chief gave his best horse to Running-Walker, and a lot of mococks or bark boxes of rice and maple-sugar. Then the Sioux and Ojibway mingled, giving presents; and the Ojibway were brought into camp, where they were told where to pitch their tents. That evening Running-Walker invited all the Ojibway to his lodge, while Jingling-Cloud singed a deer whole, and made the "chief dish" for them. The Ojibway thanked him [Jingling-Cloud], and told him that from that time forward they looked upon him as being half Ojibway.[101]

101. See page 74, above, for another version of this story. Riggs, "Dakota Portraits," 509–13), speaks of Maȟpiyasna. S. W. Pond, *Dakota or Sioux*, 14, thought Iŋyaŋgmani a better man than a chief, intelligent in conversation but "would not speak in public to people when they were excited and turbulent, so that his influence was felt least when it was needed most . . . while he was silent others ruled."

"Notes on Puberty Fasting and Dreaming" appeared at this point in the original manuscript. As it was a duplicate of a section in the ethnology, it has been deleted here, see page 90, above.

Appendix

[Editor's note: This outline contains the topics Amos Oneroad and Alanson Skinner intended to include in their publication. The material missing from the manuscript is so indicated.]

EASTERN DAKOTA ETHNOLOGY

Outline for a Monograph on the Ethnology of the Eastern Dakota Indians
A. Introduction [missing]
   1. Location, former and present
   2. Numbers, former and present
   3. History traditional and post European
   4. Future prospects
B. Civil and Military Organization
   1. Tribal Divisions
   2. Officers and their functions, government
   3. Warriors and War honors, War Regalia
   4. Functions of Warriors, duties etc.
   5. Privileges and exemptions of warriors
   6. War customs, conduct of war parties, war medicines etc.
C. Social Life and Organizations
   1. Method of camping [missing]
   2. Societies
      a. Warriors societies or military organizations
      b. Religious and semi-religious societies
      c. Other ceremonies
D. Life of the Individual
   1. Customs of pregnancy and childbirth [missing]
   2. Customs connected with infancy [missing]
   3. Naming customs
   4. Puberty fasting
   5. Courtship and marriage. Ploygamy [sic] and divorce etc.
   6. Terms of relationship, etc.
   7. Mortuary customs and belief in the hereafter.
E. Religious Concepts [missing]
   1. Pantheon
   2. Beliefs and observances
   3. Ceremonies
   4. Sacred articles

F. Material Culture
   I. Houses, costumes, etc.
      1. Dress
      2. Dwellings
      3. Manufactures, processes, etc. [missing]
      4. Household utensils
      5. Weapons [missing]
      6. Musical Instruments [missing]
      7. Ceremonial Paraphernalia [missing]
      8. Games
      9. Art [missing]
   II. Hunting and Fishing [missing]
      1. Methods and utensils, traps, etc.
      2. Medicines, lures, etc.
  III. Agriculture [missing]
      1. Products of the fields
      2. Other vegetal foods
  IV. Foods and their preparation [missing]
      1. Meats
      2. Vegetal foods
   V. Miscellaneous Customs [missing]
      1. Names of seasons, months, and days
      2. Miscellaneous. Numerical system
G. Mythology and Folklore [see Folklore table of contents]

Bibliography

MANUSCRIPTS

American Board of Commissioners for Foreign Missions. Microfilm, Minnesota Historical Society, St. Paul, Minn. Originals in Houghton Library, Harvard University, Cambridge, Mass.

American Indian Correspondence. Presbyterian Historical Society, Philadelphia, Penn.

Morris, H. S. Papers. Carnegie Library, Sisseton, S.Dak.

National Archives Record Group 75, Annuity Rolls for the Sioux, 1853–58. Washington, D.C.

Oneroad and Shepherd Family. Papers. Red Shield, Inc., Sisseton, S.Dak.

Ortley, Henry. Probate. June 15, 1922. Department of the Interior, Washington D.C.

Riggs Family. Papers. South Dakota Conference United Church of Christ Archives, Center for Western Studies, Augustana College, Sioux Falls, S.Dak.

Riggs, Stephen Return. Papers. Minnesota Historical Society, St. Paul, Minn.

Satterlee, Wiliam W., and Marion P. Papers. Prison and Trial Rolls. Minnesota Historical Society, St. Paul, Minn.

Skinner, Alanson Buck. Collection. Braun Research Library, Southwest Museum, Los Angeles, Calif.

U. S. Congress. Senate Documents and Reports. Serial Sets.

Williamson, John Poage. Papers, 1866–1915. South Dakota State Historical Resource Center, Pierre, S.Dak.

NEWSPAPERS

Devils Lake Daily Journal, August 18, 1925. Tokio, N.Dak.

Iapi Oaye (Santee, Nebr.), 1881–1935.

Milwaukee Journal, June 5, 1923.

Milwaukee Sentinel, July 29, 1922.

Word Carrier (Santee, Nebr.), 1887–1933.

Wi-Iyohi, June 1965.

BOOKS AND ARTICLES

Abrahams, Roger D. "Interpreting Folklore Ethnographically and Sociologically." In *Handbook of American Folklore,* Richard M. Dorson, ed. Bloomington: Indiana University Press, 1983.

Allen, Clifford. *History of the Flandreau Sioux Tribe.* Flandreau, S.Dak.: Tribal History Program, Flandreau Santee Sioux Tribe, 1971.

Ames, Michael M. *Museums, the Public and Anthropology: A Study in the Anthropology of Anthropology,* ed. L. P. Vidyarthi. Ranchi Anthropology Series no. 9. Vancouver: University of British Columbia Press, 1986.

Anderson, Gary C. *Kinsmen of Another Kind: Dakota-White Relations in the Upper Mississippi Valley, 1650–1862.* 1984; St. Paul: Minnesota Historical Society Press, 1997.

——. *Little Crow: Spokesman for the Sioux.* St. Paul: Minnesota Historical Society Press, 1986.

——, and Alan R. Woolworth, ed. *Through Dakota Eyes: Narrative Accounts of the Minnesota Indian War of 1862.* St. Paul: Minnesota Historical Society Press, 1988.

Babcock, Barbara. "A Tolerated Margin of Mess: The Trickster and His Tales Reconsidered." In *Critical Essays on Native American Literature,* ed. Andrew Wiget. Boston: G. K. Hall & Co., 1975.

Barton, Winifred W. *John P. Williamson:*

A Brother to the Sioux. Chicago: Fleming H. Revell, 1919.

Bascom, William R. "Folklore and Anthropology." In *The Study of Folklore,* Alan Dundes, ed. Englewood Cliffs, N.J.: Prentice Hall, Inc., 1965.

Bauman, Richard. "The Field Study of Folklore in Context." In *Handbook of American Folklore,* Richard M. Dorson, ed. Bloomington: Indiana University Press, 1983.

Beckwith, Martha Warren. "Mythology of the Oglala Dakota." *Journal of American Folklore* 43 (Oct.–Dec. 1930): 377–98.

———. *Folklore in America: Its Scope and Method.* Poughkeepsie, N.Y.: Publication of the Folklore Foundation, 1931.

Blackthunder, Elijah. *Ehanna Woyakapi: Sisseton-Wahpeton Sioux of Lake Traverse Reservation.* Sisseton, S.Dak.: Sisseton-Wahpeton Sioux Tribe, Inc., 1973.

Boas, Franz. "Mythology and Folk-tales of the North American Indians." *Journal of American Folklore* 27 (1914): 376–410.

———, and Ella Deloria. *Dakota Grammar.* Washington, D.C.: GPO, 1941.

Boon, James A. *Other Tribes, Other Scribes: Symbolic Anthropology in the Comparative Study of Cultures, Histories, Religions and Texts.* New York: Cambridge University Press, 1982.

Catlin, George. *Letters and Notes on the Manners, Customs, and Conditions of the North American Indians.* 2 vols. Philadelphia, 1841; New York: Dover Publications, 1973.

Clifford, James. *The Predicament of Culture: Twentieth-Century Ethnography, Literature, and Art.* Cambridge: Harvard University Press, 1988.

Comaroff, John, and Jean Comaroff. *Ethnography and the Historical Imagination.* Boulder, Colo.: Westview Press, Inc., 1992.

Day County Historical Research Committee. "History Is Intertwined with Reservation: By Word of Mouth." In *History of Day County.* Aberdeen, S.Dak.: North Plains Press, 1981.

Dégh, Linda. *Folktales and Society.* Bloomington: Indiana University Press, 1969, 1989.

Deloria, Ella. *Dakota Texts.* Publications of the American Ethnological Society, vol.14. New York: G. E. Stechert & Co., 1932.

De Mallie, Raymond J., ed. *The Sixth Grandfather: Black Elk's Teachings Given to John G. Neihardt.* Lincoln: University of Nebraska Press, 1984.

———. "Indians Speak for Themselves." In *Research and Creative Activity: American Indians.* Office of Research and the University Graduate School, 13 (2): 8–13. Bloomington: Indiana University Printing Services, 1990.

Dorsey, James Owen. "The Myths of the Raccoon and the Crawfish among the Dakotah Tribes." *American Antiquarian and Oriental Journal* 6 (1884): 237–40.

———. "Siouan Folk-Lore and Mythologic Notes." *American Antiquarian and Oriental Journal* 6 (1884–85): 174–76; 7: 105–8.

———. "The Places of Gentes in Siouan Camping Circles." *American Anthropologist* o.s., 2 (1889): 375–79.

———. "'Gens' and 'Sub-Gens' as Expressed in Four Siouan Languages." *American Anthropologist* o.s., 3 (1890): 320.

———. "The Social Organization of Siouan Tribes." *Journal of American Folklore* 4 (1891): 257–63.

———. "A Study of Siouan Cults." In Smithsonian Institution Bureau of American Ethnology, *Eleventh Annual Report* (Washington, D.C.: GPO, 1894), 351–544.

Dundes, Alan. "Structural Typology in North American Indian Folktales."

In *The Study of Folklore,* Alan Dundes, ed. Englewood Cliffs, N.J.: Prentice-Hall, 1965.

Eastman, Charles A. *The Soul of the Indian.* Boston: Houghton-Mifflin, 1911.

——. *From the Deep Woods to Civilization.* Boston: Little Brown and Co., 1916.

——. *Indian Boyhood.* 1902; New York: Dover Publications, 1971.

Eastman, Mary. *Dahcotah: Life and Legends of the Sioux.* 1849; Minneapolis: Ross and Haines, 1962.

Edwards, Paul M. "Fort Wadsworth and the Friendly Santee Sioux, 1864–1892." *South Dakota Historical Collections.* Vol. 31. Pierre: South Dakota State Historical Society, 1962.

Elias, Peter Douglas. *The Dakota of the Canadian Northwest: Lessons for Survival.* Winnipeg: University of Manitoba Press, 1988.

Eriksen, Thomas H. *Ethnicity and Nationalism.* London: Pluto Press, 1993.

Folwell, William Watts. *A History of Minnesota.* Vol. 1. St. Paul: Minnesota Historical Society, 1961.

Gans, Herbert J. "Symbolic Ethnicity and Symbolic Religiosity: Towards a Comparison of Ethnic and Religious Acculturation." *Ethnic and Racial Studies,* 17, no. 4 (October 1994).

Gilmore, Melvin R. "The Dakota Ceremony of Huŋka." *Indian Notes* 6 (1929): 75–79.

Graber, Kay, ed. *Sister to the Sioux: The Memoirs of Elaine Goodale Eastman, 1884–91.* Lincoln: University of Nebraska Press, 1978.

Grinnell, George Bird. "Falling Star." *Journal of American Folklore* 34 (1921): 308–15.

Hall, Thomas D. "Lessons of Long-term Change for Comparative and Historical Study of Ethnicity." *Current Perspectives in Social Theory* 5 (1984): 132.

Harrington, Mark Raymond. "Alanson Skinner; and Bibliography of Alanson Skinner." *American Anthropologist* n.s. 28 (1926): 275–76.

Hassrick, Royal B. *The Sioux.* Norman: University of Oklahoma Press, 1964.

Hertzberg, Hazel W. "Indian Rights Movement, 1887–1973." In *Handbook of the North American Indian,* William C. Sturtevant and Wilcomb E. Washburn, ed. 4:305–23. Washington, D.C.: Smithsonian Institution, 1988.

Hodge, Frederick Webb. *Handbook of the American Indian North of Mexico.* Smithsonian Institution, Bureau of American Ethnology bulletin 30, 2:945. Washington, D.C.: GPO, 1907.

Hoebel, E. Adamson. "The Influence of Plains Ethnography on the Development of Anthropological Theory." In *Anthropology on the Great Plains,* Raymond Wood and Margot Liberty, ed. Lincoln: University of Nebraska Press, 1980.

Holcombe, Return I. *Minnesota in Three Centuries.* Mankato, Minn.: Publishing Society of Minnesota, 1908.

Howard, James H. "Notes on Two Dakota 'Holy Dance' Medicines and Their Uses." *American Anthropologist* 55 (1953): 608–9.

——. "The Tree Dweller Cults of the Dakota." *Journal of American Folklore* 68 (1955): 169–74.

——. *Reprints in Anthropology: The Dakota or Sioux Indians.* Lincoln, Nebr.: J & L Reprint Co., 1980.

——. *The Canadian Sioux.* Lincoln: University of Nebraska Press, 1984.

Huggan, Nancy McClure. "The Story of Nancy McClure," *Minnesota Collections,* 6:438–60. St. Paul: Minnesota Historical Society, 1894.

Hughes, Thomas. *Indian Chiefs of Southern Minnesota.* 1927; Minneapolis: Ross and Haines, 1969.

Hunter, Peter. "The Spider and the

Ducks or How the Sheyaka's Eyes Became Red." *Word Carrier,* June 1889,
p. 4–5.

Hymes, Dell. "The Ethnography of
Speaking." In *Anthropology and Hu-
man Behavior,* ed. T. Gladwin and W.
C. Sturtevant. Washington, D.C., 1962.

——. "The Ethnography of Communication." *American Anthropologist* 66
(1964): pt. 2, p. 1–34.

Jahner, Elaine. "Finding the Way Home:
The Interpretation of American
Folklore." In *Handbook of American
Folklore,* Richard M. Dorson, ed.
Bloomington: Indiana University
Press, 1983.

Johnstone, Barbara. *Stories, Community,
and Place: Narratives from Middle
America.* Bloomington: Indiana University Press, 1990.

Kaplan, David, and Robert A. Manners.
Culture Theory. Prospect Heights,
Ill.: Waveland Press, 1986.

Karie, Karen. *Fort Sisseton (Fort
Wadsworth), 1864–1889: Our Living
Heritage.* Sisseton, S.Dak.: South Da-
kota Department of Game, Fish and
Parks, 1979.

Landes, Ruth. *The Mystic Lake Sioux.*
Madison: University of Wisconsin
Press, 1968.

Lankford, George. "The Unfulfilled
Promise of North American Indian
Folklore." In *Handbook of American
Folklore,* Richard M. Dorson, ed.
Bloomington: Indiana University
Press, 1983.

Laviolette, Gontran. *The Sioux Indians
in Canada.* Regina, Sask.: Marian
Press, 1944.

Linderman, Frank B. *Indian Why Stories: Sparks from War Eagle's
Lodge-Fire.* New York: Charles Scribner's Sons, 1915.

Long, Stephen H. *The Northern Expeditions of Stephen H. Long: The Journals of 1817 and 1823 and Related Doc-*

uments, Lucile M. Kane et al., ed. St.
Paul: Minnesota Historical Society
Press, 1978.

Lounsberry, Clement A. *Early History
of North Dakota.* Washington, D.C.:
Liberty Press, 1919.

Lowie, Robert H. "Dance Associations
of the Eastern Dakota." *Anthropological Papers of the American Museum
of Natural History* 11 (1913): 105–42.

——. "Some Cases of Repeated Repro-
duction." In *The Study of Folklore,*
Alan Dundes, ed. Englewood Cliffs,
N.J.: Prentice-Hall, 1965.

Lurie, Nancy O. *A Special Style: The Milwaukee Public Museum, 1882–1981.*
Milwaukee: Milwaukee Public Museum, 1983.

Lynd, James W. "History of the Dakotas." *Minnesota Collections,* 2:7–88. St.
Paul: Minnesota Historical Society,
1889.

Matthews, Cornelius. *The Enchanted
Moccasin and Other Legends of the
American Indians.* New York: G. P.
Putnam's Sons, 1877.

Meyer, Roy W. *History of the Santee
Sioux: United States Indian Policy on
Trial.* Lincoln: University of Ne-
braska Press, 1967, 1993.

Milroy, Thomas W. "Solomon Two Star
(We-cah-npe-no-pah) Peace Warrior."
Minnesota Archaeologist 47 (1988).

Minnesota Valley Historical Society.
*Sketches Historical and Descriptive of
the Monuments and Tablets Erected
by the Minnesota Valley Historical
Society in Renville and Redwood
Counties, Minnesota.* Morton, 1902.

Morris, H. S. *Historical Stories, Legends
and Traditions: Roberts County and
Northeastern South Dakota.* Sisseton,
S.Dak.: Sisseton Courier, 1939.

Murray, David. *Forked Tongues: Speech,
Writing and Representation in North
American Indian Text.* Bloomington:
Indiana University Press, 1991.

Neill, Edward Duffield. "Dakota Land and Dakota Life." *Minnesota Collections*, 1 :254–94. St. Paul: Minnesota Historical Society, 1872.

Nicollet, Joseph N. *Joseph N. Nicollet on the Plains and Prairies: The Expeditions of 1838–39 with Journals, Letters, and Notes on the Dakota Indians,* Edmund C. Bray and Martha Coleman Bray, trans. and ed. St. Paul: Minnesota Historical Society Press, 1976.

Olden, Sarah Emilia. *The People of Tipi Sapa.* Milwaukee: Moorehouse Publishing Co., 1918.

Pond, Gideon H. "Dakota Superstitions." *Minnesota Collections,* 2:215–55. St. Paul: Minnesota Historical Society, 1889.

Pond, Samuel W. *The Dakota or Sioux in Minnesota As They Were in 1834.* St. Paul: Minnesota Historical Society Press, 1908, 1986.

Powers, William K. *Oglala Religion.* Lincoln: University of Nebraska Press, 1975.

———. "Plains Indian Music and Dance." In *Anthropolgy on the Great Plains,* W. Raymond Wood and Margot Liberty, ed. Lincoln: University of Nebraska Press, 1980.

———. *Sacred Language.* Norman: University of Oklahoma Press, 1986.

Radin, Paul. *The Trickster: A Study in American Indian Mythology.* New York: Philosophical Library, 1956; New York: Greenwood Press, 1969.

Ramsey, James. *Readings in the Fire.* Lincoln: University of Nebraska Press, 1983.

Reichard, Gladys A. "Literary Types and Dissemination of Myths." *Journal of American Folklore* 34 (1921): 269–307.

Riggs, Stephen Return. *Mary and I: Forty Years among the Sioux.* Boston: Congregational Sunday-School and Publishing Society, 1880.

———. *Tah-koo Wah-kan: or, The Gospel among the Dakotas.* Boston: Congregational Publishing Society, 1869.

———. *A Dakota-English Dictionary.* Washington, D.C.: GPO, 1889; St. Paul: Minnesota Historical Society Press, 1992.

———. *Dakota Grammar, Texts, and Ethnography.* Washington, D.C.: GPO, 1893.

———. "Dakota Portraits." *Minnesota History Bulletin* 2 (November 1918): 481–568.

Riggs, Theodore Foster. "Sunset to Sunset." *South Dakota History Collections,* 29:90–306. Pierre: South Dakota State Historical Society, 1958.

Ritzenthaler, Robert E., and Pat Ritzenthaler. *The Woodland Indians of the Western Great Lakes.* Garden City, N.Y.: Natural History Press, 1970.

Robertson, Thomas A. "Reminiscence of Thomas A. Robertson," *South Dakota History Collections,* 20:568–602. Pierre: South Dakota State Historical Society, 1940.

Robinson, Doane. "The Fight at Webster." *Monthly South Dakotan* 3 (1901): 324–27.

Satterlee, Marion P. *A Detailed Account of the Massacre by the Dakota Indians of Minnesota in 1862.* Minneapolis, 1923.

Schell, Herbert S. *History of South Dakota.* Lincoln: University of Nebraska Press, 1968.

Sisseton Centennial Yearbook. 1992.

Skinner, Alanson B. "A Sketch of Eastern Dakota Ethnology." *American Anthropologist,* n.s., 21 (1919): 164–74.

———. "Sun Dance of the Sisseton Dakota." *Anthropology Papers of the American Museum of Natural History* 16 (1919): 383–85.

———. "Medicine Ceremony of the Menomini, Iowa and Wahpeton Dakota." *Indian Notes and Monographs* 4 (1920).

———. "Tree-Dweller Bundle of the Wahpeton Dakota." *Indian Notes* 2 (1925): 66–73.

Sneve, Virginia Driving Hawk, ed. *South Dakota Geographic Names.* Sioux Falls, S.Dak.: Brevet Press, 1973.

Spier, Leslie. "The Sun Dance of the Plains Indians: Its Development and Diffusion." *Anthropological Papers of the American Museum of Natural History*, 16 (1921): 451–527.

Thompson, Stith. "The Star Husband Tales." In *The Study of Folklore,* Alan Dundes, ed. Englewood Cliffs, N.J.: Prentice-Hall, 1965.

———. *Tales of the North American Indians.* Bloomington: Indiana University Press, 1966.

Turner, Fredrick W., III. *The Portable North American Indian Reader.* New York: Viking Press, 1974.

Velie, Alan R. *American Indian Literature.* Norman: University of Oklahoma Press, 1991.

Voget, Fred W. *A History of Ethnology.* New York: Holt, Rinehart and Winston, 1975.

Waldman, Carl. *Atlas of the North American Indian.* New York: Facts on File, 1985.

Walker, James R. *Lakota Belief and Ritual.* Raymond J. De Mallie and Elaine A. Jahner, ed. Lincoln: University of Nebraska Press, 1980.

———. *Lakota Society.* Raymond J. De Mallie, ed. Lincoln: University of Nebraska Press, 1992.

Wallis, Wilson D. "The Sun Dance of the Canadian Dakota." *Anthropological Papers of the American Museum of Natural History* 16 (1919): 317–80.

———. "Beliefs and Tales of the Canadian Dakota." *Journal of American Folklore* 36 (1924): 36–101.

———. "The Canadian Dakota." *Anthropological Papers of the American Museum of Natural History* 41 (1947): 1–225.

Washburn, Wilcomb E. "The Noble and Ignoble Savage." In *Handbook of American Folklore,* Richard Dorson, ed. Bloomington: Indiana University Press, 1983.

Waterman, T. T. "The Explanatory Element in the Folk-Tales of the North-American Indians." *Journal of American Folklore* 27 (1914): 1–54.

Wedel, Mildred Mott. "Le Sueur and the Dakota Sioux." In *Aspects of Upper Great Lakes Anthropology: Papers in Honor of Lloyd A. Wiford,* Elden Johnson, ed. St. Paul: Minnesota Historical Society Press, 1974.

Wiget, Andrew. *Native American Literature.* Boston, Mass.: Twayne Publisher, 1985.

Williamson, Thomas S. "Dakota Scalp Dances." *Minnesota Collections,* 6:409. St. Paul: Minnesota Historical Society, 1894.

Wilson, Raymond. *Ohiyesa: Charles Eastman, Santee Sioux.* Urbana: University of Illinois Press, 1983.

Wissler, Clark. "Some Dakota Myths." *Journal of American Folklore* 20 (1907): 121–31.

———. "Societies and Ceremonial Associations in the Oglala Division of the Teton-Dakota." *Anthropological Papers of the American Museum of Natural History* 11 (1916): 1–99.

Zumwalt, Rosemary Levy. *American Folklore Scholarship: A Dialogue of Dissent.* Bloomington: Indiana University Press, 1988.

INTERVIEWS AND PERSONAL CORRESPONDENCE

Ackerman, Dorothy Nancy One Road. Telephone conversation with author. Portland, Ore., Dec. 9, 1993.

Garcia, Louis. (Historian for the Devil's

Lake [Spirit Lake] Sioux Tribe). Correspondence with author.

One Road, Arlene. Interview with author. Sisseton, S.Dak., Jan. 4, 1994.

Pipeboy, Darlene. Telephone conversation with author. Sisseton, S.Dak., May 18, 1994.

Red Owl, Edward M. Correspondence with author.

——, Michael I. Selvage, Sr., and John Eagle. Interview with author. Sisseton, S.Dak., Jan. 5, 1994.

Red Owl, Karen. Nebraska Indian Community College, Niobrara, Nebr. Correspondence with author.

Torness, Harold. Sisseton, S.Dak. Correspondence with author.

Torness, Mary. Sisseton, S.Dak. Correspondence with author.

Woolworth, Alan R. Minnesota Historical Society. Correspondence with author.

Index

Acculturation: agriculture and, 9; assimilation vs. separatism, 9–10; cultural identity and, 14–15; of Oneroad family, 16–22; policies, 3; suppression of traditional culture, 7–8,11–14, 30–31, 34–35

Agriculture, 7, 11; acculturation and, 9; traditional vegetal foods, 110

Akicita (warrior societies): buffalo hunting and, 111; "challengering," 67–68; punish transgressions, 68–70, 111; responsibilities, 63, 64, 110

Allotments, 10–11

American Museum of Natural History, 38, 39–40

Animals: as dreamfast visions, 92, 189; as symbols in war bundles, 71–72. See also specific animals

Annuities, 7, 8

Arrows: bow and arrow games, 116; points for, 107–8; sacred arrow bundles, 76; witch arrows, 85

Artichokes, in stories, 130–31

Artifacts: collection of, 31. See also Tools and utensils; specific items

Axes, 107–8

Bags, 110

Bark houses, 104–5

Basdohampi game, 116

Bears: ceremonial feasts, 181, 194; custom for killing of, 76; as dreamfast visions, 92–93; in stories, 144–45, 181, 193, 194

Beloved Child, see Child of Love (Beloved Child)

Berdaches, see Winktas (berdaches)

Berry crushers, 108

Bisexuals, see Winktas (berdaches)

Bison, see Buffalo

Bladders, 169

Boas, Franz, 39, 40

Bow and arrow games, 116

Bowl and dice games, 113

Bowls, 109

Bravery, tests of, 70, 116–17

Brother-in-law relationship, 68

Buffalo: Buffalo Nation described, 162–63; as dangerous, 164–65; hunting and consumption of, 20, 111; hunting medicines, 87; Legend of Hoop Ravine, 156–66

Buffalo Dance society, 76, 82–83

Buffalo Woman, 156–66

Burial customs: mounds, 102; punitive exposure of the body, 148; scaffold burials, 99–100, 137, 148. See also Death

Burke Act of 1906, 11

Buzzards, in stories, 128–30

Caŋkuwaŋzidaŋ (Peter Oneroad), 18–21, 78; pictured, 53 (following)

Cannibalism: in stories, 132–34, 140–41, 149–51, 154, 180–82, 194; as war practice, 73–74

Canoes, war honors and, 65–66

Cat's cradle, 116

Ceremonial feasts, 80

Cheyenne Indians, 191

Chiefs and chief making, 64–65

Child of Love (Beloved Child), story, 146–55; cannibalism themes in, 154; four pets of, 148–49; Iktomi and, 147–48, 154; incest conflict with sister, 146–48; revival of the dead, 155; witch sisters and, 150–55

Children: games of, 116; naming of, 88–89

Clans, see Gentes

Clothing, see Dress

Clowns: clown songs, 79; Heyokas (contraries), 191–92

Collier, John, Oneroad's correspondence with, 36

Containers, 109, 110

Contraries (Heyoka), 191–92

Cooking methods and practices, 105, 108

PICTURE CREDITS

Frontispiece: Milwaukee Public Museum, Milwaukee, Wisc. (Huron H. Smith, photographer); facing page 54: Museum of the American Indian, Heye Foundation (William Rau, photographer); all other photographs from a private collection. The editor and MHS Press are grateful to the *Sisseton Courier* for providing scans of several of the pictures.

CPSIA information can be obtained
at www.ICGtesting.com
Printed in the USA
JSHW031130190820
7377JS00002B/43

9 780873 515306